Black Tights

Laura Robinson

Black
Tights

Women, Sport, and Sexuality

HarperCollins*PublishersLtd*

www.harpercanada.com

HarperCollins books may be purchased for
educational, business, or sales promotional
use. For information please write:
Special Markets Department,
HarperCollins Canada,
55 Avenue Road, Suite 2900,
Toronto, Ontario,
Canada M5R 3L2

The author expresses great gratitude
to the Canada Council for the Arts
and their assistance in making
this book happen.

First edition

Canadian Cataloguing in Publication Data

Robinson, Laura
Black tights : women, sport and sexuality

ISBN 0-00-200041-5

1. Women athletes.
2. Sex discrimination in sports.
I. Title.

GV709.R62 2002   796'.082   C2002-900561-2

KRO 9 8 7 6 5 4 3 2 1

Printed and bound in Canada
Set in Spectrum

This book is dedicated to the young women who told the truth in a Mississauga courtroom in September 1996.

Contents

Introduction

Black tights first entered my life in 1974.

When I started to compete in local bicycle races in southern Ontario, the only available leg coverings were men's sweatpants, and even they weren't that easy to find. Certainly there was no such thing as real sportswear for women. I rode my bike around in baggy royal blue sweatpants held up with suspenders. Eventually they took on the imprint of oily chains on the right inside calf and black dye from the leather saddle on the butt. Suspenders, chain oil, and a stained rear end—I was the picture of athleticism.

When cyclists came to Canada from Europe and brought plenty of cool clothes to sell out of their suitcases, I was at last able to trade in these not terribly practical, baggy pants for a real pair of wool cycling tights. Now, I thought, I could be a real cyclist. I saw my legs as wings, powerfully and smoothly providing strength I could use to fly into this new and wild foreign land of sport.

Years later, in 1988, I read the book *Stroke*, by Heather Clarke and Susan Gynn-Timothy, members of Canada's national rowing team. They too believed that black tights—which were worn only by rowers who had been to Europe or had European connections— were what signalled an athlete's ascent to the upper echelons of sport. In effect, these wool tights were a graduation present of sorts—and then some. "Rowing, when it comes right down to it, is about ecstasy," they wrote. And they felt that the form-fitting apparel gave them a new intimacy with their bodies that heightened that ecstasy. Much later, Sandi Kirby, another Olympic rower who became a role model for me when I was in my early 20s and a colleague and friend later, told me that when she stretched that black fabric over her taut thighs and sculled across Elk Lake in Victoria, she thought she could "slice through wind and water at the same time."

But here lies the paradox of black tights. We female athletes see these tights as signposts of strength and power—and yes, sexuality—but that's not necessarily the way others see us when we're wearing them. There are no zippers or flies to camouflage the genital area; form-fitting blackness stretches over crotches and down well-shaped thighs and calves. We become aware of our sexuality and sexualized at the same time.

Sexuality and sexualization are polar opposites; one suggests empowerment, the other obedience. The tension between these two states of being—the balance beam women and girls must walk in order to survive the sporting culture—is what *Black Tights* is all about.

Personally, I ended up having a love-hate relationship with sport. I loved it for all it gave to me and made of me, but I hated that some men used sport to get their hands on so many of my friends and competitors. And it was often such an unwelcoming place for women. When I lobbied for equal prize money for women bike racers, I was denounced as a "lesbian." A "normal" woman, it was implied, would be happy with the way things were (as if anyone in her right mind would be content to take home a bottle of bubble bath while her male counterpart walked away with a cheque for $1,000).

The same thing happened to 12-year-old Justine Blainey when she decided to fight for her right to stay on the boys' hockey team she had legitimately made. As her case made its way through the legal system—and eventually all the way to the Supreme Court of Canada—the one thing that was constantly called into question was her sexuality. It seemed impossible for people to view her as an athlete who simply believed in equality.

To an outsider, the world of sport looks like a breeding ground for confidence, empowerment, and raw strength. Indeed, it can be all of that and more. But it is also a place where young people win and lose in physical and emotional contests. Furthermore, its history is based in militaristic, hierarchical, and patriarchal practices. Taken together, these factors leave athletes highly susceptible to manipulation, exploitation, and abuse. Today, top women athletes are so often marketed not as strong, powerful individuals, but as the passive objects of some sexual fantasy or another. Thus we are faced with the disappointing dilemma that, as women finally make it onto the professional playing field, they are expected to submit to an old set of rules. All too often, these rules mistake gender for sexuality.

By "sexuality" I mean the way we interpret and present the sexual self, intimately and publicly, consciously and subconsciously. On the other hand, gender is the way society constructs sexuality—the way we learn femaleness or maleness—and there is no question that sport is highly gendered. But conceptions of gender can be dangerous. In *The Constructed Body*, French sociologist Colette Guillaumin notes how notions of what is appropriate for the female body greatly limit the physical, emotional, and cultural freedom of girls and women. Separating girls and boys in play and competition is sport's first way of teaching children that we need rules to keep their sexed bodies apart. And because boys receive the lion's share of sport's resources and attention, they grow up believing they—and their gender—are naturally superior to girls.

Yet great things can happen when bodies and spirits mix it up on the field. Sport is a place where it is possible to be just an athlete—to lose yourself in movement and be nothing but a cyclist, a skier, a runner, or a rower. The passion of sport has no gender. When triathlete Lori Bowden won the 2001 Australian Ironwoman competition, she was the third-fastest runner—female or male—of the 1,200 competitors in the marathon leg of the race. In October 2001, Kenyan runner Catherine Nderba ran the Chicago marathon in 2:18:47—a phenomenally fast time that proves that women can go under 2:20.

Yet women were barred from running Olympic marathons until 1984. What great strides have been literally made since that time.

Who knows what women are capable of? Perhaps the triathlon gives us some idea. Because it is a new sport, and women and men have competed together right from the start, it hasn't been burdened with the years of entrenched sexism that plagues most sports. At the 1989 world championships in Nice, France, male competitors discovered that their female counterparts weren't receiving equal prize money and threatened to boycott the event if this wasn't rectified. Just the kind of guys you want to have around.

But plenty of people—male and female—still need to construct masculinity through sport, and the presence of the strong female body confuses the issue for them. Sport can be a way to achieve some kind of universal understanding and respect for others, or it can institutionalize attitudes and behaviours that make these goals unattainable. What would happen to sexuality if we had an atmosphere that welcomed all? We can only guess.

Sexuality is a web that stretches, in non-linear ways, from female to male, straight to gay, and everything in between. We are attracted to others in cerebral, physical, and emotional ways that none of us can truly understand. Some people will station themselves in one area for their entire lives; others will take plenty of side trips along the way. But no one, in a free and equal world, would ever define a sexual self based on athletic ability. Indeed, if inhabiting a body were not so fundamental to being human, the right to play would not be so important. But physical competition—living fully in your body and enjoying the rich way it reacts to other physically active bodies—is part of what makes being human so wonderful, and I believe it contributes to a more whole sexuality.

Instead, we like to rationalize sport by saying that it builds character, discipline, and pride and contributes to nationalism and patriotism while simultaneously contributing to peace and international understanding. But none of this, true or not, really matters. For me, sport is important because a lived body is deeply pleasurable and humans like pleasure. Sport can also be very sensual and sexual, and, after all, our natural sexuality is not a social construct. We are first and foremost sexual beings, and much of what we do is profoundly directed by our sexuality, however it manifests itself. In spite of what some religious doctrines say, pleasure feels great, and if we had a little more of it, perhaps some of us wouldn't embrace violence so wholeheartedly. *Black Tights* celebrates pleasure, but it also examines how pleasure—and freedom—are taken away. And let me say right from the start that, as long as we define sport in patriarchal terms, women will never be completely free—sexually or in any other way.

It may seem as if a chapter on the legal implications of provincial human rights codes and how they impact on the rights of women and girls to play is not related to our notions of sexuality. But I would argue that as long as our culture teaches girls their bodies don't belong in the public sphere of sport, then they learn about female sexuality as something that isn't the norm—that the "lived" female body must ask permission to be part of our culture—and never discover their most honest sexual self. The canvas on which we paint our sexuality is indeed very broad.

Redefining sport is worth trying to do because of what we could end up with. A healthy sexual atmosphere will become possible when women and men, straight and gay, able-bodied and not, can compete together and be honest about what turns their bodies on— in both the sporting and the sexual arenas (which are bound to over-lap). As my good friend and sport historian Doug Brown says, "Straight or gay, male or female, no matter how you slice it, when you're out there surrounded by butts and thighs covered in Lycra, it all matters."

Physical activity is at once the simple enactment of a human truth and a very layered and complex cultural story. It is about celebrating a truly lived body.

Unfortunately, professional male sport today is often not about this at all; instead, it is little more than a rather large cog in the military-industrial entertainment complex. I would even argue that professional male sport is actually intensely anti-body—but that's another book.

Sport is not about testosterone. It is about being free and independent in your body and spirit, about challenging yourself and your competitors to see just how fast and strong you can be. And it is about being a sexual animal, and allowing that animal to come to the surface—to come out and play.

Part i   Denying the Whole Woman

1   Constructing the Stadium

Putting Women in Their Place

On the eve of the 1999 Pan-Am Games in Winnipeg, several top Canadian athletes came together to take part in a panel discussion on ethics in sport. The panel was chaired by Dr. Bruce Kidd, the dean of physical education at the University of Toronto and once a fine middle-distance runner. Those who spoke included Ken Dryden, the president of the Toronto Maple Leafs and a former Stanley Cup–winning goalie; Susan Auch, a speed skater and two-time Olympic silver medallist; and Dr. Andrew Pipe, a physician and outspoken advocate of ethics in sport who is internationally leading the fight for drug-free athletes.

But the showstopper was Marion Lay, a former member of the Canadian swim team and bronze medallist at the 1968 Mexico City Olympics. Lay spoke with heartfelt compassion about the case of Katie Morrison.

This then nine-year-old girl from Coquitlam, British Columbia, had been the complainant in a 1994 sex-discrimination case launched by her father. We'll examine the legal suit in more detail in the next chapter, but here I will note in passing that David Morrison was attempting to challenge his community's inequitable approach to awarding access to sport services and facilities and was spurred to action when he realized that his son's ice time for hockey was publicly subsidized, but his daughter's gymnastics facilities were not.

Sadly, Lay knew from both personal experience and her many years of involvement with sport at all levels that Katie's story was all too common. As an openly gay woman in a subculture known to treat homosexuals with less than commendable tolerance, Lay has not had an easy time of it. Yet she has spent decades trying to make sport a more welcoming and friendlier place for women and girls, and has taken considerable risks in so doing. Since 1997, she has been part of both a national collective on harassment in sport and a committee to counter homophobia in sport. Lay was a founding member of the Canadian Association for the Advancement of Women and Sport and Physical Activity (CAAWS), and she is one of the chairs of Pacific Sport Group, a network of sports centres offering facilities and services to national team athletes from a variety of sports.

On that evening in Winnipeg, Lay used her notable flair for words to weave together a story about the discrimination and unfair play that girls and women still habitually encounter in sport. "When we went to the Mexico Olympics in 1968, we had to prove we were women in order to compete," Lay told the crowd—both the participants on the panel and the members of the audience—at Place Louis Riel. "But at least the test in 1968 consisted of taking a swab of saliva from our mouths and testing it for X and Y chromosomes. It's offensive, but in 1966, women athletes had to parade nude in front of a panel of male doctors, who could check in more detail to ensure that they indeed were women. People still believe if a woman is strong, she must not really be a woman. These Pan-Am Games are the first international games since the 1960s where women athletes have not had to prove womanhood in order to compete."

Lay let the absurdity of such gender testing sink in with the audience. Then she told another story. This time, it had to do with young Katie Morrison and the everyday way in which children are taught that boys matter more than girls do. "When David Morrison compared what the city was doing for his son with what it wasn't doing for his daughter, he found that ice time for boys was subsidized 50% by the municipality, while girls' gymnastics received no funding whatsoever," Lay told her listeners. "They launched a sex discrimination complaint at the B.C. Human Rights Commission, and spent the next few years fighting for something that boys don't have to think twice about. That their sporting needs will be taken care of is simply a given." Eventually the Morrisons won the case, and the city started to investigate itself. "What they found," Lay said, "is that in one arena alone, of the 207 hours of available ice time for hockey, 200 of them went to boys."

At its heart, Lay's story was about the subtle messages given to females who want to take part in a sport: We may have to let you in now, but don't think you are worth as much as boys are. The flip side of that message—the idea that men matter more and are therefore naturally superior—is reinforced with every boy whose hockey team is given more time on the ice, every boy whose community sports facilities are publicly subsidized, and every boy who lives in a city that subsidizes male professional sport to the tune of hundreds of millions of dollars.

When it came time for Ken Dryden's address, he talked mostly about hockey and read from his book *Home Game*, an eloquent study of Canada's favourite sport. He reminisced about a childhood spent playing hockey in the backyard with the other boys in the neighbourhood, he in one goal and his brother in the other. It was a magical scene he conjured—a bonding of hearts, minds, and bodies that is familiar to men and boys from one end of this country to the other. But it was also a lopsidedly privileged scene, an experience that is effectively denied to half the population. And although Dryden appeared moved by Lay's talk, he seemed to miss this point entirely. He certainly never addressed the gross inequities females face in his favourite game, a sport that has a long history of discriminating against women.

Had the panel been on any other topic, Dryden's oversight could perhaps be excused. But to paint such an idyllic picture of a male-dominated sport on the heels of Marion Lay's story, and in the context of a discussion of ethics in sport, simply isn't acceptable. Dryden certainly knows that kids learn life lessons through sport— and that these lessons are an essential part of the process of becoming well-rounded adults. But boys will never become well-rounded men if they don't learn to play together with girls in a fair, equitable, and inclusive fashion. How can they be expected to become men who treat women as equals if they are constantly being encouraged to participate in activities that exclude females as inferior?

It's important to note here that, for the most part, men and boys don't consciously design programs that shut out women and girls. I do not for one second believe that someone with Ken Dryden's integrity would exclude women and girls intentionally. The problem is not that men have thought this all out, it's that they *haven't* thought it out at all. They never seem to notice that half of the population doesn't have the sporting rights they take for granted.

Now, just to be clear, I am not arguing that meaningful experiences cannot or should not take place among members of the same sex. Girls play together as often as boys do—albeit usually at more "domestic" activities, such as skipping, sewing, creating plays, and playing with dolls. Still, these activities are integral to their growth, and the atmosphere they create would be negatively impacted by the introduction of the highly competitive values and posturing that go along with traditional male sports. I do believe, however, that boys should be exposed to the culture of girls in a way that respects it and doesn't displace what are often more cooperative values. Most every boy would benefit from learning to wait his turn at jumping rope.

When I questioned Dryden about the exclusivity and privilege boys experience in hockey, he conjured up images of spoiled professional male athletes. He spoke of the bad-tempered, unsportsman-like behaviour exhibited by members of the American men's hockey team at the 1998 Nagano Olympics, and then contrasted it with the grace and respectability displayed by those on the American women's team. All the high salaries and star treatment didn't amount to much for the men's team, Dryden concluded; yet the women needed none of that to be true champions.

Dryden's implication was that athletes who are given too much become corrupted by greed and lose the essence of what it means to be a true athlete: someone who is able to achieve excellence while maintaining the honesty and integrity that comes from being a good person. But if that were the case, why would we pay *any* athletes? Dryden is the president of a hockey club that has spent many millions of dollars on male athletes over many decades. Let's just try to add up all the North American cities that have stadiums and arenas that are used almost exclusively by male professional sports teams. Now let's imagine the cost of those venues, each one adding up to hundreds of millions of dollars to build (see chapter 2 for details on this) and several hundreds of thousands every year to maintain. If we add in the salaries of all the players in each of those cities, the total is so astronomical, it is absurd. There is surely a great irony in Dryden's trying to argue that the "poor but pure" female athlete is a better athlete while he is completely entrenched in a system that showers male sport with money, privilege, and adulation.

Romanticizing the amateur athlete is a fairly regular exercise among those who can't justify the unfair practices of the system of which they are part. It's as if they are saying, "Why would you want to be like our guys, with their bad manners and egotism? You are better off the way you are—enjoying sport for its own sake, without the hundreds of millions of dollars and countless untold privileges to cheapen you." And as long as women accept this unspoken assertion, they will remain cheerleaders, girlfriends, groupies, wives, fans, or volunteer gophers, and male athletes will continue to monopolize virtually all public space.

As an athlete, Dryden made a salary. It certainly doesn't compare to what NHL players make today, but it was good money for the time. He had the opportunity to compete for both the Stanley Cup and the Canada Cup (the latter against the magnificent Red Army team of the Soviet Union). Today, he is the president of an "original six" NHL hockey franchise. He has parlayed a law degree and a stellar professional hockey career into a reputation as one of the country's most respected citizens. But his suggestion that women are better athletes if they remain poor but pure harks back to the days when women were advised not to clutter their minds with thoughts of suffrage or the right to work for equal pay in safe environments, and certainly not the right to equal play.

And, of course, the women hockey players he so admired can hardly be considered true amateurs. The United States Olympic Committee spent millions of dollars training them to win the gold in Nagano, and the National Collegiate Athletic Association (NCAA) now offers top scholarships to women hockey players. They may be poor in relation to their male professional counter-parts, but compared with most other women athletes, they are well-off indeed. If he believed his own argument, Dryden should most admire the members of the Russian, Brazilian, and Ghanaian teams at the 1999 Women's World Cup of soccer, for example. These women didn't win gold, but they overcame more obstacles and did it with fewer advantages than the Americans who defeated them.

The three teams I mentioned above did extraordinarily well at the World Cup, but of course the poverty of the countries they came from—which particularly affects the female population—should never be romanticized, should never be painted as a means of producing a purer athlete or a more authentic human being. The fight to survive and then even perhaps escape poverty can very often teach the kind of discipline, tenacity, and dedication that is needed in sport. And there is no question that avoiding a life of destitution provides a huge incentive to succeed as an athlete. But being denied the privileges that male athletes enjoy doesn't make women more noble; it is simply an unfair distribution of wealth, resources, and public space. And of all the panellists meant to address ethics in sport, only Marion Lay spoke of this fundamental imbalance.

A Long History

So how did we get to where we are today? Well, if we were to take a very quick survey through time, from the hippodromes of ancient Greece to the sports arena down the street from you today, we would see that one message recurs: In the public domain, the sporting body is strong and primarily male. While it has a wonderful history of freeing the body, sport is also significantly rooted in war, so to understand why it is still so often dominated by men, we must look briefly at the role the male body plays in the military. Sport and the military have been and continue to be so inextricably linked in the minds of most people that the concept of the male athlete and the male warrior are interchangeable. And this perception is formed when we're young. For those of us who remember the Cold War, we also remember an Olympics where comparing medal counts between the United States and the Soviet Union was everything. Athletes became metaphors for the armies that defended the ideologies of capitalism and Communism, and not surprisingly, few Olympic events were open to women in those dark days. Real defenders, real soldiers, were men on the athletic field, while any attention paid to female athletes went to figure skaters and gymnasts, who did not challenge the masculine status quo of the hard, warring body.

But this practice of seeing the athletic body and the soldier's body as one and the same has deep historical roots that date back to ancient Greece, and particularly to Roman times, when the balance the Greeks practised between the body and the mind was replaced by ugly, violent public spectacles. We may have packaged the product differently today, but we remain a product of our past. Each era has managed to replicate the male athlete-soldier as a reflection of its own idealized male. In North America, I believe much of our sporting roots are found in the pre-Victorian era.

During that time, there were many ways for boys to learn how to be good little soldiers, but I would argue that the blueprint for North American sport comes from the fields of Eton, where the upper classes of England sent their sons to be turned into leaders of the British Empire. As the Duke of Wellington famously exclaimed, "The battle of Waterloo was won on the playing fields of Eton."

I would further argue that we in North America inherited this hierarchical, elitist, militaristic, and patriarchal structure for sport. In Canada, the Strathcona Trust system was a series of militarily based physical exercises for schoolchildren that had its roots in the Boer War. Canada's Minister of Militia and Defence, Frederick

Borden, persuaded Lord Strathcona (otherwise known as the railway magnate Donald Smith) to finance the program, which sought to build stronger soldiers by incorporating Prussian military exercises into school exercise regimens. The Boy Scouts were founded on similar principles when Sir Robert Baden-Powell, himself a veteran of the Boer War, organized boys into "troops" and "platoons" and divided them into classes, much as the military does with its soldiers.

In organizations like the YMCA, religion got added into the mix. Founded in London, in 1844, at the start of the Victorian era, the YMCA perhaps best exemplified the doctrine of muscular Christianity. This movement was based on a concern for the moral health of all the young men who had come to live in the many cities that had cropped up in the wake of the Industrial Revolution. The idea was that these men were likely to be morally swayed unless they were preoccupied with both physical activity and good works. Meanwhile, adherents of a related and purportedly scientific theory known as vitalism believed the body had only a limited amount of energy to expend. Sexual activity especially had to be limited, and no sperm was to be spilled in a frivolous manner, because then it couldn't be "reabsorbed by the blood and carried to the brain from whence growth and creativity would be stimulated."[1] Masturbation, sex with anyone other than one's wife (and then for the purposes of procreation only), and anything else that might stimulate a male were deemed sinful. Even maintaining physical contact with a dance partner could be construed as promiscuous sexual behaviour.

In this context, it's no surprise that the beautiful, fit male body was seen not as a source of pleasure or fun, but rather as a walking billboard for the positive values of Christianity. Instead of indulging in sins such as sex and masturbation, men would learn to be obedient, well-trained soldiers for Christ.

In today's secular world, all we need to do is listen to any football, hockey, or baseball broadcast, or even to the instructions many parents and coaches give their sons and players in community sports facilities, to understand how ideals of militarism and obedience are passed on to boys. We are supplied with one combative metaphor after another, and highly gendered language is often used to denigrate teams that lose. In other words a losing, impotent male is also a female. To quote hockey know-it-all Don Cherry, when boys aren't playing "hard," they "should give their skates back to their sisters." When they don't perform well enough in a workout, they are asked "if they think they're at a ballet practice." In the United States, football coaches have been known to put sanitary pads and tampons in the lockers of team members when they lose. There is no bigger insult than to be told you "play like a girl."

According to this school of thinking, a man is a "man's man" when he pulverizes the competition. When male teams win, their "virility is intact"; they were able to "stay hard until the end." And this mixing of warfaring and sexual terms to describe traditional sporting behaviour sells male professional sport today. Inevitably, it suggests a borrowed and aggressive sexuality. Greg Malszecki, a sport sociologist at York University in Toronto, calls this "man talk" that combines "the erotic with the combative." The male athlete is the public face of the soldier, and each is a metaphorical phallus, a physical representative of patriarchy. In her book *The Reign of the Phallus: Sexual Politics in Ancient Athens*, American classics professor Eva Keuls defines "phallocracy" as "a cultural system symbolized by the image of the male reproductive organ in permanent erection, the phallus. It is marked by, but is far more particular than, the dominance of men over women in the public sphere."[2] As I argued earlier, I don't believe we have moved beyond this state as a civilization. We have just learned how to integrate 21st-century norms into a culture that is centred around the phallus.

In this theatre of maleness, which is acted out not just in America but worldwide, the female body's softness is banished. Remember, we only get to be wives, girlfriends, groupies, fans, and gophers in male professional sport. And in war, on those rare occasions when the female body is present, it is part of the territory to be penetrated. There is such an entrenched belief still that the female body is there for male use, or to describe the worth of the man to whom it is attached. Rape was not considered an official war crime until February 2001, with the investigation into the atrocities that took place in the former Yugoslavia. This delay in justice for half the world's population demonstrates just how long-standing is the belief that men have a territorial prerogative over women's bodies in a patriarchy. The female body is seen as nothing more than material to be raped and bartered. In more progressive but still patriarchal climates, this practice is acted out in far less ruthless and violent ways, but women's bodies nonetheless remain largely the territory of men. In my own experiences as a journalist in hockey arenas, I was mistaken for a fan, a girlfriend, and a secretary. Not once was I asked if I was a sports writer. Somehow I could be there only as an appendage of a male.

In modern society, the idea of the warrior-athlete has been taken to an extreme. Even in ancient Greece, there was a belief that the physical and the intellectual must be given equal weight, that there must be balance in all things—a concept called homeostasis. We can see this belief reflected in how the male sporting body was depicted in frescoes, sculptures, and other art works. The athletes portrayed had highly defined, muscular frames, of course, but the body didn't replace the mind in the space it occupied. There was a place for the thinking man—he wasn't all reactive anger as so many heroic figures are in our present-day cinema.

That's not to say that such representations were not idealized, however. Greek philosophers and artists might have publicly espoused the principles of balance and harmony, but most of their compatriots had lives that were far from harmonious. The practice of slavery thrived, boys and women were used as sex slaves, and women were not considered citizens of the so-called democracy. And neither women nor slaves were allowed to participate in the philosophical discussions that often followed sporting events. In other words, most of the population couldn't even consider a place in the scheme.

As the societies of western Europe matured and developed, the male body became ever more idealized. During the Renaissance, even Christ and his disciples were depicted as taut, muscular soldiers locked in an eternal battle with evil. Meanwhile, the female body was polarized. A woman could be Eve, and cause man's expulsion from Eden; she could be Mary, the exalted virgin; or she could be Mary Magdalene, the fallen woman who needs to be saved.

In the Victorian era, women became what sport historian Patricia Vertinsky calls "eternally wounded." There were two sets of rules for women—one for those in the middle and upper classes, and one for those in the working class. Middle- and upper-class women were seen as fragile and easily excitable and were not to be overtaxed by strenuous physical effort. Their raison d'être was to produce heirs for their husbands, so any physical activity that might jeopardize their wombs was forbidden. But working-class women were even less fortunate. They could be physically taxed until they dropped dead—and many, many did. Exhaustion and childbirth frequently claimed the lives of women in the 19th century.

These puritanical beliefs eschewed physical pleasure—particularly for females. Furthermore, as science gained a foothold in social practices, "experts" tried to link moral directives with scientific "research." Theories abounded that those in the working class were better suited to physical labour because of their limited intellectual capacity. Women—if they were white and from the same class and perhaps the same families as the men in power—were far too delicate and morally upright to concern themselves with the corrupting spheres of politics, suffrage, and, of course, sports.[3]

Canada was influenced by both Victorianism and social Darwinism, but in such a harsh land, surviving was first and foremost in most people's minds. The physically and mentally tough European women who moved into the young country belied the notion of the fragile female. Aboriginal women, when they have been mentioned at all in the "official" history of Canada, are seen as "squaws," the exotic other, and the exact opposite of the fragile white female— they are in fact the backbone of every First Nations community.

In the United States, not only were Aboriginal women the exotic other, so were African-American women. This coincided with the

Victorian shift from rural to urban living. As industrialism swept through the eastern states and into the Midwest, massive changes disrupted the traditional power structures. Fathers physically dominated the family when most work was at or near to home, but they began to be displaced as the Industrial Revolution took hold and work sent them farther afield.[4] Middle-class women assumed greater importance, not only in the home, where they were often the only remaining adult, but also in the church, where they began forming ladies' auxiliaries and charitable organizations.

Of course, these newly powerful women couldn't be seen as the equals of men. They were said to be morally superior, however, and their increasing influence in the home and at church was thus made acceptable. But this moral superiority would be harmed by such manly pursuits as politics and sports. It was deemed unseemly for a middle-class woman even to be present at a men's sporting event. Thus the myths of female fragility and male superiority were maintained, and a Victorian paradox remained intact: Women were supposed to be innately morally superior, but this characteristic could vanish if they entered a man's world.

This set of ideas was reflected in the way women were expected to dress. Their apparel all but bound and gagged them. Corsets could be pulled so tightly that ribs were broken, lungs were punctured, and organs were squashed. Necklines were high and skirts long. When the bicycle came along, women couldn't open their legs wide enough to ride one. But a revolution was born when women's bloomers were introduced. Suddenly, women had not only two legs, but something at the top of them: movable, sexual bodies. Little wonder the moralists warned of uteruses falling out and women developing the repulsive "bicycle face" that would make them spinsters for life.

Is it any wonder that sport, with its history of combat, was destined to act out these highly gendered roles in the secular stadium? And this role would become a lot easier when representations of the body could be more readily reproduced. In the early 19th century, the invention of photography and the later advent of photojournalism meant that ordinary working people gained access to mass-produced images. We rarely question the truthfulness of photographs—it is a cliché that cameras don't lie—but in fact they are mediated reproductions that are frequently manipulated by the photographer to distort the reality of the subject matter. By mediated, I mean that the image is, by definition, a subjective reproduction of reality. Photographers quickly learned to make the best use of a technology that gave them the power to manipulate, intensify, or modify reality in the service of art. And as the technology became more advanced and the images sharper, embarrassing flaws and aesthetically pleasing details both became more apparent to the casual observer. Images that would sell, whether they were aesthetically pleasing or repulsive, became essential in a highly commercialized medium. But if photography signalled a dramatic shift in our ability to see ourselves, television ushered in a virtual revolution in self-consciousness. Static bodies were definitively lifted off the page to create a moving and talking imagined world.

And what a world it was, too. In this post–Second World War era, the threat of Communism occupied the American imagination, and television helped to create an ultra-conservative, patriarchal, and patriotic society that would stand tall against the red scourge. Women had proved they were more than capable of doing "a man's job" during the war, but now they were hustled back into the kitchen where they belonged. Rosie the Riveter was supplanted by Harriet Nelson and June Cleaver: women who needed the protection of their men, and who were entirely fulfilled playing the role of wife and mother. Even Lucy Ricardo, who can perhaps be considered one of the more liberated of the 1950s female television icons, found herself in the deepest trouble whenever she dared to venture out of her apartment. By the end of the show, however, she and her sidekick, Ethel, had always learned their lesson and retreated home to take care of Ricky and Fred—who had told them in the first place that their plans had been hare-brained.

Meanwhile, the Cold War demanded a "man's man," someone who would defend his country and safeguard his helpless family.

Women—weak, overly emotional, in need of protection—were clearly not up to the fight. Instead, they were to bear the children (preferably boys) who would fuel the great American dream of boat-like cars and sprawling suburbs—the ultimate proof that capitalism was far superior to the evils of Communism.

Forced out of the workplace, women soon found that public sporting facilities had also shut their doors to them. Sports in which they had been participating for decades, from softball to hockey, once again became the exclusive domain of men. The playing field or ice rink became the ultimate proving ground of a man's virility, and his participation symbolized his loyalty to the ideals of war and the triumph of a competitive economy.

Televised professional sport, with all the concomitant imagery of aggressive maleness, was the perfect metaphor for an American society that was fighting for all that was true and good about capitalism. The professional athlete became larger than life, and he ran with every other American male at his side. All the beaten-down Ozzie Nelsons out there had figured out, if only subconsciously, that they were really just replaceable cogs in a giant machine, but they triumphed when he did. Their wives, meanwhile, were portrayed as content to stay at home to do their laundry, cook their meals, and raise their sons[5]—as little more than constant consumers of products, particularly domestic ones. And, as Betty Friedan observed in *The Feminine Mystique*, they were expected to fill any "extra" time with yet more domestic labour. Is it any surprise that prescription drugs became one of the biggest consumer products for these women?

But the transformation of America was just beginning. The next step was to take all those sedated Harriets and isolate them in huge tracts of land that were (and still are) as sterile as their scrubbed kitchens. While city life allowed women to live somewhat publicly, suburban life squirrelled them away in the ultra-domestic privacy of lawns, double garages, and rumpus rooms. The 1950s effectively eliminated women from the public stage.

Of course, with a few, usually early exceptions, North American cities were built to accommodate not humans but their vehicles—

and this is especially true of the suburbs. There, vast stretches of asphalt discouraged people's movements unless they were suitably enclosed in steel and fuelled by combustion. Most men needed the automobile to commute to their jobs in the city, and the car soon became a public masculine symbol.

In Europe, things didn't evolve in quite the same way. Television and the cult of the automobile haven't dominated European culture to the same degree. Europeans still rely on conventional forms of cultural delivery—though this is rapidly changing—such as books, theatres, opera halls, museums, and art galleries. Public life there is also different from that in North America. Europe has a long tradition of the plaza, of an outdoor communal area where people can meet. Men have dominated these spaces, but women and children have not been banished to the suburbs as they have been in North America. Europe also built virtually all its roads well before the advent of the automobile, and most of them are narrow and don't accommodate large vehicles. Public transit is far more advanced and gas prices much higher, so the public landscape is not dominated in the same way by hulking metal forms and combustion engines. All of these factors result in a more welcoming public space for women. And women's sport, for the most part, has had a higher status and is better understood in Europe than in North America.

This is not to say that discrimination against women doesn't exist in Europe, but the fact of being a woman is seen on a canvas that stretches beyond the very taut and tiny one allowed on this side of the Atlantic. For instance, people in the European sporting world know who the world's top women athletes are in just about any sport. They know who Silken Laumann and Marnie McBean are, and they know that Canada's women's cycling and kayaking teams are among the best in the world. In fact, during my many trips to Europe to ski or to cycle, I didn't once encounter the North American practice of questioning the normalcy of a female athlete. In my experience, European men have a genuine respect for "sportswomen."

And Europe is in some ways a more welcoming place for women

even beyond the sports arena. Beauty, for instance, doesn't end at age 25 or size 6, as it does in the super-mediated culture of North America. Smart and sophisticated women in their 50s exude a confidence and a presence that few women in North America are ever allowed. In Europe, there is no particular narrow corridor the female body must somehow inhabit.

Some would argue that this balance of power is changing in the U.S. because Title IX has so greatly influenced women's sport. Title IX was a landmark piece of equity legislation that the American Congress passed in the 1970s; we will examine this important piece of legislation in chapter 9. But while we have seen the rise of women's professional basketball and soccer for young, very talented women, we have also seen a much greater increase in the way public funds are used to subsidize male-only stadiums and arenas. And as the case of Katie Morrison will show, this practice occurs even at the municipal level when it comes to sports and recreation for boys and girls. We must face the fact that, in so many ways, North America will continue to script a story that is only for boys—unless we successfully challenge it.

2   Show Me the Money

How the Economy of Sport Controls Women

Karen Strong, of the National Sport Centre in Calgary, and her colleague Shirley Voyna-Wilson, the harassment officer at the University of Calgary, introduced a workshop designed to address all forms of harassment in sport—racial, physical, and sexual—in the fall of 1999 at the annual general meeting of Athletes CAN, the association of Canada's national team athletes. Called "Out of Bounds," the seminar was meant to give athletes some strategies for recognizing and preventing abuse of all kinds. Mark Tewksbury was an Olympic gold medallist from 1992, and he attended just months after he had first acknowledged his homosexuality on national television. But few other athletes did.

Where were they? Everyone had flocked to the "How to Market Yourself" workshop. It seems that in our modern sporting culture, physical ability, while still necessary, has taken a back seat to marketability—and every athlete knows it. If you are Anna Kournikova, it matters not one whit what your Women's Tennis Association (WTA) ranking is or how many tournaments you've won (or even attended). No, all that really matters is your coy smile, your long, beautiful blonde hair, and your Lolita-like presence. Kournikova has the great distinction of being the most downloaded athlete in the world, ahead of even Michael Jordan and Tiger Woods, but as of January 2002, she had competed in 94 WTA tournaments and won none of them. Let's face it. The world's interest in her has little to do with her athletic ability—she is always depicted in ultra-passive poses, never smashing a cross-court winner. As the WTA's director of player promotions, Jim Fuhse, told author L. Jon Wortheim for his book on women's tennis, *Venus Envy*, "We're never going to stop selling sex. If anything, I'd like to see us be more risqué and take more chances. Look, if a player doesn't sell tickets because of her tennis, she has to do something else to contribute."

Today, what limited sponsorship funds are available for women go almost exclusively to particularly attractive athletes. (Complacency and compliance also come in handy. If you want the cash, don't talk about issues like racism, sexism, and the environment—just keep smiling and say nothing of substance.) This means that the bulk of women athletes do without—regardless of ability. While this may not be "sporting," it's the reality of the marketplace—as all those athletes flocking to the "How to Market Yourself" seminar could tell you.

So how do we measure this kind of attractiveness? Well, you're out of luck if you don't fit within the very narrow parameters of conventional North American standards. If you're a woman, you need to look fit, but not *too* fit. Strong, but not *too* strong. And you can forget it altogether if you don't look "heterosexual" enough. We'll see in chapter 4 how individual athletes and even whole sports have gone to great lengths to remove the taint of homosexuality, the death knell of any sponsorship deal. And this goes for men too. Even before he came out, Mark Tewksbury lost a six-figure sponsorship deal because he "was just a little too gay."

Colour matters too in this game. At the Sydney Olympics, I asked the bronze medallist in the women's 100 metres—the marquee event for women in track and field—how she felt about seeing the Olympics turned into the Glam Queen Games. "I love my body," Jamaica's Tanya Lawrence told me. "I love what it can do, and if someone else doesn't like it, then that's too bad for them." Unfortunately, this commendable attitude is probably not very realistic. All too often, women like her are left behind in the race to win sponsorship dollars in spite of their top performances.

For black athletes like Lawrence, there can be another complicating factor. "What is considered acceptably black for black women is very narrow," I was told by a black assistant track coach from the Australian Olympic team. "She has to be a light-skinned black woman and have white features. Her body has to be long and lean, and she can't say anything about being black or about racism. Lawrence is too black, too short, and too muscular to get a big sponsor. And she's not American, so she really doesn't matter to these guys. That's the way this game is played, and anyone who denies that is denying the truth."

Kevin Blackistone is a columnist for the *Dallas Morning News* and is also black, and he came to a similar conclusion once the Games were over. "All around the world, there are different perspectives on what are good looks and not good looks. In the European world, it's blonde hair, blue eyes, and fair skin. This raises questions," he told me from his Dallas office, "as to what are our standards of beauty. The mass media has perpetuated the European standard, though I don't think you will find this in Africa and the Caribbean. There are other aesthetics, such as the Asian aesthetic, that I think people find attractive too, but in the homogenized world that we live in, the European standard is the ultimate one. I think young girls looking at sport today may think they have to look a certain way just to play. It would be very unfortunate if this turned out to be the case."

But if we never move beyond conventional Western models of attractiveness, can the blame be placed entirely on the international sponsors and their advertising firms? I believe that sometimes women themselves perpetuate the problem. In the hypermasculine world of sport, women, no matter what their ethnic or cultural backgrounds, frequently play up or exploit their own femininity to gain acceptance. As the great Women's National Basketball Association (WNBA) star Lisa Leslie once said, "When I'm playing, I'll sweat and talk trash. However, off the court, I'm lipstick, heels, and short skirts. I'm very feminine, mild-mannered, and sensitive."[1]

Why all this emphasis on femininity? When all is said and done, it is wholly a social construction. And isn't sport about being a real human, not a constructed one? Unfortunately, many women feel a strong conflict between being an athlete and being a woman. They want to excel in their sport, but they don't want to be perceived as "freakish," somehow not normal, mannish. At its most extreme, the fear of being pronounced too masculine can keep women from taking up sports in the first place. Those who do compete often take pains like Leslie's to announce their heterosexuality to the world. In *The Frailty Myth: Redefining the Physical Potential of Women and Girls*, Colette Dowling writes, "Many female athletes have a vested interested in proclaiming their femininity. The theory of 'sex-role conflict' argues that … [women who participate in sport] often experience debilitating conflict between their roles as athletes and women. Some athletic women try to resolve the conflict by overemphasizing their feminine side with lots of jewelry, short skirts, and references to their boyfriends."[2]

So what's wrong with a woman understanding and profiting from the culture she lives in? Perhaps the biggest problem is that even conventionally attractive women athletes must display their bodies in extremely passive and vulnerable ways. Those poses of course rob them of power—including the power they had gained from being elite athletes in the first place. And facial expressions are equally important. Women athletes who become glam girls are not allowed to express the intensity, concentration, determination, or fortitude that faces bear in the heat of competition. There is nothing the least bit challenging, passionate, sweaty, or strong about the facial expressions of glam athletes once they have become mediated images. These women could be any other vacuous cover girl.

As Dowling points out, "There is no quicker way to put women in their place than to portray them as sex objects." And when women do it to themselves, they're not reclaiming any of their lost power, they're simply making it easier for men to go on objectifying—and therefore discounting—them. As an example, let's take a look at the story of the Canadian women's Nordic ski team.

Nordic Nudes

During the buildup to the Sydney Olympics, several women's teams posed in the nude to raise some of the significant amounts of money needed to compete internationally today. First it was the Australian soccer team when its members put together a calendar with full-frontal nudity. Then it was New Zealand's eight in rowing. Soon even individual athletes caught on to the trend. Sweden's swimming ace Therese Alshammar had a "Diva" tattoo installed at the top of her buttocks and was happy to reveal it for any camera—as long as the photo would be distributed internationally. American swimmer Jenny Thompson appeared in a *Sports Illustrated* shoot standing on a beach with her legs apart, in red go-go boots and stars-and-stripes hot pants, holding her fists over her bare breasts. Many of these women got paid nothing for their shoots, but the simple act of taking off their clothes—of surrendering their own power to the power of the man gazing at the female body—increased their stock. Women who want sponsorship deals must show that they're willing to do what they're told.

Not about to be left out in the cold, the members of the Canadian women's Nordic ski team soon decided to produce their own nude calendar. Like centuries of women before them, they too were struck by the brilliant idea that they could make money if they took off all their clothes. They even obtained private sponsorship for each page; this way, they said, they would at least break even if the calendars didn't sell well.

I should stress that the calendar is in no way pornographic. Equipment or arms and legs coyly cover breasts and genital areas. Sponsors' skis, bindings, boots, and running shoes are prominently displayed. The skiers do not smile or gaze in the "come hither" way so common in porn, nor are there any "do me" poses. In fact, the women who participated believe the calendar will help girls develop a positive body image. "We're strong women with a little bit of fat, and we don't have breast implants," one told me. "I think this is good for girls to see because they get the opposite image all the time." It's true that the calendar is a lot better than the Britney

Spears–Anna Kournikova kiddie porn that proliferates in mainstream culture—but I don't imagine many girls are forking out $30 to buy it—and if they have $30 to spare, there's better material than this to spend it on.

In the end, the calendar is all female, all naked, and all passive. If it had included male skiers, at least the calendar's gendered nature would have been wiped out, and perhaps it really would have been a tribute to the skier's body. Instead, these women have internalized cultural norms that reward females for looking passive and isolating themselves before the camera lens.

To make matters worse, the calendar also includes Pollyanna-ish yearbook-style motivational slogans with each shot. One reads, "I dream of things that never were and ask why not?" While I remembered John F. Kennedy saying this at the height of the civil rights movement, I didn't know if that was the original source. When I asked the relevant athlete where she got it, she wrote back and said her coach had told her it was from "a 19th-century English playwright named George Burner [sic] Shaw." Sure enough, in *Back to Methusela*, Shaw has the serpent in the Garden of Eden utter these words. In their use of the line, both Shaw and Kennedy show a deep understanding of the human condition. And what did it mean to the cross-country skier? "I dream that there will be a Canadian woman on the podium at the Olympics or the world cup races," she told me, "and it will be me." Well, I don't think it was this kind of individual triumph that either Shaw or Kennedy had in mind, but there is nothing inherently wrong with dreaming big dreams for yourself. The problem for me is that the dreams of these women, and those of the types of athletes who flood the "How to Market Yourself" workshops, don't ever seem to reach beyond personal gain. And of course the whole idea of co-opting such lines as the Shaw quotation when you haven't the slightest awareness of their historical significance is disturbing. Many younger women athletes seem to have no understanding at all of important events in history, even when it is as recent as the Kennedy era, the civil rights movement, and the contemporary phase of the women's movement.

Today, it often appears that all those who fought the good fight have been supplanted by a New Age, "motivational seminar" philosophy that revels in self-congratulatory individualism. The Nordic skiers may be go-getters when it comes to raising funds, but only when they sell a version of womanhood that in no way threatens traditional patriarchal values, and only when the money goes to them and their sport. Unfortunately, there are only so many sponsorship dollars, and as long as women athletes continue to promote themselves according to the narrow definition of how women are supposed to look and act, many others will lose out.

I should stress here that patriarchy is an ideology that doesn't necessarily appeal to all men. In fact, individual males are not usually the problem in this sexual power paradigm; instead, the problem is the mindset with which men—and women—get indoctrinated under patriarchy. One male coach from Alberta told me that he admired the Nordic skiers for going out and getting the sponsors for the calendar, because funding for sport is so dismal in Canada. However, he was concerned that the girls he coached would receive the wrong message. "I wondered if girls would draw from this that taking your clothes off is the way to get ahead. That's not what I think girls should take away from sport. None of the girls I coach brought it up with me, but perhaps they did with the woman who coaches with me. I always coach with a woman so girls have someone they can go to."

When I spoke to one Nordic ski team member, Jamie Fortier, in the fall of 2000, she was about to leave for competition in Alaska and discussed how difficult it is for national team athletes to finance travel costs because of drastic funding cuts by Sport Canada. Did they protest to the government about these cuts, I asked, or lobby to have them reinstated? No, they just decided to try to raise money for themselves via the calendar. "Sarah Renner and Becky Scott [two other team members] were in Britain last year and they saw this calendar of British housewives posing nude," explained Fortier. "It was for leukemia research or something, and we talked about doing something like that ourselves, and eventually we went for it."

I asked her if they'd been harshly criticized for posing nude. "Not many people have criticized us," she insisted. "It was surprising, but some men were very critical … and we were attacked by feminists. They said it's sad that you have to do this to make money, but we said it's a good idea. We weren't pressured. We came up with the idea completely on our own. I'm a very strong anti-feminist. I think a lot of them have gone too far. I'm looking out for myself, and I'm thinking for myself. We definitely were not told to do this calendar. We decided for ourselves."

There's a tremendous irony in Fortier's remarks, of course. Women's Nordic skiing was added to the Olympics only in 1964, and even then, it was only because women fought for its inclusion. It wasn't until 1984 that women were allowed to ski any farther than 10 kilometres. Fortier calls herself "a very strong anti-feminist," but without feminism, not only would she not have an Olympic event to compete in, she wouldn't have the vote, the right to own property or hold public office, or the freedom to work at the job of her choice and be properly paid for it. She wouldn't be able to go to university, and she would have to quit her job—if she'd been lucky enough to get one in the first place—when she got married. In fact, it was because of feminists in 1929 that women legally became people in Canada, so I had to wonder what exactly did Fortier not like about the legacy she'd been left.

Despite Fortier's perfectly valid complaints about Sport Canada cutbacks (though some funding has been restored of late), she is actually one of the lucky ones. Most Canadian athletes—male and female—never make it to national teams because they simply can't afford to continue to train and compete at the level needed today. White, economically privileged athletes are the ones most likely to make national teams as costly as Nordic skiing.[3] Yet there is no correlation between economic privilege and athletic ability.

Now that I've said all this, how did the calendar do in the end? In January 2001, Sarah Renner confirmed that they had indeed sold out and netted approximately $80,000. "Thirty percent of the proceeds will be donated to the Nordic Advocates Guild [NAG], which is a non-profit foundation for Nordic skiing," Renner told me. "The rest will be divided among the five women on the team." While it's admirable that the women donated some of their profits to a charitable cause, I should point out that NAG projects are directed not at skiers at the grassroots level, but at athletes who are close to making the national team (or in some cases already on the team). And all this belies Fortier's claim that the women used as their inspiration the calendar put out by Britain's Rylstone & District Women's Institute (WI).

That calendar was a fundraiser in memory of John Baker, the husband of one of the women, who died of leukemia in 1999. The women in it are not young, svelte athletes, but middle-aged, ample, voluptuous members of this regional chapter of the national WI organization; their ages range from 45 to 61. And unlike the skiers in the Nordic Nudes calendar, the Rylstone women are far from passive. They are pictured playing the piano, singing, working in the kitchen, reading, sewing, attending meetings, wearing wonderful hats, and generally having great fun with their campy role-playing of what people imagine WI members do all day. And every photo includes Baker's favourite flower—the sunflower—as a tribute to the man and his work in environmental conservation.

The WI calendar is a politically and socially aware parody that doesn't take itself very seriously. The Rylstone women come across as self-assured, confident people displaying a relaxed attitude toward the body. It's as if they are saying, "Hey, this is the real female body—like it or lump it." Fortier and the other members of the Nordic ski team claim their calendar is an attempt to do the same thing: show teenage girls real female bodies—ones that are strong and powerful, not skin and bones, with bloated, artificial breasts. But the truth is that few teenage girls are going to buy a $30 calendar, and anyway, it is clearly aimed at men, not girls. And while the women on the team may believe they are depicted as powerful role models, they aren't once pictured skiing and displaying any of the strength they show in competition (except on the last page, in stamp-sized photos). So I'm not sure how joining the long line of women who have posed with next to nothing on does anything but perpetuate the message that the female body exists only to be looked at and assessed by men.

But can the calendar be considered a success? It sold out, of course, and the women earned themselves a substantial amount of money. And it also increased the profile of Nordic women's skiing in the bargain, a not inconsiderable feat given how little media attention this sport receives. Isn't that all for the good? Well, it would be, had the media actually been paying attention to the athletes' achievements. They received plenty of coverage (pardon the pun) when they were nude, to be sure, but there was a complete lack of interest in these athletes once they had put their clothes back on and were actually engaged in their sport. The team had its best season ever during 2000–01, winning a silver medal in the relay at a world cup event in Utah and a sixth place in the relay at the world championships in Finland. Becky Scott had third- and fourth-place finishes in two world cup races, and she finished 11th at the world championships. Yet despite these best-ever performances, the women were ignored in the national media. For reasons those of us who ski with our clothes on can only guess at, Fortier and her fellow team members seemed to think posing nude was a way to bring cross-country skiing to the masses. But this unintentional little social experiment should make it obvious how much the media value compliant women over athletic success.

It is frustrating to see women like the members of the Nordic ski team retreat to traditional, conservative, and highly mediated images of their own bodies. As we will see in upcoming chapters of this book, women have had to fight long and hard to get even the small piece of the pie we now have. We have had to stand up in courts and before human rights commissions and demand rights we are legally entitled to. We have had to endure insults, harassment, and insinuations that have always been about one thing—our sexuality. We have been made to submit to gender tests and sexual abuse. We have been pushed back two steps every time we take one step forward. And why? It all has to do with not allowing women autonomy over their own bodies—and under a capitalist system, the best way to do this is to deny funds to those who insist on autonomy and reward those who willingly hand over their bodies to the male gaze.

Different cultures design this body–power exchange in different ways. In the next chapter, we will see how, all over the world, various all-male control committees—in sport and in all other areas of life— dictate what women can and cannot do with their bodies. Indeed, this is what's at the root of the most contentious female body issue in North America: freedom of choice. The Republicans in the United States and the Canadian Alliance party are both anti-choice, and a significant portion of their election war chests comes from far-right, Christian, anti-abortion organizations. The fact that North American—particularly American—gender politics are still ultimately defined by a woman's right to choose whether she will remain pregnant tells us a great deal about the realpolitik of our patriarchal states.

But both male and female bodies are defined by their traditional gender roles. And once again, we can see that money, and the way it's distributed, keeps everyone in line. In sport, public funds are used to enhance the role awarded the strong male body, while they quickly diminish if girls and women try to gain access to them. In his book *Major League Losers: The Real Cost of Sports and Who's Paying for It*, professor Mark Rosentraub of Indiana University argues that the public subsidization of professional male sport costs North Americans hundreds of millions of dollars each year. He gives plenty of examples of how municipalities, in their desperate attempts to be considered "world class"—which they interpret as having a professional male sports team—roll over and do whatever the team owners ask.

The city of Denver originally thought it was subsidizing a stadium for the Colorado Rockies baseball team to the tune of either "$100 million or 70% of the cost," Rosentraub reports. But by the time the deal had been ironed out, the citizens would have been lucky to get off that easy. "Although the team's contribution [in the final contract] never matched what was originally expected, this did not stop the public sector from providing even more revenue for the owners," Rosentraub writes. "The city [even] permitted the team to retain the $15-million fee for naming rights charged to the Coors

Brewing Co."[4] Of course, what's a few hundred million when Denverites get to live in the shadow of a few dozen men who are good at throwing balls or passing pucks?

Rosentraub devotes several pages of his book to Toronto's SkyDome as well. The stadium cost in excess of $625 million to build, he writes, which was "2.5 times more than taxpayers were told," and daily interest on loans amounted to $60,000 a day. While the SkyDome was still under construction, the board of directors decided to add more "restaurants and recreation venues, which increased costs by $36 million." And how much of this cost was shouldered by the public sector? Rosentraub quotes the *Toronto Star*'s final estimate of $262 million.

The SkyDome project was initiated by Bill Davis's Conservative government, but in 1995 it was inherited by the New Democratic Party. The NDP eventually sold the stadium to the private sector for the bargain-basement price of $151 million, plus $20 million in interest (to reflect the delay in finalizing the sale).[5] Meanwhile, most of the employment opportunities ultimately created were McJobs—minimum-wage positions in the service industry, often part-time, and with little to offer in the way of training or promotion.

In the first chapter, we looked briefly at why male professional team athletes are so much admired by other men, but the deeply embedded psychological attachment some men have to the publicly powerful male body is the stuff of another book. For now, let's see how our patriarchal society has made public sports facilities infinitely accessible to males and almost completely inaccessible to females.

Katie Morrison and the Fight for Equal Access

"Why have women had to struggle so hard to be included in competitive sports?" asks Colette Dowling. "It isn't so much that men don't *want* women playing, they keep insisting, they just don't want funds taken away and their own opportunities compromised."[6] This was exactly the argument nine-year-old Katie and her father, David Morrison, faced when they began asking why hockey arenas used mostly by boys are subsidized while gymnastics facilities used mostly by girls are not.

Katie's father started to research gender issues in 1992 when he first realized that his son's ice time was publicly subsidized. The systematic discrimination against female children became crystal clear to him when he looked at a family photograph of his own kids with his nieces and nephews. "My nieces, they dance, play the piano. And I realized these things were private, while the boys have hockey and lacrosse and baseball in the community," he told his local newspaper, the *Tri-City News*. "It grew from there. When I was a director at Omega [Katie's gymnastics club], we were trying to get equal access; we were a group of parents trying to keep our kids in sports, and we had to pay property taxes to keep them in."

The gymnastics club, which primarily served girls, had to pay property taxes on a building in an industrial area because there were no public facilities the athletes could use. For three years in a row, the parents asked the city council in Coquitlam, B.C., a suburb of Vancouver, to waive the property taxes, but to no avail. The city did offer the parents a public facility, but because of the kind and size of equipment needed for gymnastics, it was not suitable. All told, the Omega Gymnastics Club was paying $9,000 a month in rent, utility costs, and property taxes.

"A lot of kids drop out [of gymnastics because of the cost]," Morrison told the local paper. "If it was 50% subsidized, like hockey, it would probably be more reasonable. ... It's not about creating champions—there are so few, there's not 10 in all B.C. But if gymnastics could be more affordable, there would be more participation."

It soon became evident to David Morrison, however, that the city wasn't going to budge. Then he read another article in the *Tri-City News*, this one written by Tammy Lawrence, and he knew what he had to do. Lawrence was then the executive director of Promotions Plus, an organization that advocates on behalf of girls and women in sport, and she said in the article that equity is synonymous with fairness. That was all Morrison needed to hear. He launched a complaint with the B.C. Human Rights Commission under section 8 of the province's Human Rights Code. Section 8 states:

> A person must not, without a bona fide and reasonable justification, deny to a person or class of person any accommodation, service or facility customarily available to the public, or discriminate against a person or class of person regarding any accommodation, service or facility customarily available to the public, because of the race, colour, ancestry, place of origin, religion, marital status, family status, physical or mental disability, sex or sexual orientation of that person or class of person.

At first, the commission refused to hear the complaint, saying the Human Rights Code didn't ensure that people would have access to the sport of their *choice*. This was a public policy, the commission concluded, not a human rights issue. Morrison believed this analysis was wrong, so he got in touch with Gail Dickson, a lawyer he found through the Women's Legal Education and Action Fund (LEAF). Dickson wrote to the commission, arguing that because Coquitlam provided public funding for sport and physical activity, the city had a responsibility to distribute such funds in a fair and equitable manner. At present, she maintained, funds were being administered in a way that favoured boys over girls. After receiving Dickson's letter, the commission members revised their original opinion and agreed to hear the case in August 1994.

The first step was for an investigator from the commission to compile data provided by the city on levels of male and female participation in sports and physical activities. The city's legal advisers argued that *all* recreational facilities and services should be considered when looking at funding allocations, and they tried to include arts and crafts and other sedentary activities attended mainly by females. According to those numbers, the participation rate was 55.6% for boys and 44.4% for girls. But the commission dismissed this biased accounting and asked for statistics that included only physically active programs. The revised numbers showed that 69% of services and facilities were devoted to boys, while girls received only 31%. In certain sports, the contrasts were even greater. Sports fields were used by boys 74% of the time and by girls just 26% of the time. In one arena, boys received 200 of the 207 hours of available ice time.

In the eyes of the Morrisons, and plenty of other parents, the city of Coquitlam was in clear contravention of section 8. And they soon found a powerful ally in Harinder Mahil, the deputy chief commissioner of the Human Rights Commission. "The B.C. Human Rights Code protects the fundamental rights of British Columbians by prohibiting discrimination on the basis of race, colour, ancestry, place of origin, political belief, religion, marital status, family status, physical or mental disability, sex, sexual orientation, age, and criminal or summary conviction unrelated to employment," Mahil states simply. "The Supreme Court of Canada has held that human rights legislation is of a 'quasi-constitutional' nature and should be interpreted accordingly. This means that the Human Rights Code takes precedence over other provincial statutes. It also means that the rights contained within the human rights legislation must be given their full recognition and effect, without attempts to minimize those rights or interpret the protections they offer in a narrow fashion."

Like the Morrisons, Mahil felt the case was an example of rights being interpreted in the narrowest of fashions, so he took the extraordinary step of becoming a party to the complaint. He did not want to see it get buried among the many cases that have languished at the commission for years, uninvestigated and unresolved. Yet even with Mahil in their corner, the Morrisons had to wait nearly five years to win their case.

How was that possible? Human rights disputes are usually heard by a tribunal and the process to get to the tribunal is filled with backlogged cases due to a combination of an over-burdened bureaucracy and a very underfunded department. The Coquitlam dispute was headed to a tribunal, but at the last minute, the city asked for mediation instead. With mediation, both parties get together and try to come to an agreement. But the first day of mediation in this case didn't last long. Coquitlam's lawyer said the city had made positive steps, and therefore there wasn't anything else to discuss. The city flat-out refused to comply with any more of the demands made by Mahil and the Morrisons. "We were shocked," said Tammy Lawrence of Promotions Plus, still a party to the complaint. "After all that, the city still didn't get it. We knew we were in the right, and we weren't about to let them off the hook."

After a lunch break, the parties met again. Mahil and the Morrisons said that they believed the city hadn't taken their complaint seriously, and that they would prefer to shut down the mediation so the case would go to arbitration. They quoted from the *Provincial Policy on Girls and Women in Physical Activity and Sport* report, which had been adopted by the government in 1992. "Equity implies that girls and women at all levels of the physical activity and sport system should have the same opportunities as boys and men to participate in activities of their choice," read the report. "This means that women do not necessarily need to participate in the same activities as men but that programs should be provided and administered in a fair and unbiased way."

"All of a sudden, things switched around," remembers Lawrence, "and they were willing to negotiate." The lawyers for the city agreed to consider the changes the Morrisons were asking for. The most important of these was the establishment of a six-part gender equity program that would see Coquitlam maintain and release gender equity statistics, appoint a gender equity committee, designate a gender equity coordinator, and establish a fund that would provide annual grants to predominantly female, non-profit sport user groups that do not have access to publicly funded facilities. According to an internal memo from Promotions Plus, "The long-term goal of this program is to attain gender equity in sport (and physical activity) in Coquitlam. The short-term goal is a 50% reduction in gender inequities in sport and physical activity in Coquitlam within five years; including a similar increase in young female participation rates relative to current participation rates."[7]

Although Mahil and the Morrisons were thrilled when the city signed off on the agreement on March 31, 1999, they knew that because of the quasi-judicial nature of all provincial and federal human rights commissions, it would have no impact beyond their own jurisdiction. "This is not a binding decision outside of Coquitlam," Mahil explains. "My advice to other municipal offices was to ask the following questions:

"(1) Who are your users and members? How many use the facility in a given year? How many are male? How many female? What are their ages? What kind of families do they live in? What income levels do they have? What is their ethnic background?

"(2) Where is the money going? You should analyze your budget. How much budget is spent on programming for boys and men and how much on girls and women?

"(3) What are you promoting? Examine your brochures, publications, and advertisements. Determine programs that are aimed at boys, girls, men, and women. Also, review visual images representing females and those representing males, and the times that males or females are portrayed in stereotypical ways. How diverse are your images?

"(4) Are your facilities friendly? Take a hard look at your facilities. Is the lobby area welcoming? Where are the public phones? Where are the dark corners that are difficult to secure?

"(5) What does the community look like? Review information about your community from your planning department and Statistics Canada. ...

"(6) Make the comparisons. Compare the information you have gathered about your users, facilities, promotions, and budget with what you found on the community as a whole. Do they match? If not, where are the gaps? Are equal numbers of females and males using your facilities? Does your budget assign money equitably to programs for girls and women, boys and men? Do the people using your programs and facilities accurately reflect the population of your community in gender, age, ethnicity, income, family status, disabilities, and employment status?"

As I was listening to Mahil rattle off this list of questions, I started to add up how much time and effort it takes to ensure that human rights are not being infringed upon in the sporting world—or anywhere else, for that matter. But surely it is worth it. "There are phenomenal benefits," says Mahil, "just, for instance, in what we spend on health care. First of all, if you look at cities or municipalities and their bottom line, if you can attract more people to your facilities, you generate more revenue. You get young women active, and they become more aware and understand their bodies, have respect for the body. It enhances self-esteem and helps with body-image issues such as eating disorders. When we work together, women and men can learn to build equal partnerships which benefit all of society."

Mahil's vision of the future sounds promising, but we will see in upcoming chapters of this book that we have a long way to go to get there. Things may have changed for the better in Coquitlam, but in communities across the country, other women and girls are still being discriminated against every day. As Colette Dowling writes in *The Frailty Myth,*

> By century's end the myth of the weaker sex lay in tatters,
> but that didn't bring an end to inequity. ... Male college
> athletes [in the United States] receive over $179 million *more* in
> scholarship dollars every year. Men's sport programs
> command 77% of athletic operating budgets. Clearly there's
> much to be done if women are to have equal training, equal
> funding, equal acceptance. And gaining these is not in itself
> the ultimate goal, but rather the underpinning required for a
> much larger paradigm shift: the change that has to take place
> if girls are going to throw off the shackles of restrictive
> gender conditioning and fly out the door and run and kick
> and throw as early in life as boys—and not stop when they
> enter puberty.[8]

Mahil says there is more to equity than just providing programs for girls and women who are already in the system. "Sport is for the rich now," he asserts. "If you play any sport, it's increasingly too expensive for most people to play. Our resources are limited at the commission. I wish we had the resources so we could look at what's happening in all municipalities—so they will themselves look at sports and equity—but we don't. This *has* to be addressed. This *must* be addressed."

As far as David Morrison is concerned, the time he spent fighting for equity was well worth it. "I'm just a dad with two daughters looking for fairness. When I take my son to a hockey game, I am reminded to take my daughters. My wife and my daughters are always reminding me, and we always joke about being gender-equitable."

3   Sex and the Single Chromosome

How a Biological Test Turned into a Social Test

X Marks the Spot

During the mid-1960s, major women competitors at international track and field meets and games were forced to parade naked in front of a panel of male doctors who would decide their sex for them. If they didn't pass this cursory visual test, they were expected to submit to a more probing, gynecological version. Today, one member of the 1960s Canadian track team compares this invasive examination to rape. How wonderful it seemed for women when, in 1968, the International Olympic Committee (IOC) introduced the buccal smear test (also called the Barr test) at the Olympics in Grenoble and Mexico. Now all they had to do was supply a sample of tissue scraped from the cheek to receive their "femininity card," a piece of identification bearing their photo, height, weight, and accreditation number.

Spanish hurdler Maria Patino was assigned her first femininity card at the World Athletic Championships in Helsinki in 1983. Unfortunately, she left it at home when she went to Kobe, Japan, to compete in the 1985 World University Games. The day before she was to run the 60-metre hurdles, she was told there were problems with her buccal smear and she would have to report to the hospital to have the test repeated in the morning, before the race. On the way to the stadium, she was told she had failed both tests and should fake an injury. "I could barely comprehend what was happening. I was scared and ashamed, but at the same time angry, because I couldn't see how my body was different from the other girls,"[1] she told Alison Carlson, who was one of the first journalists to write about the issue and went on to lobby against gender testing.

It turned out that Patino had a condition called androgen insensitivity. She was infertile—but no less a woman than any other. She had a normally proportioned woman's body, external female genitalia, and a vagina, but no uterus. One psychologist commented at the time, "The assumption is that there are two separate roads, one leading from XY chromosomes at conception to manhood, the other from XX chromosomes at conception to womanhood. The fact is that there are not two roads, but one road with a number of forks that turn in the male or female direction. Most of us turn in the same direction at each fork."[2]

In Patino's case, she took the first turn toward becoming male: She had an XY chromosome configuration. But because of a genetic mutation, she never produced testosterone. Without that hormone directing the additional changes that would make it male, the fetus automatically became female. The tiny testes that were originally produced eventually atrophied and retreated, and Patino became unequivocally female. "I knew I was a woman—in the eyes of medicine, God, and most of all, in my own eyes. If I hadn't been an athlete, my femininity would never have been questioned," she said.

Although she knew what was in store for her—Spanish track officials had told her they would expose her secret to the world—Patino insisted on running in the national championships. She won, and soon she began reading about herself in El Pais, Madrid's daily newspaper. Endless articles about her sexuality were printed, and in short order, she lost her academic scholarship, was expelled from the national athletic residence, and was barred from training with her coach. Her boyfriend left her, most of her friends likewise deserted, and people gawked at her in the street. All her athletic records were disallowed, and she was banned from sport for life.

But Patino refused to give up. She was convinced that science could show how ludicrous gender testing was, and that people could be convinced that her genetic disposition did not give her an advantage (in fact, without testosterone, which most women produce, she was at a distinct disadvantage). "I was erased from the map," she told Carlson, "as if I had never existed. I have given 12 years to sport, it never came easily. I was no 'superwoman.' If I had any advantage it was from my mind, not my body."

In 1988, the IOC finally formed a working group to address "how and when to look into the sex test issue." Patino's case was argued successfully, and her "womanhood" was reinstated. She was allowed to compete again. "I have new sensibilities," she said at the time. "Women must fight, and not just for a day or a year. What happened to me was like being raped. I'm sure it's the same sense of incredible shame and violation. The only difference is that, in my case, the whole world was watching."

Patino came back at the 1989 Spanish championships and made it to the finals. Two months later, she set a national record in the indoor hurdles and qualified for the 1991 world championships in Seville. At the time, one expert in gender research commented, "It seems just fine in our society to have a birth defect of any organ—as long as it isn't the sex organ."

Taking on Sport's Stepford Wives

In the 20 years since Patino failed her Barr test, has much changed? Dr. Berit Skirstad, an associate professor at the Norwegian University of Sport and Physical Education, Dr. Sandi Kirby, a former Olympic rower and the chair of the sociology department at the University of Winnipeg, and several other sport activists have lobbied for years to have the tests banned because of their intrusive nature and the high number of false results, as well as the stigma they attach to being a female athlete. "The results from the tests have been treated confidentially," Dr. Skirstad told the European College of Sport Science conference in 1999. "They are handed over to the team doctor by the president of the IOC Medical Commission. The uncertainty of the first test was approximately 20%."

Can you imagine what would happen if tests for performance-enhancing drugs registered false positives in 20% of cases? No athlete, sport governing body, or Olympic association would stand for it. But when it comes to female sex tests, no margin of error is apparently too large.

And why *are* there so many false positives? The short answer is that gender issues are far more complex than single X and Y chromosomes suggest. As Dr. Skirstad explains, "There exists no simple laboratory test that decides gender. The difference between male and female is not black and white. It is a biologic continuum. Any dividing line is a matter of context." Women who appear to be female might test male because of a chromosomal abnormality that gives them two X chromosomes and a Y. Ironically, this condition often prevents them from absorbing testosterone—or the synthetic testosterones we call steroids—as was the case with Patino. If anything, these women are at a *dis*advantage.

In 1992, at the Barcelona Olympics, 11 of the 2,406 women tested had Y chromosomes but were not anatomically male.[3] So why all the hype over a Y chromosome that doesn't give its possessor any of the advantages normally associated with male athletes? And why did most female athletes support the tests despite the demeaning premise behind them?

Annika Sorensen of Sweden, a freestyle skier and the athlete representative to the International Ski Federation—the only governing body that was still employing biological gender tests as recently as 2000—says they are just meant to help make sport as fair as possible. "We felt that some of the Nordic skiers looked quite muscular, even masculine, and thought they may be doing steroids, and so we support gender testing."

I asked Sorensen if she knew whether something as fundamental as a person's genetic composition could actually be changed by the use of steroids or other performance-enhancing drugs. She did not know the answer to this. Still, she insisted, gender testing was fair and not in any way an insult to women. What do they have to fear, she asked, if they are indeed women? Obviously, Sorensen had not read Dr. Skirstad's work, nor did she understand basic biochemistry. The ingestion of steroids, or any other performance-enhancing drug, will never change the genetic imprint that is carried in the X and Y chromosomes.

Like many women athletes today, Sorensen seems to feel the need to apologize for those who have dared to blur the gender borders by being confidently and unapologetically strong. To compensate for the threat to men that these women represent, Sorensen and others like her adopt a self-righteous femininity. They point the accusing finger of blame—"She doesn't look like what I think a female is supposed to look like, therefore I'm going to question whether she is one"—to mark themselves as different. They are the Stepford wives of sport. As Gloria Steinem would say, they have become female impersonators, acting in ways that won't threaten male power.

The Sydney Olympics was the first international sports meet since 1966 where women didn't have to genetically prove they were women before they were allowed to compete. From the 1966 European Athletic Championships to Atlanta in 1996—and at all world championships and world cups in between—female competitors had been forced to endure testing by medical personnel to ensure they weren't really tarted-up males.

The gender tests, which were justified as a necessary evil meant to protect women from "female impostors," subtly told women athletes that there was something deviant about them. The IOC always argued that it was looking for men posing as women, but only Stella Walsh, who competed for Poland in 1936, was ever found to have male genitalia (which in her case were tiny and remained undiscovered until she died years later). In truth, the gender tests really had nothing to do with protecting women from men. Rather, the tests were about the social control of women who had dared to step beyond the boundaries designated for the passive female. And it's no coincidence that they were instituted in exactly the time period when women were starting to question gender issues and civil rights in the political sphere.

Indeed, it wasn't until June 1999—on the eve of a new millennium—that the IOC finally decided it would cease administering tests to women to qualify them for their "female carding"—at least until it came up with a better solution. But even when these tests had been banished, if only temporarily, the underlying question remained: If a woman is an active, strong, physically skilled athlete, then just what kind of a *woman* is she?

This question is hardly new. For as long as there have been women athletes, there have been debates about whether competition is "natural" or "feminine" (two of the most gender-laden words in the English language). University of British Columbia sport historian Patricia Vertinsky is just one of the many researchers who have written on the Victorian era and its influence on gendered beliefs about women. In her essay "The Social Construction of the Gendered Body: Exercise and the Exercise of Power," she asserts that "gender has ... become a way of signifying cultural construction—'a social category imposed on a sexed body.'"[4] Later in the same essay, she writes, "I have argued that during the latter part of the nineteenth century a formidable body of theory related to sex and gender difference was brought together and disseminated by scientists and the medical profession and effectively put to the use of an ideology of female bodily incapacity—an ideology from which women, especially sporting women, have had difficulty escaping."[5] This body of theory gave birth to everything from Victorian notions of fragility and frailty to Freud's views on female hysteria and penis envy. As Vertinsky reasons, it is an ideology women are still trying to escape.

Nevertheless, I would agree with Freud's assertion that the sexual self is paramount to the real self—that humans are first and foremost sexual beings, and that much of what we do in our "other lives" is directed profoundly by our sexuality. The problem is not that we are sexual, but rather that sexuality and gendered behaviour—which is learned—get mixed up in people's minds. The fact that we are sexual beings doesn't mean our behaviour revolves solely around sex. The actual biological act of intercourse is just one aspect of being sexual. And as we will see, sport can either enhance female sexual agency or be constructed in ways that rob us of it.

Gender Testing by Any Other Name

The International Ski Federation is the last organization that has yet to eliminate biological tests , but I would argue that the gender testing of women in sport has simply been switched to the public, or social, domain. A governing body like the International Volleyball Federation might not be as brazen as the ISF, but it has found an equally harmful way to make women prove their femininity.

The International Volleyball Federation—or Fédération internationale de volleyball (FIVB)—is the umbrella organization responsible for beach volleyball; it has been heavily involved with the promotion of the sport, both internationally and at the Olympic level. But this is a sport unlike any other, and its packaging reflects a distinctly American, "Daytona Beach" flavour. Although it now has defined rules of organized play, it maintains its allegiance to rock music, beer, and female skin. And, ironically, the group tasked with overseeing the sport internationally is the aptly named Control Committee.

There are no women on the Control Committee, but its decisions directly affect women athletes, who must abide by them or lose their right to play internationally. It is the Control Committee that decides that women athletes must wear bikinis or high-cut one-piece bathing suits—or not step onto the court. It is the Control Committee that decides that female players can cover their backsides with a slice of Lycra no more than seven centimetres long at the hips. And it is the all-male Control Committee to which women players must appeal if they want to put on a pair of tights and a T-shirt in cold or windy conditions.

Beach volleyball proved to be one of the most popular sports at the Sydney Olympics. Indeed, its television ratings were exceptionally high, given that it is a relatively new sport. Yet the most desirable television sports fan is male, between the ages of 18 and 35, and a follower of male team sports. He tends to like athletic contests with frequent male body contact and bone-crunching injuries. So what is the attraction of a sport with no body contact, where teams of only two players, separated by a net, hug and kiss each other during the match, and then do the same to their opponents at the end of the game?

Easy. This is a sport that keeps women in their place. No matter how strong and athletic they are, no matter how much prize money they earn, they still must do what they are told by the Control Committee. And what they are told to do is to compete in skimpy uniforms. Of course, the women themselves aren't blameless. They willingly accept a physical power imbalance that disadvantages them. And what's most disturbing is that none of them appear to be complaining.

I asked Kerri Pottharst, a member of the Australian team that won the gold in Sydney, if she thought women were intelligent enough to decide for themselves what to wear. She bristled. "Of course we are intelligent enough to decide what to wear. There was an issue in Toronto [at a world cup event] when it was really cool—not even 13 degrees—and it was the first time we went to the International Volleyball Federation and they allowed us to wear leggings. I think that they would have allowed us that here [in Sydney] if we'd asked. The health of the athletes is foremost for them—and to sell the sport too. I don't think any of the women have ever complained."

Even after our conversation, I still wasn't sure where Pottharst stood on the issue. She said she felt women were intelligent enough to dress themselves, yet she supports a system that doesn't allow them to exercise that intelligence. Significantly, Pottharst also posed for the book *Sydney Dream*, a collection of black-and-white nude photographs of Australian athletes that was released during the games. She asked her partner, Victor Anfiloff, if he would pose with her because she was "a bit chicken," and she was surprised when she realized there were other people at the sand dune they'd chosen for the shoot. She rationalized her embarrassment by mentioning the skimpy suits women must wear in competition, as if she should have gotten used to that sort of thing by now. "It wasn't as deserted as I thought it would be!" she recalled. "But when you think of what we have to wear in tournaments ..."

In fact, plenty of control committees throughout the sporting world are continually dictating the role the female body is to play. In Canada, our national game is overseen by the Canadian Hockey Association, which has a board of directors of 35 people. As of the 2001–02 season, just three of them are women—and only two have a vote. There are no women at all on the powerful seven-member executive committee, and even the CHA's 13-member female council has six men on it. Five men have a vote on this committee, while the other one represents women to the executive committee.

Ironically, the International Volleyball Federation (FIVB) believes it is a governing body that recognizes gender equity because it distributes prize money equally among men and women (though women receive none of the significant amounts of money earned in television revenues). The federation's spokespeople insist they are looking out for the best interests of their female members. After the gold medallists' press conference in Sydney, Allan May, a Toronto promoter and member of the world council for the sport, asked to speak to me. He wanted to talk about the uniform issue. "The FIVB, as an organization, is very sensitive to the uniform issue," he told me. "The players can also wear a one-piece uniform, and I've never seen any of the athletes choose to wear one. It's an evolutionary perspective—I've questioned this a number of times. As a promoter, it was brought to my attention in Toronto that the weather may be hazardous to the athletes. They said, 'We'd prefer to wear cold-weather clothing,' and the Control Committee agreed."

When I asked him why the players should even have to ask for someone else's permission, he made the same excuse as everyone else: Things have to look uniform. The word "uniform," however, seems to be code for revealing attire. Do track and field athletes, triathletes, rowers, or cyclists look bad, I wondered, when they wear slight variations on a theme, depending on how they feel that day?

Do they all need control committees of their own to look out for their "best interests"?

I believe this insistence on a "uniform look" really masks a desire for beach volleyball to have a highly gendered appearance. Women are obliged to wear revealing Lycra bathing suits, while men wear baggy cotton shorts and tank tops. There is no mistaking who is who. Clothing acts as a social dividing line.

With its all-male membership and its ridiculous rules, the Control Committee may strike us as funny, but the ideology behind it continues to threaten the autonomy women should have achieved years ago. Whether the issue is reproductive freedom or the freedom to dress as they please, women all over the world can't seem to escape men who feel the need to tell them what they can and cannot do with their own bodies.

In many ways, the men on the beach volleyball Control Committee reminded me of the mullahs, or religious leaders, who control women's dress in fundamentalist Muslim countries, where even a bare wrist or nail polish can be punished as an act of promiscuity. Just like the men running beach volleyball, the mullahs constantly argue that they have the well-being of their women at heart.

De facto control committees exist outside of sport as well, and not only with the mullahs in the fundamentalist Muslim world. In the United States, one of the first international moves made by the new Republican president, George W. Bush, in 2000 was to deny funding to aid organizations that operated in countries where abortion and birth control counselling were available. The 1973 *Roe v. Wade* decision is under attack by this government, as are many other pieces of legislation that have sought to deliver equality to women, including Title IX. In Canada, we have our own control committee in the guise of the Canadian Alliance, with strong ties to the Christian right. Of course there is a great deal more freedom awarded women volleyball players than those under the absolute control of religious police. However, one man's religious text is another man's sport rulebook—it just depends on in which culture a woman finds herself.

The Road from Here

Beach volleyball's women certainly are not alone. Female athletes willingly cast themselves as sex objects in plenty of other sports as well. At the women's mountain bike competition at the Sydney Olympics, the Italian Paola Pezzo, who had won the gold medal in 1996, showed up in a silver lamé skinsuit accessorized by pink shoes, a pink helmet, and a pink bike. Even a section of her blonde hair was dyed pink. Her bio on the official Olympic Web site quotes her as coyly saying she is better known in Italy for her cleavage than for her athletic abilities. In 1996, she rode with her skinsuit unzipped; cameras zoomed in on her chest for most of the race. Since then, Pezzo has played up the sex kitten angle and been very well paid for it. On one occasion in 1999, she stepped up to the world cup podium in go-go boots and a gold lamé miniskirt, accepted her medal, and sped off on the back of her coach's motorcycle.

When I asked Pezzo, at the post-race press conference in Sydney, if she was surprised to find that someone who presents herself as a sex object is then treated like one by others, she recoiled and said she was an athlete first. Like some other female athletes, Pezzo seems to like to play the game of "What? Me sexy?" She acts the role of the virgin-whore, crossing herself at the start line before pedalling off in her revealing, skin-tight suit. This is an act that has sold well for centuries, and it has won Pezzo many sponsors and endorsement contracts.

Before the Salt Lake City Olympics in the winter of 2002, two members of Canada's women's hockey team posed for *Ohmm* magazine in the United States. This time, it wasn't a lack of clothing that made the shots seem pornographic, but the pose of the athletes and the context of the shot. Becky Kellar is standing up, legs apart, in a glitter tube top and tiger-print pants. Kendra Fischer is sitting with her legs wide open and her top undone, a pair of standard-issue "fuck-me" shoes on her feet. She looks vulnerable, weak, and spacey. But what is most important about these shots—besides the fact that they take pains to erase the women's physical strength—is that both players are backed into a corner between walls that appear

to be made of plywood, like those found in basements and unfin-
ished rooms. Interestingly, when I was researching gang rapes
committed by members of male hockey teams between 1992 and 2000,
I found that the ones that happened in private homes all took place
in basements, where noise is muffled and there is only one small
avenue of escape for a victim.

Kendra Fischer took over in goal for the national team after
Manon Rheaume, who brought a certain fame with her because she
was the first woman to play in the NHL (albeit only in one exhibition
game). While the sports pages heralded Rheaume's major-league gig
as proof that women were making it in hockey, not many of the
players felt that way. They knew of at least three other women who
they thought were better goalies than Rheaume but didn't get
invited to play in the NHL. And they believed it was because those
goalies weren't as attractive. Many felt that Rheaume's good looks
were being cashed in on by pro hockey to the detriment of other
women, and sometimes they had mixed feelings toward her. They
thought it was great that she brought the profile of women's hockey
up, and they welcomed her on the national team, but they were
critical of how all of this was achieved. In *Higher Goals: Women's Ice
Hockey and the Politics of Gender,* University of Waterloo sport sociologist
Nancy Theberge writes,

> [I]t is generally agreed that Rheaume's "success" was a
> publicity stunt, owing in good measure to her appearance
> rather than her ability. Players feel that the publicity she has
> garnered detracts from the respect due them for their
> athletic accomplishments. Some were scornful. When
> players who attended the 1994 national team selection camp
> returned, it was reported that one of the Blades had beaten
> Rheaume on a penalty shot. A player remarked, "I always
> said that Rheaume is vulnerable through her legs."[6]

Of course, we have seen that Rheaume was hardly the first
woman to be objectified and then hope it would help her get ahead.

Nor will she be the last. The October 2001 issue of *Maxim* magazine featured several female extreme sports athletes in soft-core porn poses; on other pages, meanwhile, their male counterparts are shown in a multitude of action shots. The male spread, titled "Blood Sports," shows athletes base jumping (jumping off cliffs with parachutes that are opened at the last minute), rock climbing, big-wave surfing, free-snowboarding (where you're dropped by a helicopter onto a mountain ridge), whitewater kayaking, downhill mountain biking, and paragliding. Then we turn to the women's spread, "Action Figures," which has a group shot of three American surfers—Amy Cobb, Malia Jones, and Lana Papke—taking a shower together. Topless. Snowboarders Tara Dakids and Victoria Jealouse come next, and they are both shown reclining in bikinis—hardly typical snowboarder attire. Base jumper Lottie Aston is also in a bikini bottom, though no top, and is standing in what looks like a change room. Mountain biker Tara Llanes is again wearing a bikini, as is rock climber Steph Davis. Accompanying these large photos are postage-stamp-sized shots of the women actually doing their sports. These images are so tiny that not one woman can be identified—but then isn't the point *not* to acknowledge the active, strong female body? And even in the larger, posed shots, not one of the women has any leg or arm muscle definition. All of which leads you to believe that either *Maxim* chose to profile women who aren't in fact very fit, or the magazine's makers airbrushed all the strength out of these bodies.

But should Fischer and Kellar—and all of the others—be blamed for their inability to read the subtext of these photographs? When they're competing at the international level, athletes have little time to go to public debates or mix with cultures that are out of the mainstream. Few read critical essays on the very subculture in which they participate. They are far more likely to be cocooned in their own little world, and they are often actively discouraged from discovering points of view that may be contrary to their sport's ideology. So how do we combine sport and culture in a way that gives people the opportunity to become both good athletes and better thinkers who will apply a little critical analysis to the vast amounts of information that threaten to overwhelm everyone these days?

Sport at the elite level is now so commercialized. The IOC has signed multi-million-dollar contracts with companies such as Coke and McDonald's, who are hardly representative of the holistic values that at one time were part of the sporting culture. I'm not sure we will ever again see the mind–body balance the ancient Greeks considered important. But perhaps we should try to look beyond Western culture for guidance. First Nations people, for example, have always considered it imperative for human beings to strive for a balance in the physical, spiritual, cultural, and intellectual aspects of being.

After the Sydney Olympics, I went to interview several Native Canadians who were top runners in the 1960s. Without exception, they told me how disappointed they were with today's Olympic athletes. In their tradition, the most important characteristic for a good athlete is the ability to be humble. Flaunting one's body—especially for economic gain—is frowned upon because it smacks of arrogance. William Merasty, who grew up in northern Saskatchewan and was once a great long-distance runner, told me that he didn't watch any of the Sydney games because he believes most athletes no longer earn respect because they have lost the ability to be humble. "*Kawitha mistayi etethimisu*," he said to me. "Directly translated, it means, 'Do not think lots of yourself.'"

"We look at sport today and it's very competitive," said another former runner, David Courchene Jr. of Sagkeeng. "There seem to be only three winners in the competition. They're pressured so much to win, rather than developing their skills collectively. Our way of life means we work collectively with the gifts we have. Some people could do things in the canoe that the runner could not do. Athletes should not take this competitiveness seriously." Like Merasty, Courchene believes many of today's athletes have lost their way.

Have we forgotten the reason sport mattered to so many of us in the first place? The idea of sport as a quiet, humble experience, as an inspiring display of simple human effort, is rarely written about or even acknowledged among the athletes themselves. And, unfortunately, very few women athletes have spent any real time examining what it is they are doing when they allow themselves to be transformed into sexualized and mediated objects. This process may reward them financially or help convince them that they are "real" women, but I believe it robs them—and anyone else who cares about both sports and women—of their very humanity.

4 The Love of a Strong Woman

The Lesbian Athlete

What female athlete in a non-traditional sport hasn't been told that she must be a lesbian? For me, it started at 14, when I began competing in local cycling time trials. I had short hair, a flat chest, and a pair of awfully strong legs, and my best friend's brothers immediately found a new name for me: Lesbie Laura. Soon all their friends called me that too. At that age, I had no idea what a lesbian was, but I could tell by how they spat out the words that it was meant as an insult.

What a surprise, then, when I grew my hair long enough for a ponytail and joined the cheerleading squad. The boys who called me a lesbian were two grades ahead of me—and of course they were the ones I most wanted to impress. I was sure that if they saw me cheering on male athletes, they would realize the baselessness of their accusations. (I later handed in the cheerleading uniform after I read Germaine Greer's *The Female Eunuch*.)

But the "lesbian" tag wasn't going to go away. It reappeared years later, in the late 1980s, when I began campaigning for equal prize money for women cyclists in Toronto. Some real wits even mockingly renamed the Cycling Women's Committee of the Ontario Cycling Association—the group spearheading the drive for equality—Dykes on Bikes. Obviously, only lesbians could believe in anything so audacious as equity and fair play.

Even as recently as the spring of 2001, at the end of my year as writer in residence at the University of Calgary, I found that my sexual preference was up for debate. An employee of the university told me that the media had been very curious about me that year: an athlete, a sportswriter, a feminist … a lesbian, right?

Why is there so often an assumption that women athletes must be gay? And why do so many women athletes—both straight and gay—consider such an assumption an insult? I believe that when any woman wants to compete in her own sport, with her own body, in the same arena as a man—instead of for that man's affection—she challenges the notion that she is a "real" woman. Women who are strong and self-reliant, and therefore don't depend on men for physical support and protection, are suspect, and women athletes certainly do not have frail or passive bodies. Indeed, women athletes are capable of physically matching or outperforming most of the men in their lives, a fact that gives those men—unless they are secure enough in their own sexuality—no small measure of grief. The athletic woman is an autonomous woman because of her physical capability. Her body exists not to give pleasure to men, but for her own pleasure. And because theoretically she doesn't need the attention of men to confirm her status, the female athlete represents a threat to masculinity that must be marginalized. She may choose to have men in her life, but her relationship with the "sporting world" is through her own body, not theirs. She is a dangerous agent.

At the annual general meeting of the North American Society for the Sociology of Sport (NASSS) in 1995, American sportswriter and former pro basketball player Mariah Burton Nelson suggested that this marginalization is something all women athletes feel. "How many women athletes are lesbian?" she asked audience members. "One hundred and ten per cent."

Unfortunately, sometimes women athletes silence themselves. We saw an example of this in the previous chapter, with the beach volleyball players who defended the very system that controlled and exploited them. But they are by no means alone. At all ages, and all levels of play, we female athletes—both straight and gay—tie our hair up in ponytails, as if to say, "Look, I'm not a dyke—I have long hair." We drop the names of boyfriends (fake or real) or make a point of mentioning how good-looking we think some guy is if we sense we've been placed in "the wrong box." We employ all kinds of subtleties—smiling nicely, wearing makeup and "feminine" clothing, not correcting a man when he's wrong, laughing at jokes that aren't funny at all—just to reassure the men around us that we are heterosexual, that we do still need them for something. But we're just another example of Gloria Steinem's female impersonator.

Some women believe that these tactics are justified. After all, to bring about change, you have to play by the rules to some extent. I did it for years, and still do it on occasion. In meetings in Ottawa during the 1980s, when I joined with a number of other women to try to find ways to make sport more equitable, I was extremely outspoken and never minced words when I wanted my male colleagues to know what I thought of the system. But, away from those meetings, I was always a "nice girl"—happily accommodating them and complimenting them whenever we went cycling, skiing, running, or out to dinner together. It was as if I wanted to assure those egos I had beaten up in the meetings that I was harmless outside the boardroom.

But others can't countenance such behaviour. "I could have never done it," says Dr. Sandi Kirby, chair of the sociology department at the University of Winnipeg, a former Olympic rower, and an out lesbian in both sport and academia. "First of all, I just couldn't have lied in that way, and secondly, even if I could have forced myself to lie to someone ... I couldn't have passed. I don't look straight enough to pass."

While I was able to expose the "other side" of my personality—the person who could put aside, for at least a few hours, the skills needed to challenge inequitable policies and programs—Kirby was stuck with her "boardroom personality." She explains it like this: "While I was still in the closet, I always had to make sure the meetings were absolutely focused on the task at hand. I couldn't risk getting into personal kinds of conversations because I couldn't expose my personal life. As soon as the meeting was over, I left. I didn't socialize." Given how many decisions are made not at the boardroom table, but on the ski hill, the squash court, and the golf course, Kirby's behaviour put her at an extreme disadvantage. And this is true of any lesbian who believes the culture she lives in is homophobic.

Look, for instance, at what tennis star Martina Hingis has tried to do to French player Amélie Mauresmo, who came out while on the WTA circuit when she was still a teenager. At the Australian Open in 1999, Hingis described Mauresmo as "half a man," while she refers to herself as tennis's "spice girl." I wonder how Martina Navratilova, Hingis's namesake, feels about this uncalled-for disrespect and prejudice?

One lesbian who has been involved with Canadian hockey for years had lived a lie in a cover-up marriage. I asked her why she bothered when she'd had such great affairs with women. "Do you think I'd go anywhere in hockey if I showed up at the annual golf tournament with a woman?" she asked me angrily. "You can't do that in my sport. I intend to go places in my career."

This woman was engaging in what American coach and author Pat Griffin calls "the protective camouflage of female drag,"[1] which is part and parcel of a self-silencing and denying behaviour that women learn especially well in misogynist sports. Sport sociologist Nancy Theberge tells a particularly galling story about just this kind of behaviour taking place on a boat cruise for one of the top women's hockey teams in the country. "A player entertained the group by singing a misogynistic song," reported Theberge, "of the sort that is part of the male rugby culture, about a woman being violently assaulted sexually. Complete with rhythmic verse and refrain, the song was performed to apparent good cheer."[2]

Unlike these women and so many others like them—both straight and gay—Sandi Kirby has simply refused to be silenced. She came out in sport in 1982 at a leadership weekend on Saltspring Island. Her own experiences have given her great empathy for others who are pushed to the margins in sport, and today she writes extensively about lesbian struggles for human rights and is an advocate for all athletes—straight, gay, disabled, Aboriginal.

"The way lesbians get to where they want to go is to be twice as good," she says. "I knew I had to be the best athlete, then the best coach, the best administrator, because there wasn't any other vehicle to use except being really good at what I did. That way, you are unassailable on these fronts. ... It may look like this takes a lot of energy, but no more than it takes to pretend to be something you aren't, or pretending someone said something brilliant when he didn't."

Of course, Kirby is luckier than most, as a tenured professor, and although she was out before she received her tenure in 1992, she made a conscious decision to wait until then to start researching and writing about lesbian issues. For many lesbian athletes, however, there is the very real threat of job loss or other financial hardship, and also of being ostracized from the community they have called home. All too often, it is homophobes who are making decisions about sponsorship, carding status, and future coaching positions. Lesbians worry that a decision to come out will come back to haunt them, like a ghost from a past that continually needs to be banished.

Coming Out of the Sporting Closet

In the early 1980s, when it became public that American tennis great Billie Jean King was lesbian, she lost all her sponsors except one (and even that one put so many conditions on the sponsorship, she turned it down). And it also happened to Martina Navratilova, arguably the best female tennis player ever. She lost all her sponsors when she came out in 1981, and it was 1999 before Subaru finally picked her up as a spokesperson.

Many of the pioneers in this area know exactly what price can be exacted. Betty Baxter was the captain of Canada's volleyball team at the 1976 Montreal Olympics, the first female head coach of the sport, and one of country's earliest out lesbian athletes. In the 1980s, when the Canadian Volleyball Association found out she was gay, she was fired. She recalls that one member of the board of directors smashed his fist into the boardroom wall when he confronted Baxter about her sexuality. "If I'd known you were a dyke, I never would have hired you!" he screamed.

At a 1999 fundraiser during Gay Pride Week, Baxter told the audience, "The athletes are better today, but the system isn't. ... It's about power. Ultimately, sports, teams, leagues, who's the captain—that's all about figuring out who gets power. And being queer throws that. Unless you're quiet and ashamed and going to toe the line, you're a threat to the whole system."

Baxter went on to say that an athlete has to judge for him- or herself if it's safe to come out. Physical danger and the elimination of a gay athlete through backroom politics are still very real threats. She advised young athletes to go "like guerrillas" into sport. "You have to say, 'We're here, we're queer, and we're good. Do you want us on your team or not?'"

New Brunswick–born boxer Savoy Howe spoke at the same fundraiser. Howe had inadvertently outed herself in 1993 when she appeared in a TSN documentary, "For the Love of the Game," about gays and lesbians in sport. She was still in the closet to most of her family, which was how her parents wanted to keep it, but she figured the chances of any of them seeing one 45-minute segment of TSN were slim. Ironically, the documentary was so powerful that it was replayed many times—enough for all of her 68 Maritime cousins to see it. "That was probably the best thing that happened to me," she told the audience. "I had no choice. I'd outed myself, and people had to deal with it." Howe went on to win a silver medal at the Ontario boxing championships and become a high-level coach at a Toronto gym. "Most of [the women boxers at the gym] are gay," Howe told the audience, "and we let it be known that the straight world has to adjust to us."

More and more lesbian athletes are adopting Howe's attitude. Leslie* and Marsha* are long-time sports enthusiasts. Leslie's first love is golf, while Marsha's is hockey, and the two women met playing a pickup hockey game on a Friday night in rural Ontario. "I was flat on my back," Leslie told me, to describe the first time she saw Marsha. "I had never been on hockey skates until 1993, so I was still

* pseudonyms are being used here

learning. Marsha had been playing forever, and my girlfriend at the time introduced us. The three of us hung out together—the lesbian community in small-town Ontario is quite closed—but eventually Marsha and I became a couple. Now we live together, and we don't make any excuses for it."

I interviewed the two women at their favourite sports bar in rural Ontario. Sharing the booth was the couple they golf with—Jen and Brad. And they made quite the foursome. Marsha plays on the same hockey team she co-coaches with Brad, and Leslie and Jen also play on the team. The four socialize outside of sports as well. "Jen is our straight buddy," said Leslie affectionately. "She sticks up for us."

That night, Marsha and Leslie let Jen and Brad in on a secret neither of them had known: More than half the team is gay. Both initially looked a little shocked, but they quickly recovered and said it didn't matter to them; they only wanted to have good people in their lives. Still, they wondered why they hadn't known this before. "There's a separate social life for lesbians," Marsha explained. "We have our own dinner parties, our own way we socialize with each other. Especially up here, because in public it's not easy for us. Our neighbours shun us, turn their backs when we say hello. I lose business because I am a lesbian, and we certainly don't go walking down the street holding hands. It's nice to just be who we are with these other women."

I wanted to know why Marsha and Leslie thought so many lesbians feel attracted to sport. Certainly, gay people are in every walk of life, but it is unlikely that half of the National Ballet of Canada or the Toronto Symphony Orchestra is lesbian. "It's the social life," said Marsha. "When you've got to hide all your life, it's a relief not to have to do so. If we have a dance, I can dance with Leslie. In our group, there are more gay couples, but there are straight couples too, and they're completely accepting of us."

"It's a comfort level," added Leslie. "When we are aware of the comfort level of the other players, it feels good."

Still, I wonder, why sport? Why not bridge, or … well, what else is there? When you think about it, how many places *are* there where women can get together purely for their own interests, pleasure, and the satisfaction of being among other women? And let's face it, gay lovemaking is about pleasure, not procreation. Many straight women, on the other hand, find much of their lives taken up with childbearing and the subsequent needs of the family. They help out at funerals, weddings, and births, and in the past, they have joined the auxiliary arms of male organizations, particularly religious organizations. Would a gay woman want to join a ladies' auxiliary? Would she even be allowed to without a husband providing her with some legitimacy? So many traditional female organizations aren't about female pleasure and living life richly, but about helping others and submerging the self. We learn to be dutiful women in such organizations—not pleasure-seeking athletes.

Today, women still have next to no public venues in which they can gather in groups for their own benefit. Men have always had baseball diamonds, hockey rinks, soccer pitches, basketball courts, bars, taverns, street corners, religious edifices, service groups, corporations, boards of directors—the list goes on and on. Perhaps this is one of the reasons behind the success of all-female book clubs and the growth in women's organized sport. Women had to create these spaces and occupy them without any male intrusion. It doesn't happen very often. They may not literally own these public spaces, but their bodies take ownership over them.

If a woman feels like an outsider in the first place because of her sexual preference, and if, as Sandi Kirby points out, she has to develop great strengths to achieve her goals through merit instead of through her relationships with men, why wouldn't she be attracted to sport? It's a great place to be a strong woman and meet others like you (especially in team sports, where you are guaranteed a minimum number of potential friends and lovers). As University of Minnesota sport sociologist Mary Jo Kane says of team sports, "At their best, they foster a sense of community based on cooperation, mutual support and group identity."[3]

In *Higher Goals*, Nancy Theberge found several lesbians on the team she studied and the teams it played against. In the 1980s, the coach admitted, he had had a policy of excluding lesbians, but his thinking started to change as he began meeting more lesbians—and liking them. He soon also realized that he would be at a competitive disadvantage if he continued practising his policy of exclusion, which is now against the law. Now the players' lovers—male and female—travel with the team and play valuable supportive roles. Theberge also found that the team had a lesbian following, women who sat as a group at certain games. She defined the present atmosphere on the team as "liberal humanistic," an environment where straight and gay women are seen as "the same." This is certainly a welcome change from being fearful and closeted, but Theberge quotes two lesbian sport sociologists, Helen Lenskyj and Mary Jo Kane, who argue that this attitude still "denies the more radical political potential of sport as an arena where women learn respect, love, and a passionate commitment for one another as women."[4] And more and more lesbian athletes are beginning to view sport this way. They are determined to be themselves and have people accept them as they are.

Georgette Reed, a bobsledder and 13-time Canadian shotput champion, is a good example. "The women on the bobsled team did a photo spread with a Canadian fashion magazine," she told me. "I wasn't asked to be in it, and I wouldn't [have wanted] to be because some of the women pile on the makeup like Tammy Faye Baker. Women's sport is not about being a stupid Barbie doll and playing up to the coach. It's about embracing life, being yourself, and living for your dreams."

Reed is the daughter of legendary CFLer George Reed, and fans who know them both say she's bigger and stronger than her father. She says she didn't have to come out, because she was never really "in." Still, she knows that homophobia in sport is real, and she believes it has had a devastating impact. "They [other female athletes] don't let me put my arm around them anymore in the weight room," she said. "There's no closeness that used to be so much a part of sport."

Another internationally recognized athlete I know says she's been out to her friends and close teammates for several years, but she wouldn't do as Mark Tewksbury did and come out nationally. Interestingly, she says it's not the public's homophobic attitude that worries her. "The only homophobia I have to be afraid of is my own," she says. "I've never been discriminated against or threatened because I'm gay, but my own homophobia … keeps telling me to be quiet."

If her own homophobia is keeping her from being fully honest about herself, why doesn't she simply face it and come out? "I don't want to get hurt," she replies immediately. Even though she hasn't personally had any discriminatory experiences, she admits that she doesn't know "who's really out there."

This attitude is fairly typical, and you hear such comments from the mouths of just as many straight women as gay. After all, the more public a woman is, the more she places herself in the line of fire. Isn't this why so many women stay quiet about their lives and beliefs? Take what happened in 1998, when Canadians saw firsthand what can happen to a woman who dares to challenge the male power structure in sport.

The Case of Shannon Miller, Angela James, and the Canadian Hockey Association

Shannon Miller had been the coach of the national women's hockey team for three years. For most of that time, she worked as a member of the Calgary Police Department and was expected to combine her full-time job and her coaching duties—the latter paying an annual honorarium of less than $6,000—and produce a team of world champions. (One former men's coach, Andy Murray, told me he was paid $70,000 at the time.) When women's hockey became an Olympic medal sport in 1998, the Canadian Hockey Association finally decided it might be time to start paying the team's coach an actual salary. In return, Miller knew she was expected to put together a team of "uncontroversial" women to bring home a gold medal from Nagano.

In the fall of 1997, every woman who was invited to the six-month training camp prior to the Olympics had to sign a contract with the

CHA. Anyone who didn't sign wouldn't be covered by the CHA's insurance policy, and therefore would not be allowed to step onto the ice. CHA spokespeople had earlier said the association would "pay the women what the men were receiving, $15,000 to $20,000," for the pre-Olympic training camp. But that wasn't quite how it worked out.

Each woman who played on the team in 1997 received $5,000 from the Canadian Olympic Association as a bonus for having won the world championships. Somehow, the CHA came to view this money as part of its contribution to the women's training camp salaries. No one from the 1997 team had ever imagined that she would in effect have to give her $5,000 to the CHA before she'd be allowed to play on the Olympic team. It was like working two part-time jobs, only to have one employer tell you that he was going to count the salary paid by the other employer as his.

In the end, veteran players received just $237 a month from the CHA, for a total of $1,422 for the six months of the training camp. With their Sport Canada carding money, the total came to $6,282— considerably less than the $15,000 to $20,000 the CHA had been bragging about. Even if the COA grants were included, the total for the entire training camp still came to only $11,282.

Shannon Miller says the women were shocked and felt cheated, but in the end, they decided to sign the contract anyway. "I told them they had every right to be angry, every right to refuse to play," Miller said months later. "But we had six months to prepare to win a gold medal, and who knew what would happen if they protested."

The women were already on shaky ground. One lesbian on the national team estimated that one-third of the team, at the time, was gay. There is an unspoken rule in much of sport and the military: Don't ask, don't tell. Don't ask me if I'm gay, and I won't tell you that I am. But when 20 women stand up and tell an all-male organization that they've been cheated, the homophobic innuendos about dykes and ball-breakers start to surface. If you're going to be a woman—straight or gay—in such a culture, you learn how to be silent—or take the fall.

Unfortunately for Miller, she had soon been singled out by the CHA as a troublemaker, a rogue female missile who had obviously lost her way. She didn't advise the team to go public with their complaints about the CHA; she told them their job was to win a gold medal. But Miller always carries a certain confidence and body language that says in no uncertain terms that you'd better not mess with her. When she made the decision to cut a veteran player, Angela James, from the team, all hell broke loose. James had a meeting with officials from the CHA to appeal Miller's decision. The next day, sports pages across the country began publishing allegations that Miller was having an affair with one of her team members. James repeatedly declared that she had made no such claims, and that she had simply passed on a rumour that a CHA staff member was involved with a player on the women's team. She also stressed that the meeting was supposed to be confidential, and alleged that the CHA itself leaked the details of the meeting to the press.

"I told Bob [Nicholson, the CHA's vice-president of operations] I would take a lie detector test to prove that I did not have an inappropriate relationship with a team member," says Miller, who still bristles when the subject of her integrity is brought up. "He kept brushing it off, but it was someone in the CHA who floated those rumours to the press in the first place, and that person should have taken the test with me, because what [he] said was completely false."

In the end, the talented but troubled Canadian team lost the gold medal to the feisty Americans, Miller lost her job, and the full-time coaching position was axed. The team members did eventually challenge the CHA and demand the return of their $5,000, but they were able to get only half of it back. And the whole sordid story became a perfect example of how allegations of lesbianism in sport can be used to put athletes and coaches in their place.

HP, LP, and NP

Angela James must have been particularly horrified to find herself at the heart of the controversy surrounding Shannon Miller. James first came out in Scott Russell's book *Ice Time*, published in the fall of 2000, where she is unapologetic about her sexual preference. "I've always been honest about who I am," she told Russell. To have been partly the cause of Miller's downfall, albeit unintentionally, must have been difficult for her. And while she was devastated when she was cut from the 1998 Olympic team, she later learned why her performance fell short: She had been suffering from Graves' disease, which causes hyperthyroidism, and in James contributed to significant fatigue, weight loss, and general ill health. Eventually, James had her condition diagnosed and treated, and she made the team again for a series of exhibition games in 2000. She popped the final goal in the deciding game of one tournament before she retired from international competition for good. But what's most important about the Angela James story is the fact that she was a pioneer of women's hockey in Canada.

James was one of five children from a single-parent home in the low-cost housing projects of Toronto's Flemingdon Park neighbourhood. Her mother is white, her father black. When she started playing hockey in the early 1970s, there were no teams near her for girls, and her mother didn't have a car to drive the long distances girls had to travel then if they wanted to play. James initially played on the local boys' team, but when she became the leading scorer, the fathers of her teammates demanded she be banned from playing. Officials agreed, and James and her mother were reduced to catching buses to the forlorn outskirts of the city, where girls were granted ice time at dangerously late hours. The teams she played on couldn't match her skill level, so as soon as it was possible for her to do so, she graduated to senior women's hockey and the Toronto Aeros (now the Beatrice Aeros). Eventually, James became the winningest woman in the history of international hockey.

All the time she was playing international hockey, James studied and worked to make a future for herself when her playing days were over. She attended Seneca College's sports administration course, and also organized and coached several hockey camps. Today, girls and women from all over clamour to attend her camps, and she runs the recreation program at Seneca. She is as good a coach as she was a player.

With her quick comebacks, saucy smile, beautiful bronze skin, and athlete's body, James had no trouble attracting legions of fans. But she's no Barbie doll. When I interviewed her in the winter of 1999, she weighed nearly 170 pounds, something she viewed as a sign of her strength and power. Her hair was so short it was nearly a brush cut, and she walked with a John Wayne swagger that cut a swath through the bar at the rink, where I met her after a game. Hockey bag in tow, she threw out friendly barbs to the guys who had just watched her play. She couldn't have been more a hockey player if she'd tried.

But Angela James, greatest of the great, pioneer of the pioneers, role model for all children—male and female, gay and straight, black and white—has never attracted a single major corporate sponsor who wanted to promote her as an individual. For all she has meant to women's hockey, she is not viewed as a desirable product to endorse.

Why? Hockey is certainly one of the most popular women's sports in Canada. But even as the sport has grown and sponsorship emerged, the unspoken ponytail rule has been enforced, not to mention the preference for a white face to accompany it. Women on the national team speak of high-profile, low-profile, and even no-profile athletes— HP, LP, and NP, in the language of sport marketers. "The high-profile ones are usually the pretty ones," said one athlete who did not want to be identified. "They get most of the contracts and sponsorships."

The CHA chose Cassie Campbell, a former fashion model, to adorn posters promoting both the 1997 world championships in Kitchener and the CHA's own anti-harassment policy. She also appeared on the covers of *Elm Street* and *Chatelaine* before the 1998 Nagano Olympics. Not surprisingly, as the public became more familiar with her image, Campbell received even more sponsorships; meanwhile, the less conventionally appealing women went without.

In the fall of 1999, the director of the CHA's High Performance Program, Denis Hinault, told me that the organization would not be using Campbell to advertise its programs again. Instead, it would give some of the other women on the team some much-needed exposure.

But in the spring of 2000, the CHA came out with yet another promotional video starring Campbell. This one paired her with Bobby Orr and Mike Bossy—great former NHL players. The program this video was promoting, "Chevrolet Safe and Fun Hockey," was also publicized in full-page ads in popular Canadian magazines. Campbell was even featured on a TSN series on Canadian sport history, although there are other women on the team who have outperformed her who were not included in the documentary.

No one acknowledges it publicly, but the "dykier" women will probably always remain LP or NP because they're not straight, or at least not perceived as straight. And that alone keeps them out of the running for sponsorships. The decision-makers believe parents won't send their daughters into a sport that has lesbians in it, so sponsors will not back gay women. One coach of a top women's team told me that he would lose hundreds of thousands of dollars in sponsorship money if the women on his team came out. A national team member who wouldn't be named said it's a given that lesbians won't receive sponsorship money: "It's just something you live with if you want to play."

In contrast to this is how heterosexuality is rewarded. One of the most common ways for a female athlete to assure acceptability for corporate sponsorships is to have a public, sexual relationship with a man, particularly a man in a position of power in her sport. It gives a heterosexual stamp of approval, and effectively ensures that she'll never be stigmatized with the dreaded lesbian label.

But what the CHA—and so many other organizations like it—has overlooked is female players' appeal to any fan who puts athletic ability above traditional physical attractiveness. Indeed, one wonders why any of this even matters in a sport where players wear helmets and significant body padding. At the 2000 Women's World Hockey Championships in Mississauga, Ontario, the packed stands held some pretty diverse groups of fans. In terms of gender, they appeared to be split pretty much down the middle, and there were as many people over the age of 30 as under. Many groups were adults with male and female children, and the girls were often decked out in their own team jerseys, screaming the names of their favourite players. And, of course, there were many groups that were all female adults.

With its strong homophobic sensibility, sport continues to deny the lesbian and gay market despite the fact that these groups have strong purchasing power. Even sports that have traditionally been a big draw among lesbians, such as women's golf, have opted to change their image rather than embrace the lesbian presence.

Every year in Palm Springs when the Nabisco Dinah Shore LPGA event occurs, this Republican town becomes a gay-positive, happening place. As 20,000 lesbians arrive, all the rental cars are snapped up, hotels are completely booked, and restaurants are packed; lesbians now contribute one-eighth of Palm Springs's annual tourist revenue.

Still, despite being a capitalist's dream, the LPGA has distanced itself from its own lesbian following. Lesbians are referred to as "an image problem," and in 1995 CBS promoted the LPGA's "Mother's Day Special," saying they wanted to promote "family entertainment."[5] Last year, The Globe and Mail ran a feature on how women golfers have taken to travelling with beauty consultants. Lori Kane talked about how important it was for her to have the consultant along, and how she could never get along on the green without hairspray. I couldn't help wondering if the article was meant to counterbalance the lesbian look of the sport.

And we certainly don't see a culture that fawns over women golfers the way tennis, for instance, has done over so many of its female players. Women golfers tend to be older, heavier and squatter, and wear far more clothes. They are not easily objectified sexually because they don't fit the limited definition of what a female athlete is supposed to look like these days; that is, the athletic version of a fashion model. Yet this is precisely why golf—and hockey, for that matter—has such a strong lesbian following. Both sports are so un-Barbie-dollish and so unconstrained by heterosexual rules.

In Los Angeles, the new women's pro basketball team has realized just how silly it is to appeal only to conventional heterosexuals. In May 2001, Diane Pucin of the Los Angeles Times reported that the Sparks had partnered with Girl Bar, a lesbian social club that meets at the

Factory, a West Hollywood bar. After one game, the team members headed over with free pennants, keychains, and team notebooks. By the end of the evening, they'd signed up a new batch of season's ticket holders.

Pucin also notes that, in the past, TV cameras had managed to ignore the magic of women's basketball—but that all changed when the players showed up at the Factory. That Friday night, they were the talk of the town on TV, radio, and in the print media. Sandy Sachs, co-founder of Girl Bar, was surprised when Sparks general manager Penny Toler first called and suggested they work together. Whenever Sachs herself had suggested that women's sports and lesbian organizations were a good fit, she'd received a rather cool reception. For years she has approached the organizers of the Dinah Shore tournament in Rancho Mirage with the idea of jointly promoting weekend packages for spectators. But "the LPGA wants nothing to do with us," Sachs said.

But Toler is perhaps more pragmatic. "This isn't about marketing to sexual lifestyles," she said. "It's about marketing to a group of people we think will buy tickets." She believes the Sparks are making the most of people who live a particular lifestyle and are normally overlooked.

And Toler must be on to something. Like the Women's World Hockey Championships, Sparks games attract a diverse crowd. Both boys and girls wear Lisa Leslie jerseys, and lesbian couples come with their kids. They're families—and even if certain religious groups would never include them, the Sparks do.

"We've gotten a couple of negative calls," says Sparks president Johnny Buss. "That's too bad, but all we're doing is adding to the marketing we've always done. We've reached the point now where we can be smarter about our marketing. We can target particular groups. Our market is girls age 12 to 14. It's also these women."

DeLisha Milton, a Sparks player, said it made perfect sense to her that the team would join with Girl Bar. "We're in Los Angeles, which is one of the most diverse places in the world," Milton pointed out. "We want everybody to come to our games: blacks, whites, men, women, people who have alternative lifestyles. We've got plenty of room for anybody who wants to watch us play. If we want to keep getting paid to play basketball, we've got to get fans. That's what we're doing: getting fans to come to our games. That's all."

Toler says that people who can't accept that sport should be as diversified as the culture we live in need to discover the new millennium. "Women's sports have moved beyond the old stereotypes," she explains. "We don't sell tickets for section D, rows 1 to 4, for black fans, and section C, rows 1 to 4, for white fans, and section F, rows 1 to 4, for lesbian fans. We just want fans. We've reached out to many different parts of this city looking for fans."

And if moral values are going to be debated, Pucin added in her original article, let's talk about men's sport for a while. "How many basketball fans would ever have a problem taking their daughters and sons to Laker games?" she wrote. "Say a Laker–Trail Blazer game? A game where Shawn Kemp plays? You know Kemp? He has fathered a number of children by a number of mothers. His season came to an early end when he entered a drug rehabilitation program."

The Sparks are doing something exciting and positive, and the Women's National Basketball Association (WNBA) now has what is called "an inclusive marketing strategy" that is gay-positive. And I don't think they're alone. As Sandi Kirby and I end a long-distance conversation and she can finally go back to giving the doubles tennis match she's been watching her full attention, she tells me, "You know, Martina [Navratilova] has this amazing vein that runs the length of her bicep. She is truly unbelievable. Forty-five and still such a phenomenal athlete. I love her Subaru car commercials too."

I think Martina's vein and bicep are amazing too. In fact, when I think about it, Martina's been one of my superheroes for decades. Just imagine how incredible it must feel to be Martina Navratilova.

Part ii   Exploiting the Whole Woman

5   Whose Body Is This?

Women Athletes in the Media

Gabrielle Reece didn't make the U.S. Olympic beach volleyball team for the Sydney Games, but she did make the cover of the January 2001 issue of *Playboy*. In the text of the piece, Reece says, "I don't think of the images [in the interior spread] as sexual. ... Our goal was to shoot the body as a form. They're more a statement that a woman can be really powerful, really feminine, really natural and really confident and just put it out there. No big deal. I'm not trying to say, 'Check me out.'"

But of course *Playboy*'s whole raison d'être is to be checked out—at the checkout counter, by millions of men around the world each month. And does anyone really believe the magazine is interested in showing women as powerful, natural, and confident? It's not like it intersperses nude shots of women with images of them debating in a legislature, taking down criminals, or presiding over the World Court. Nor does it offer in-depth articles about women fighting the religious right or protesting cuts to health care. It doesn't even tell its readers how women performed at the Olympics. It's quite amazing that there is a never-ending demand for *Playboy*, given that it has been delivering the same product, over and over and over, for so many years. The magazine offered to pay tennis player Anna Kournikova $10 million to do a photo spread because they knew the issue would sell out. She refused. But Kournikova would probably have been the 5,000th pretty blonde woman to pose nude for them.

By the time all the computer enhancements are done, she will look, more or less, identical to the 5,000 other blonde *Playboy* bunnies who've turned up in the magazine. Why don't these eager guys just get a back-issue—any one would do—and paste in Kournikova's face? It would be about as realistic as the photo spread, should one ever appear.

I looked at Gabrielle Reece's spread with an American photographer, and he candidly told me how he and his colleagues convince women to do what the photographers want. "The most important part of the process is to make her think everything is her idea," he said. "So when [Reece] uses the [first-person] plural, as in 'our goal,' she's doing exactly what the photographer wants. She's imagining she has some say in the shot. The whole idea, though, is to get her to do things she wouldn't have thought of herself, and wouldn't necessarily initially want to do."

This does seem to be the case. It's pretty hard to imagine how Reece could think the words "really powerful" describe the woman in the photos. The facial and bust shots have the typical "come hither" look found in all *Playboy* spreads. One photo has a fully nude Reece, a former model, backed up against a wall, dripping with water and staring at the camera—a symbolically trapped woman if ever I've seen one. The male fantasy behind these shots—one with her bending over and the other with a cactus leaf (looking like a set of serrated knives) pointing to her rectum—needs no explanation. There is no question that Reece is strong and powerful, but in these shots she looks limp and completely lacking physical power. In fact, there is only one image of her doing anything remotely active— running on the beach—and even then we get to see none of her muscles or sinewy strength.

By contrast, in her 1997 autobiography, *Big Girl in the Middle*, Reece looks like most elite women athletes. In the cover photo, she has obvious muscles, a determined, angry look on her face, big thighs, and a flat chest (courtesy of her sports bra). Photos inside the book show her as forceful, active, grimacing and wincing as she returns shots.

Somewhere along the line, Reece seems to have come to believe that she needs to qualify the fact that she is strong and confident. When she tells *Playboy* that women "can be really powerful, really feminine," it's an apology—subtle reassurance that she's not so strong that she can get by without male approval. And she's not alone in this. As women athletes become stronger, many compensate by trudging out that old chestnut, "But I'm feminine too." Nearly every woman in the *Maxim* shots I described in chapter 3, for example, used this phrase as a qualifier. But if they are apologizing for having stepped out of line by being strong, where exactly is this power that Reece wants to refer to? Or is she talking about the power to manipulate herself to please others? She has certainly learned how to place herself on the public auction block.

In the past, people went to watch athletes play. The Sunnyside Ladies Softball League had thousands of fans in the 1930s and '40s. In some years, their gate receipts surpassed those of every men's team in Toronto. But an outing to the ball diamond was a real social event; it was centred around watching a sports event, but when the game was over, people strolled along the beach, they danced at the Palais Royale ... citizens were highly social beings who loved to watch a good ball game.

Since the advent of television, we now live in a culture that has become obsessed with the "watching" part of the equation and not the "doing" part. Traditionally, many sports were rooted in transportation. People ran, skied, canoed, rowed, swam, rode horses—and later bicycles—mainly because they had to get from A to B, not because someone wanted to watch them. There were no "fans" as we know them—vicarious, passive consumers—but that didn't keep the body and the spirit from responding fully to the sensation of being free in space and time. Nor did it hinder many impromptu competitions.

When sport is about taking the body somewhere, it often also becomes about transporting the spirit into what I call the foreign land that athletes visit, where time stands still and great human effort takes precedence. This is a place of poetry and near perfection, but it's also a land that's intensely private. The athlete must focus on his or her race to the exclusion of all other distractions. If you watch the slow-motion replay of any Olympic race, you will see the focused faces of athletes. They are aware of other people in the race, of course, but the experience of the movement is paradoxically a highly private endeavour.

Few people understand sport this way. Today, fans think of it as intensely public, even to the point of believing they are part of the team they are watching. I believe television images that show the effort in an athlete's body and face create an intense but unconscious intimacy. These images are presented to viewers who are all too often starved for intimacy in their own lives and have to settle for fleeting moments that disappear when their televisions are turned off. Most people have lost the "realness" of their own bodies. So sport has become a place that is not about celebrating the athletic body—male or female—but about *borrowing* the athletic body to try to satisfy an insatiable hunger in the spectator. I don't know why there is such hunger for the sporting body, why people want to watch instead of participate. They could get the realness of their own bodies back if they tried living in them instead of just existing. But in our exceedingly sedentary, mechanized, and voyeuristic culture, this suspension of realness has become the norm.

In our present mediated sporting culture, it is not the athlete who matters, but the person who watches the athlete. Demographic studies tell us that most viewers of sport are men, and all those who are in the business of marketing sport understand that the athletic body—particularly today's emerging female athletic body—is a valuable commodity, a product to be sold like any other.

It wasn't always this way. Historically, representations of the human form tended more toward idealization than commodification. Michelangelo, for one, believed that "the artist is not the creator of the Ideas he conceives, rather he finds them in the natural world, reflecting the absolute Idea, which for the artist is beauty." Nature did not just inspire, it created, and the artist acted as the interpreter or conduit.

Today, the idealized body, which is most often the athletic body, is understood in a much different way in most mainstream Western cultures. Athletes are on public display: They exist to excite and entice the viewer. And even when they are not competing, athletes are treated as little more than a means to an end. They are sexualized objects whose main use is to sell track shoes or expensive tennis rackets.

This "publicization" of athletes can be especially damaging for women. We have already seen that women take great chances when they decide to live aggressively and vigorously in the public realm (though it is important to note that a woman is still safer in the public realm than in the domestic domain, where most of the abuse of women occurs). Once a woman enters the public realm, she no longer belongs solely to herself. All too often, if her body meets the very confining set of physical standards that are currently exalted, our culture steals her very sexuality, transforming her into an object of male fantasy. And while some women athletes read this culture correctly and use it to their financial advantage, others find themselves reduced to little more than products to be consumed and forgotten once a new and younger product comes along.

Of course, there *is* power in being able to command a significant amount of money for photos of your body, and this should not be discounted in a culture that revolves around money and idealized bodies the way ours does. But is this the kind of power that actually aids women? We get paid only if we open our legs, reveal our breasts, bend over, or stand silently looking like schoolgirls who couldn't pass a simple spelling test. Why is this called power? Is it not just the power we imagine we have over men when they are sexually attracted to our bodies? Ultimately, what kind of power is that in a world that is still so dominated by men? Added to this is the poisoned environment that's created when so much sexual objectification takes place. As we shall see in the next chapter, sport has a terrible history of coaches sexually abusing female athletes. Do we want to put another generation of girls at risk by teaching them that good girls cooperate and do what they are told by the men in charge?

And there is something else going on here—something that, as a female athlete, I find very disturbing. Because so many women have chosen to be portrayed as sex objects, life is more difficult for those of us who would prefer to be seen as whole people.

As a female cyclist, I have noticed a difference in male attitudes over the past few years. In the summer, I like to ride early, before the day gets too hot and too many people are awake. By the time I'm nearly finished a few hours later, more people are out and about on Toronto's streets, and there will inevitably be a guy in a car who needs to insert his presence into my experience. He will invariably cut me off, honk very loudly, gun the engine as he passes me, or just yell, "Get off the fucking road!" Sometimes he will also feel compelled to comment on how I look. And no matter how many times this happens, I am always taken by surprise. Why do so many men feel the need to comment openly about a complete stranger's body? Do they not understand sport as a private experience that should be respected as such? Or is the mere presence of an active female body in the public realm reason enough to believe one has some sort of right to it?

In his book *Human Rights as Politics and Idolatry*, Michael Ignatieff argues for a "negative liberty," one that gives people freedom to not be interfered with. He believes that human rights are of such great importance because they protect human agency, which subsequently allows us to live our lives fully and pursue our goals. One would think that the simple right to ride a bicycle without a man inserting himself into that experience—especially in a pig-headed way—would, by now, be something women could take for granted.[1]

Given how women, and especially athletic women, are sexualized by our culture, I wonder if it is possible for men to interpret a sweaty female body in Lycra as anything other than a sexual fantasy. Have we ever asked the question: How does the constant objectification of the public female body rob that body of its own agency? Does it ever occur to our culture that a strong female body has the right to take up public space without being subjected to public comment from men? Is it because public space has always been dominated by men that the strong female body seems an intrusion? When women are exhibiting strength, men may feel displaced or diminished. In response, they diminish the women in turn by using sexual and sexist language, thus putting them "in their place" and negating the power that sport has bestowed. Do those men feel better now?

Be a Good Girl and Smile

Sadly, I believe that every time a woman athlete poses nude, she makes it harder for the rest of us to have a respected and private experience while we try to enjoy our sport. And Gabrielle Reece has plenty of company these days when it comes to the publicly mediated body. Two days after the Sydney Olympics ended, the *Calgary Herald* quoted the organizer of the 2001 World Track and Field Championships in Edmonton as saying that women's pole vault, a new event at both the Olympics and the world championships, would "get good billing." And why was that? "The Australian Tatiana Grigorieva, the absolutely gorgeous Australian pole vaulter," would grace the cover of the official program for the competition, Jack Agrios told the *Herald*. "The attraction of the women's pole vault will help the promotion of our event considerably," he explained.

As the world championships wound up, *The Globe and Mail* ran a story entitled "Pole Vaulting Fashion Is All T and A: Technology and Advancement." The accompanying photograph of Grigorieva was shot from a camera position below her, emphasizing the crotch area as she prepares to vault in what the cutline refers to as "some of the skimpiest fashions in sport." In the body of the article, a Nike spokeswoman, Michelle Noble, is quoted as saying, "The sports where you see the most bare middles are the ones where overheating is a factor, and you want as little restriction as possible."

This is simply untrue. In cycling and rowing—two sports where overheating is a far greater problem than it is in pole vaulting (extremely low on the overheating scale)—competitors cover their midriffs and manage to do just fine. In the marathon, which is perhaps the worst sport for overheating, many great athletes—male and female—have been able to complete the run successfully without wearing bikinis.

But of course Jack Agrios was not wrong: The women's pole vault did "get good billing," at both the world championships and the Olympics. Grigorieva's face was everywhere leading up to and during the Games. In one ad, she is shown with her eyes closed lying back on a cloud—not vaulting powerfully over a high bar—in what look like her bra and underwear. She also did a full-frontal nude spread for the *Sydney Dreams* book of Australian athletes. Even during competition, Grigorieva and most other female athletes didn't cover up when the camera was on them, despite some nights of cold, constant rain in Sydney. But at least they had a choice. Unlike the beach volleyball players, they could have worn longer shorts, a top with sleeves, or tights if they'd wanted to.

Grigorieva ended up fourth at the 2001 World Championships and won a silver at the Olympics, and while she received much more attention than any other finisher—do we even remember that the American Stacy Dragila won the gold?—Grigorieva must still be looking over her shoulder. Sooner or later (and probably sooner), she will be replaced by a younger woman who will wear something skimpier or do more revealing nude shots, and then what? None of these pin-up types will ever be a Wilma Rudolph or an Evelyn Ashford—elegant, beautiful athletes who made it on talent and hard work, and therefore have earned a place in our hearts forever.

Kevin Blackistone, a columnist for the *Dallas Morning News*, argues that it's fruitless to try to separate sexuality from the athletic body—it's there whether we are talking about men or women. He believes that it's how this reality is accepted by both athletes and the media that matters. "I think it's very unfair to women, and I also think it may suggest to younger women athletes that this is the only way you can succeed in sports—by your looks. I still think women athletes are taken seriously when they achieve, and if they're not on a good team, no one pays any attention. The exception to this, of course, is … Grigorieva. She cashed in on her perceived good looks before the Games by posing in the nude photo shoot with a number of other Olympic athletes."

This isn't to say that Grigorieva was victimized in any way. She voluntarily entered into agreements to pose nude, and she was no doubt well compensated financially. But did it cost her in other ways? I doubt that any man who viewed her nude photos could say how high she vaulted in the Games, or even where she placed. And among the male journalists I talked to, she was dismissed with either mockery or self-righteous anger, though they all wanted a chance to check out her nude photos in *Sydney Dreams*.

The Managed Woman

Tatiana Grigorieva is still luckier than most, because she had a choice. Many female athletes have no control over how they are depicted and are not financially rewarded when their images are reproduced. On November 4, 2000, *The Globe and Mail*'s coverage of the annual Skate Canada competition included a photo of a female skater, legs spread wide, with her crotch as the focal point. Although the newspaper's editors surely had plenty of shots to choose from, they chose one that turned the skater from a powerful, artistic, sensual athlete into a sex object. Yet it's unfair to reproach only *The Globe*; virtually all commercial images of young female bodies in our culture show them as sexual objects.

This trend got so out of control in ice dancing that in January 2002, the International Skating Union (ISU) held a press conference to express their dislike of what they call "obscene" and "gynecological" moves by skaters and the subsequent photographs that are printed the next day in newspapers around the world. U.S. judge Nancy Meiss commented, "If I want a young man waving his partner's assets in my face, I can rent a porn movie. The males are acting like pimps."[2]

A quick flip through a coffee-table book called *The History of the Olympics* shows how the female body has been portrayed through the past century of the Games. The first crotch shot is a 1972 photo of Heide Rosendahl of Germany winning the long jump. But even that image conveys Rosendahl's great power and concentration, and the uniforms athletes wore at the time didn't make the crotch a focal point the way skimpy Lycra shorts and leotards do today.

As the Games became increasingly commercialized, women's outfits grew smaller and smaller, and photos that focused on their crotches and butts became ever more frequent. In 1976, *Maclean's* magazine printed an absolutely pornographic photo of the Soviet gymnast Olga Korbut on the balance beam. By then, female gymnasts were wearing smaller, higher-cut leotards with only centimetres of Lycra over the crotch. In 1996, the same magazine ran photos of two sprinters, the American Michael Johnson and France's Marie-José Perec. But while Johnson was photographed from the front, looking powerful and strong, Perec was photographed from behind. Her shorts might as well have been a G-string for all they covered.

Most shots of female athletes focus exclusively on the crotch and butt, while breasts are the focus when non-athletic women are depicted. Typically, women athletes are quite small-breasted—a byproduct of greater physical efficiency and leanness, but not the North American ideal when the female body is offered up for male viewing and consumption, so those who serve up images of female athletes usually downplay their "disappointing" busts. The watcher is not always accommodated when reality, as opposed to fantasy, takes centre stage.

Crotch shots, however, do fit the fantasy bill. Sport is so dynamic and the movement so diverse that legs are going to fly in all directions, depending on the sport. Gymnasts, figure skaters, and synchronized swimmers in particular have their legs splayed during much of the performance. Costumes in all three sports have grown so small that now only a few centimetres of Lycra cover the genital area. And more and more often, the people performing the revealing routines in these revealing costumes are no more than girls—a highly disturbing trend I will discuss in more detail in the next chapter.

Were all these crotch shots used as just part of a series of photo-graphs showing women athletes in a full range of human movement, perhaps there wouldn't be such a problem. But women athletes disappear from the media's radar screen once the Olympic Games are over, so these shots are never seen as part of a whole. This type of isolating photography pretends that there aren't strong female bodies playing sports all the time, and instead suggests that just these few parts of the female body are engaged in what can be seen as sexually objectifying acts.

One variation on this theme, which I believe is fun and gives sexual power back to women, is the trend in sports where aerodynamics is crucial and therefore male and female uniforms are identical. Canada's long-track speed skating team leading up to the 2002 Salt Lake City Olympics had near-transparent yellow suits and they took to wearing colourful underwear underneath. They all look sexy and in charge of their bodies. Speed skaters, male or female, have extraordinarily strong glutes that look somewhat androgynous. The suits and underwear combination tells us a lot about a group of athletes who know they're strong, and want to have some fun with this fact. After all, these great butts are attached to massively strong legs that leave no question as to who is really in charge of this body

Where else can we find a model for media, both print and electronic, that will encompass the athletic female body in its entirety? When I went to address graduate students at the Norwegian University of Sport and Physical Education in Oslo in December 2000, I was amazed to see that women athletes are front-page news in Scandinavia. As I walked around the Copenhagen airport, waiting for my Oslo flight, I noticed that the cover story of every Danish newspaper was about the national women's handball team. Photos of women looking big, strong, and aggressive greeted international travellers. I have seen similar images that celebrate the strong and brash female athlete in all the Scandinavian countries, especially Norway.

Could this be due to the fact that women play a much greater role in Scandinavian public life? By the mid-1990s, the parliaments of Sweden and Norway were approximately 40% female. Finland was the first country in the world to have a woman sitting in parliament, and in 1980, Vigdís Finnbogadóttir became the first female president of Iceland. Sports coverage reflects this greater acceptance of women in Scandinavian society. Total equality has not yet been achieved, but these countries are far more advanced than the rest of the world.

Unfortunately for those of us in North America, women here don't, for the most part, hold positions of power, and they are certainly not accepted as strong, aggressive individuals the way Scandinavian women are. Until that changes, I fear we'll continue to find our female athletes gracing the covers of *Playboy* and *Maxim* or being sold at McDonald's as Olympic Barbies.

The Disappeared Woman

At least women receive some attention while the Olympics are on. But if you were to check the sports section even two days after the Games have ended, you would see that everything is back to abnormal.

What will it take to push women athletes onto the front page of the sports section even when they aren't competing at the Olympics? It's evidently not good enough to win the International Ice Hockey Federation's World Women's Championship for the seventh straight time, as Canadian women did in Minneapolis, Minnesota, in the spring of 2001. It's not good enough to win the World Curling Championships, as Colleen Jones's rink did on the same spring weekend in Lausanne, Switzerland. And it's not even good enough to win the season's first international triathlon by more than half an hour, as Lori Bowden did in Forster, Australia, also in that same weekend. These tremendous champions were relegated to page 3 and beyond. And who did grace the front page of *The Globe and Mail*'s sports section on Monday, April 9, 2001? Someone who really needed the publicity: Tiger Woods.

Is there really any athletic contest between a golfer and a triathlete? Amazingly, Bowden had the third-fastest time among *all* competitors (male and female) in the running leg of the triathlon. Since 1999, she has performed consistently well in countless international events. She logs massive amounts of training time each week in three sports—the Ironman triathlon includes a 3.8-kilometre swim, a 180.2-kilometre cycling leg, and a 42.2-kilometre run.

At least Tiger Woods did actually win a major golf tournament that weekend. Randy Ferbey's rink placed fourth and completely out of the medals at the World Curling Championships, but it rated 95 lines and 20 paragraphs (with just a passing mention of Jones's tournament-winning rink stuck incongruously in the middle of the Ferbey story). And how did the women compare? In total, the one world cup and two women's world championship wins merited just 100 lines and 15 paragraphs. Can you imagine a female team's fourth-place result showing up anywhere but in the microscopic print of the scoreboard page?

This trend—trumpeting men who can't get themselves onto the podium over women who do—went on throughout 2001 at *The Globe and Mail* and other papers across the country. On March 10, for example, *The Globe* reported that speed skater Catriona Le May Doan had once again smashed her own world record for the 500 metres, and that alpine skier Melanie Turgeon had climbed onto the winner's podium for the fourth time that season in a world cup event. Once again, these extraordinary athletic achievements were relegated to page 3. And what graced the front page? The continuing soap opera surrounding Eric Lindros and who he would or would not play for. Lindros doesn't even have to set foot on a cold, slippery surface and he's news. Isn't sports coverage supposed to be about physical movement—or at least about something that happens?

The constant speculation around Lindros in 2001 was similar to the hype that surrounded the Canadian men's hockey team before the 1998 Nagano Olympics. Countless column inches were devoted to theories about how the team was simply unbeatable. When one veteran hockey writer got really brave and suggested the team might be vulnerable, he asserted that the country's sense of self was at stake. Canadians could take losing at something like ... well, women's hockey, he said, but not men's. Not when we have the best team the country could possibly field. But we all know what happened: The team came home completely empty-handed.

From the spring of 2001, the chorus rose again. Canada failed to win a medal in hockey at the last Olympics, so we must look to Salt Lake City for redemption. What's that again? Canada didn't win a medal in hockey in Nagano? Then what were those shiny silver things hanging around the necks of the players on the women's team? *Globe* columnist Stephen Brunt even wrote that "no North American" hockey team had won an Olympic medal, though American and Canadian women had won the top two places on the Olympic podium.

In the years since Nagano, journalists had mainly deserted our women's team. When that team won the last two world championships in North America, almost all the newspapers in Canada used the Canadian Press reports instead of sending people of their own to cover the event. Most newspapers carried far more extensive and varied coverage of the men's championships in Europe, where once again the men's team finished out of the medals. On May 12, *The Globe and Mail* used the front page of its sports section to let us know that the Canadian men's team had been bounced after a disappointing loss to the Americans. "Inexperience Catches Up to Youngest Team at the World Hockey Championships" read the headline, whereas most of the articles until then had touted the team as a shoo-in for the gold or silver medal. On the same page, a column headed "Cinderella Story Comes to an End" lamented the fact that the Toronto Maple Leafs were out of the playoffs. That loss had come *a week earlier*, and the Leafs wouldn't be playing hockey again until the fall. So why were we still reading about a team that didn't win?

The constant reinforcement of the male sporting ethos—even when a win doesn't occur—dominates almost all sports reporting around the world. But the invisibility of strong women is not a natural occurrence—journalists have to purposely ignore great successes they would never overlook if men were achieving them. Erasing women is an intentional act.

In her book *The Frailty Myth*, American author Colette Dowling describes the male backlash against women's hard-won rights to access the playing field in the first place. "It isn't just fairness that's at issue here, but, once again, gender identity," she writes. "Sport is male. Muscle is male. Power is male. And as the male power mystique is slowly but surely being punctured, men feel that something is being taken away from them. They feel that something is very definitely at risk, that something very unnatural is happening, and that they are at the mercy of some huge, powerful mechanism that is fraught with injustice—injustice to *them*."[3] In other words, the more women win, the more we will hear about the poor male souls who lost.

It is sad and frustrating to think about all the stories that aren't told about women in sports. Why can't we meet the strong women of our country? Why can't we have an in-depth feature about how it feels to be a lesbian athlete—and not to be able to come out? Or one about how it feels to go faster than any other woman has gone before on a lightning-fast sheet of ice? Or what it's like to be facing a marathon run after spending the rest of the day swimming in an ocean and cycling up mountains?

Sport is normally a terrain where all-out efforts are celebrated. Paradoxically, the brand of journalism served up on sports pages and in televised sports reports smacks of timidity and mediocrity. In 1989, the Amateur Athletic Foundation of Los Angeles (AAF) did a comprehensive study of television and newspaper coverage of women's sport. When it came to newspaper coverage, they found that 90% was of male athletes, 4% was of female athletes, 4% was mixed, and 2% was of neither men nor women.[4] In 1998, they decided to look at newspaper coverage again. They followed the *Boston Globe*, the *Orange County Register*, the *Dallas Morning News*, and *USA Today*, measuring length of stories, number of stories, placement of stories, and number of photos. Men received 28.8 times as many column inches. The ratio of articles about men to women was 23 to 1. (Even when baseball and football were eliminated, the ratio was still 8.7 to 1.) Front-page stories on women athletes accounted for only 3.2% of the total number of page-1 stories. In total, women were the subjects of 3.5% of all print stories. In 1993, the television study was revisited, but the foundation found no change from 1989. Ninety-four per cent of television sports coverage focused on men and 5% on females; 1% was gender-neutral. There were 137 interviews with male athletes and just four with female athletes. Action sports had 545 seconds of the male body in motion and 45 seconds of the female body moving.

The Australian Sports Commission did three similar studies, one in 1980, one in 1992, and one in 1996. The resulting report, called *An Illusory Image*, showed that in 1980, newspaper coverage of women athletes was just 2%.[5] In 1992, it had increased to 4.5%, and in 1996 to 10.7%. This is a 400% increase, but there was still six times as much coverage of male sport. Television coverage of women's sport, meanwhile, "remained relatively static." In 1988, it amounted to 1.3%; in 1992, it was 1.2%; and in 1996, it was a whopping 2%.

The Canadian Association for the Advancement of Women and Sport and Physical Activity (CAAWS) used to do an annual report on newspaper coverage, but over the years, nothing changed. Coverage went from a low of 2% to a high of 8%, depending on the paper. Because these numbers never altered, the CAAWS eventually ceased to measure them. In a study released in the fall of 2001, however, they did show that girls' participation in sport is decreasing. "Between five and 12, half of all boys are considered active, compared to one-third of females," reported the CAAWS. "Between 13 and 17, activity levels drop for both sexes—to 40% of boys and 25% of girls."[6] It appears that all the sexual objectification of girls and women in sports has not convinced more of them to join. And what about boys? They get served up larger-than-life images of male superheroes and learn to live not through their own bodies, but through the bodies of professional male athletes. No wonder they drop out too. There is no realness to any of this, and it's all highly dysfunctional.

Sport sociologist and York University professor Greg Malszecki believes our culture is obsessed with obedience and maleness, and therefore can't possibly allow women in. The only role for women in what he refers to as the "hypermasculine" world of sport is as caregivers to men:

For a man, the attention of any man is more important than the attention of women. The only relationship that really matters is one between a minimum of two men. The role of women is to nourish the man emotionally so he can withstand the dysfunctional relationship he has with men. Not only are women out of the loop, but they end up contributing a great deal of labour to sustain such relationships because the dysfunctions men have with each other are never-ending.[7]

Michael Robidoux, a sport sociology professor at the University of Lethbridge and a former junior and varsity hockey player himself, also writes about the obsession with male approval. In his book *Men at Play*, Robidoux argues that hockey players learn to be obediently violent and sacrifice the body "for the love of the game" because they are so replaceable. "Violence is part of the process," Robidoux argues, "because they need to sacrifice themselves in order to maintain their position on the team. This is an emotionally, intellectually, and socially stunted group of men. What's at stake is tremendous. It's not only a way of living, it's all they are about."[8]

Both scholars link this behaviour to the military roots of sport, as I also argued in chapter 1. Furthermore, when I think of how this public display of male violence is seen as natural and "part of the game," I can't help linking it to the subconscious way in which women learn that we don't have a right to public space. Colette Guillaumin writes in her essay "The Constructed Body" that from the time men are boys, they are actually encouraged to take up large amounts of public space with physical play:

From infancy on, playing is not an activity shared equally between the sexes. While girls and boys each have their own games, boys play more than girls. For example, the time available to boys for play is greater than that for girls. On top of this, the space open to boys, and which they use freely, is considerably greater and subject to fewer borders or limitations.[9]

Guillaumin goes on to argue that even conflict in public space, in the form of physical violence, is a form of cooperation among men, in that it strengthens a social contract that favours them. She writes:

[C]lose bodily contact among men is a confrontation with peers. However antagonistic they may be in childhood, adolescence, or in the sports of adulthood, those combats (because we are indeed talking about combats) introduce solidarity and cooperation. Material coordination between individuals is thus learned. Men have an experiential knowledge of parity, which they put to work constantly in public places. For, in effect, the bodily contact of men is an affair of public space, a space which is theirs and from which they exclude women.[10]

As long as the idealized male sporting body is defined as violent and aggressive, I believe that all women and girls will know in our hearts that no matter how strong we are, as we run on city paths and country trails and ride our bikes across continents, we are still not safe.

6   Cornered by the Coach

The Sexual Abuse of Female Athletes

The barn where Noel Dockery trained his animals seemed like a dream come true to Elizabeth.* She was 15 years old, and she had been horse-crazy since she was eight. Her parents were far from rich, but they wanted the best for their daughter. They said she could have a horse, but they couldn't afford lessons, so when an older friend, Amy, told her about a barn where she could ride for free if she helped muck out the stalls and groom the horses, she jumped at the chance. "My parents didn't have much money or interest in horses, either," Elizabeth told me in the fall of 1999. "They didn't understand how addicted I was. It wasn't like a family passion. My parents were English and reserved, but guess where their opposite was? It was in that barn where people boarded horses from the United States that were worth small fortunes. Of course I wanted to be there."

Elizabeth was overjoyed when her parents agreed to let her work at the barn, starting in 1970. The other people who worked there were very nice to her. The atmosphere was laid back and welcoming, a perfect place for a young person who wanted to work hard and improve her riding. But after about a month, she met Noel Dockery and everything changed. Dockery had a lot of energy; he was loud, told big stories, and promised big things to a lot of people. He only coached at the stables—he didn't own them—but Elizabeth would later describe him as having "a following of people who thought he was next to God."

Elizabeth was at the barn after school nearly every day. She'd go home, saddle up her horse, and ride over. At first, there were only chores to do, and she loved them. But then Dockery started to single her out. Now, she thought, the lessons would begin.

Very quickly, she noticed there was something odd about Dockery. He had a peculiar way of adjusting the saddle, for example. He'd put his hand on top and then tell the girl he was coaching to sit on it so he could tell if she had the right position. He'd also tell "his girls" they weren't allowed to gain any weight—and to make sure they didn't, he'd roll up their shirts so he could "test" their pectoral muscles and fat ratio for himself.

But Elizabeth was just one of Dockery's girls. From 1970, when he established himself in Canada, to 1996, when he was arrested on a total of ten sex-related charges, dozens of girls went through his various riding establishments. Looking back, Elizabeth said that "the whole process starts very slowly. It was very insidious. ... It starts with comments, hand gestures, body language, adjusting my saddle and doing these things with his hands. Once you're in the saddle, then he's mauling you a bit and making comments about your body, particularly about your breasts. I was ripe for the picking. I was 15 and he was 36, and my parents weren't paying for lessons."

Elizabeth felt indebted to Dockery, and he very quickly transformed that indebtedness into a physical relationship. She told herself that this was what romance was supposed to be and didn't tell anyone, even though she had an excellent relationship with her mother. Soon she wasn't cleaning out stalls at all because "he had other intentions for me," she said. He took her up to a living space on the second floor of the barn whenever he felt like it. When no one else was around, he attacked her in the barn. "He wasn't a sensitive guy," she told me. "He was abrasive and rough with me. I didn't know anything about romance and sex. I'd never had a boyfriend or sex. Even though he was really aggressive and it was wrong, I thought this must be what 'fooling around' is like. Later I would lie awake at nights, thinking about if I'd go to someone and turn him in. But I never imagined that anyone would believe me. Now I feel plenty of guilt because it happened to others after me and I didn't stop it. But I didn't know who I would talk to."

Elizabeth continued to visit the barn nearly every day, and Dockery's aggression escalated. "He started grabbing me and very aggressively throwing me against the wall. He was completely in control. You're not participating, and he really seemed to enjoy his performance. After he threw me against the wall, he'd tear my shirt off. We'd always end up there alone; now I'm sure that was engineered. All I can truly, clearly remember is thinking, 'This will resolve itself.' Soon I felt this big, big weight that it would all be my fault. As women, we take so much responsibility. We'll take responsibility for everything, even when there's a manipulative man in our life."

The abuse continued into the spring of 1971, becoming, if anything, more violent. "He did rape me," said Elizabeth. "It was very aggressive, very violent. Most of the time, he liked to control me—hold my hands above my head and aggressively fondle me. There was a part of me that knew he wanted that—to be violent and controlling, like he couldn't get off if he didn't do that."

She remembered one rape in particular. Dockery pinned her hands with one of his, "and then he would use his other hand to fondle you and, you know, undo your jeans and drop them, and you'd be up against the wall and he would be rubbing himself against you. And I remember one incident of penetration, and he penetrated me vaginally and I yelled out for—I don't know what— 'Don't' or 'Stop' or 'Help.' I don't remember the exact words ... but I remember him putting his hand over my mouth and pushing my head against the wall."

Now Elizabeth says she sees his behaviour as "bizarre and perverted," but as a 15-year-old, she was confused. "You know, it's just so weird to look back on it now. I don't know how I could have thought any of this was normal or okay or whatever, but ... I guess I did in some ways. I thought it was like the ... I don't know, maybe [I thought] that's the way it was or it was like those romance novels, you know, where the guy throws her over his shoulder and carries her out and forces her to whatever. … I can't explain that 15-year-old thinking anymore. I'm just so far away from it now."

During the first rape, Elizabeth says she was terrified of becoming pregnant. "Just horrified. Oh, my God, what if, you know. So I was trying to get him to stop, and he did, he withdrew his penis, and I remember it because he came down my leg and I thought it was horrible, I was like … oh, you know, I mean 15-year-olds don't think that kind of thing is cool." She said he also made her perform oral sex, which added to the control he had. "What I perceive now, looking back on it, is [that] he enjoyed this captivating you, holding you sort of hostage or prisoner or whatever, fondling you, and that's what brought him his excitement." In total, she believes she was the victim of 40 to 50 sexual assaults during that year.

Elizabeth also said that Dockery was terrifying in other ways she couldn't forget. He treated the horses with the same anger he showed toward her. "I saw him be violent toward horses," she recalled. "I saw him take a horse that kicked another horse and literally beat that horse until it was on the ground. I saw him—there's a thing they call bitting a horse. They'll put a bit on a horse and run the reins up and let it stand in its stall for a period of time. Most people go for about half an hour. Noel [would] leave the horse in there all night." And this was typical of how he treated the animals.

Elizabeth is now a woman in her 40s with a calm, friendly, generous manner. She became a social worker, and sometimes she finds herself counselling other survivors, and occasionally perpetrators. But she says she's been permanently damaged. "That was my first sexual relationship. It hasn't given me a normal sex life. I don't think you're normal anymore. I think there's a part that never heals. Will any of us be repaired? No, I'm damaged. It's sort of like losing your mom. It's like a death. You can't have that type of sexual experience and not be affected. I still have a lot of trouble with things around my mouth. I don't like anybody … touching my mouth, or I don't like anybody putting their hands—like even that game, you know, where people put their hands over your eyes from behind.

"I have to wonder what happened to Noel as a child. … We can

assign blame to him—after all, he was twisted, angry, self-focused—
he was a taker, a predator. [But] that had to come from somewhere.
It doesn't come out of the blue."

Dockery had been raised in Ireland and sent to a Christian Brothers school for boys, then arrived in Canada as an adult after coaching
in the United States. His departure from Canada in the spring of 1971
to return to the States via a ranch in Omaha, Nebraska, was
surrounded by bad debts and what Elizabeth and others called
"shady horse deals." But Elizabeth was set free. Her next relationship
was with a boy her own age who also worked at the barn. Then
Dockery contacted the boy and convinced him to come to work for
him in Nebraska. One day, Elizabeth received a frantic phone call
from the boy. Could she come down right away and pick him up, he
asked. He had a great urgency in his voice, so Elizabeth and a friend
left immediately and drove to Nebraska. "[Dockery] was very angry
with me for coming," she remembered. "Angry with [my friend] for
coming. ... I think he was quite fond of [my boyfriend], so he didn't
want him to go either, I'm sure." In 1972, Elizabeth's boyfriend died in
what was described at the time as an accident. But having seen as a
social worker what happens to young people after they've been
abused, Elizabeth now believes he was a victim too.

Her journey from frightened teenage girl to professional woman
who helps others in the same situation has been very difficult.
"[Survivors] drive themselves crazy seeking that normalcy. I'll never
be normal. I have accepted that, but my husband and I have created
a home where our kids can tell us anything. ... It just crosses the
line when someone as manipulative as Noel gets into a girl's life."

For Elizabeth, discussing the case prompted the same reaction as it
did for all the other women I interviewed who'd pressed sexual
assault charges against Dockery and other men like him. She was
reminded not only of that terrible time, but of all the other destructive men she had relationships with until she met her husband.
Talking to me wrecked her day, but she did it in the hope that
another generation of young girls wouldn't be destroyed by their
coaches.

Crossing the Line

In 1992, two years after I'd retired from competitive cycling and started a new career as a sports journalist, I asked a friend if she'd ever had a coach who had crossed the line. Heather Clarke was a fellow athlete who'd retired from the Canadian rowing team after the 1988 Olympics. A funny look came over her face, and she told me she thought she knew someone who might have been involved intimately with a coach. She'd get back to me.

That spring, I had written an article for the *Media Watch* newsletter. "Why Can't We Talk about Sexual Harassment in Sport?" was the first article in Canada to address the subject, but I'd been inspired by American sportswriter Mariah Burton Nelson. In her book *Are We Winning Yet? How Sport Is Changing Women and Women Are Changing Sport*, she describes a swim coach who sexually assaulted her when she was a teenage athlete. When I read this book, I was overcome by a wave of familiarity. I knew exactly what she was talking about. I began to calculate how much energy I had expended choreographing my movements so I wouldn't end up in a room alone with certain coaches or have to sit beside them at meals during training camps or on long road trips. I thought of how often I had tried to avoid being kissed and hugged at the end of a race because of the liberties certain men took. Yes, Nelson's story was all too familiar.

Soon Heather called and we met again. This time, she brought along her sister, Suzanne, and the story came out. During high school, the two sisters had joined the Woodstock Rowing Club in southern Ontario. The club was coached by Doug Clark, a former Pan Am Games rower and successful stockbroker. Members of the crew were known as "Doug's girls."

Clark demanded total dedication, discipline, and devotion. There was intense competition among the girls for their spot in the boat, which pitted the girls against each other. Heather wasn't sexually abused, but she did suffer through plenty of emotional abuse, and endured workouts so physically demanding she would pass out. Suzanne said she did have an intimate relationship with Clark. Seventeen at the time, she described Clark as her "first love." She says he would visit her when she was babysitting and take her for drives after practice, when they would kiss and hug and touch each other. Another former teammate, Christine Cybulski, also came forward. She said that she too had been sexually involved with Clark, and that she eventually had intercourse with him. She thought they were in love, and that they would one day get married.

Clark, who stopped coaching in 1988, wouldn't return my phone calls for this book, but when contacted for a CBC show broadcast in 1993 he denied ever having a sexual relationship with any of the young women on the Woodstock Rowing Club.

In December 1992, I wrote a piece for the *Toronto Star* called "Sexual Abuse: Sport's Dirty Little Secret." I used no names, and no coach was identified, but it must have triggered a lot of memories for a lot of athletes. Women started to come to me with stories about coaches and sexual abuse. The *Dini Petty Show* called, and Heather, Suzanne, Christine, and I did a panel discussion soon after the piece ran. The following spring, in 1993, I started working on a documentary called "Crossing the Line" with Susan Teskey, a senior producer at CBC-TV's *The Fifth Estate*. The Clarke sisters had very bravely agreed to go on the air, as had Christine, but we didn't want to focus on just one sport. Did this situation exist elsewhere? I wanted to find out.

That same spring, I went to cover the Canada Summer Games in Kamloops, B.C. There were a few thousand young female athletes there, and it wasn't difficult to find clusters of field hockey players, soccer players, track and field athletes, and plenty of others from a variety of sports. I approached each group of girls as both a member of the media and a former athlete. I asked them all exactly the same question I had put to Heather Clarke: Did they ever have a coach who had crossed the line?

In every cluster of girls, I found at least one who answered in the affirmative. Not all had personally had this kind of experience, but many had had teammates or friends or sisters who did. It didn't matter if I was speaking to girls from team or individual sports, outdoor or indoor sports—as soon as I asked the question, they looked at me the same way as Heather Clarke had.

Susan Teskey and the crew joined me a couple of days into the investigation, and I told her I felt the swimming pool would probably provide a strong story. I believed there was a certain kind of man who would be particularly interested in watching girls go through puberty in nearly transparent swimsuits. So I entered the aquatic centre and sat down beside the first two girls I could find who were free of adults who might want to shut the interview down. And as soon as I asked my standard question, I could tell that we'd found our story. This question often causes young women to sit literally speechless as they replay memories, but as soon as the girls were able to speak, one of them told me that her club coach had been charged with sexual assault after girls on her swim team went to the police.

But I didn't want to stop there. That summer, through the incredible bravery and cooperation of several women volleyball coaches and a physical education professor at one of Canada's universities, we found two athletes who had trained under the assistant national coach for Volleyball Canada and had suffered abuse at his hands. In "Crossing the Line," we ended up telling the stories of athletes from these three sports—volleyball, swimming, and rowing. But once the word got out that we were interested in knowing of girls and women who had been sexually assaulted by coaches, we had no end of stories we could have used. The behaviour I had spent so much energy avoiding in cycling was rampant in every other sport as well.

"Crossing the Line" went to air in the fall of 1993. It broke a 10-year ratings record for the broadcaster, and in the spring of 1994, it was nominated for the Michener Award for meritorious public service journalism and won the Investigative Researchers and Editors Award in the United States for best investigative journalism in North America.

Sport Canada formed a committee of athletes and staff to address the many troubling issues the documentary raised. Heather Clarke was on that committee, and she did great work, pushing people to look into all the dark and dirty corners they had long been avoiding. In September 1994, the CAAWS, in conjunction with numerous other Canadian sports organizations, published *Harassment in Sport: A Guide to Policies, Procedures and Resources*. This document defined harassment in a broad way that included physical and sexual assault, outlined in ethical, legal, and social terms why harassment is unacceptable, and listed reasons why harassment occurs in the first place. Given that it was the first official statement by government and sports associations in the country, it was strongly worded. "The relationship between an athlete and a coach, administrator, or official is inherently unbalanced. ... The potential for abuse of power in this relationship is very great. Abuse can take place at any point, from showing favouritism to exploiting conflicts of interest, the subtle violence of eroding a person's self-esteem, or the blatant violence of sexual abuse," wrote Tom McIllfaterick of the Canadian Sport Council, one of the sponsoring bodies.

Unfortunately, no one seems to be able to track how this very good piece of work was actually integrated into the sport system. The document was called a "guide," not a policy statement, and its authors acknowledged in 1994 that sports associations didn't legally have to have harassment policies. At the time, only the Alpine Ski Federation specifically disallowed coaches from having sexual relationships with their athletes. While women athletes continued to warn of certain coaches, this was a very haphazard approach to the problem, and the word wasn't getting through to many athletes. But in 1997, the Canadian Professional Coaches Association finally agreed on a policy of conduct. Section 30 of this policy states:

> Notwithstanding the procedures set out in this policy, any member who is convicted of a criminal offense involving sexual exploitation, invitation to sexual touching, sexual interference, sexual assault or aggravated assault shall face an automatic suspension from CPCA for a period of time corresponding to the length of criminal sentence imposed by the court, and may face further disciplinary action by CPCA in accordance with this policy.

In other words, abusers can't coach while they're serving their jail term, but nothing prevents them from coaching once they've finished the sentence unless the CPCA chooses "further disciplinary action." It appears that the CPCA believes convicted sex offenders should be able to coach again, since nothing in their policy statement allows for the lifetime decertification of sex offenders.

When criminal charges have not been laid but the director of the CPCA believes there is enough evidence for a hearing, the tribunal will consist of two coaches and a lawyer appointed by the alternative dispute resolution program for amateur sport, which few athletes have ever heard of. Furthermore, I believe the fraternity of coaches in Canada is far too tight for this process to be fair to athletes. But even this biased tribunal came a year too late for women cyclists.

The story of national cycling coach Desmond Dickie began in 1996, when he was put on trial for sexual assault after three female cyclists went to the police to complain about his behaviour. Two of them charged that he locked them—one at a time—in an isolated gym and offered to massage them. One said he touched her breasts during the massage and pulled her shorts to the middle of her hips and massaged above them.

The complainant, who was a teenager at the time of the alleged assault said she felt "uncomfortable" and "very vulnerable."

She testified that Dickie lifted her bra "so he could see my chest," and used his saliva to get the heart-rate monitor he was attaching on her to work.

Her teammate said he massaged her topless, telling her to trust him, that trust was very important, that he usually gives full massages to national team members, both male and female.

The third complainant alleged that during the national cycling championships in Thunder Bay, Dickie sexually assaulted her while massaging her in a hotel room.

Another cyclist, who gave similar evidence, said Dickie had forced her to sleep in his room during a training camp in the United States. He told the then teenager that there wasn't room for her anywhere else. (Her evidence was discounted because, among other things, she admitted on the stand that she was still having traumatic flashbacks.) In his defense, Dickie denied altogether massaging one of the complainants and said that the massages done to the other two were sport massages and not for his sexual gratification. Dickie was eventually acquitted, although the judge found that "his conduct . . . certainly calls into question his ethics and his right to remain as national cycling coach. Another forum may properly decide that he is in violation of the ethical standards expected."

In the end, no one took responsibility for determining whether Dickie should be barred from coaching. The Canadian Cycling Association, the Canadian Olympic Association, the Coaching Association of Canada, the Canadian Professional Coaches Association, the Canadian Sport Council, and Sport Canada all managed to avoid setting up the recommended tribunal. Eventually, Dickie quietly moved to the United States, where USA Cycling hired him as the junior national coach. When I interviewed USA Cycling's media liaison, Richard Wanniger, at the 1999 Winnipeg Pan-Am Games, he admitted that no one from the organization had read the judge's decision, and therefore no one knew there were questions about Dickie's ethical behaviour and his fitness to coach. No one had even bothered to phone the Canadian Cycling Association for a reference. If they had, former executive director Patrick Healy says he would have given a detailed explanation of why he believed the CCA should never hire Dickie again. By the time the Sydney Olympics rolled around, Dickie was the head sprint coach for the senior American cycling team.

What did Dickie's case tell us? It seemed that very few of the recommendations in the CAAWS's harassment guide were implemented in Canada, and it was business as usual south of the border. And then, in January 1997, that all changed.

The Graham James Case

On January 4, 1997, perhaps the best junior hockey coach in Canada pleaded guilty to 350 counts of sexual assault after two former players went to the police. Sheldon Kennedy was the first to go public, and his story of having been abused by Graham James took over the front pages of all the newspapers and absorbed much of the sports sections as well. Canadians were shocked. How could the sport that so defined Canadian masculinity have facilitated male-on-male sexual abuse? The questions only multiplied as men and boys across the country began to come forward and talk about the abuse that they too had suffered at the hands of their coaches.

Although we had been exposing the systemic sexual abuse of female athletes since 1992, the problem had been virtually ignored. A handful of female sportswriters had written about the issue, but I never once read an article or column by a male journalist. All of a sudden, however, we were talking about men and boys. Now the sexual abuse of athletes by coaches mattered. Sportswriters who had completely disregarded stories about female athletes who had been raped were tripping all over themselves in their indignation over what James had done. Suddenly, sports associations announced it was crucial to devise a strategy to deal with the inherent power imbalance between athletes and coaches.

Once Sheldon Kennedy had come forward, most sport governing bodies couldn't move fast enough to protect their athletes. A collective was formed under Sport Canada's direction to address sexual harassment, and its 1999–2000 report began by stating, "The issue of harassment and abuse in sport came into the public's eye in January 1997."[1] The many brave young women who had told their stories to a national audience years earlier didn't merit a mention, nor did any of those who had shared their stories since then. Interestingly, Marg McGregor, the executive director of the CAAWS, chaired both the working group that put together the 1994 guidelines on harassment and the 1997 collective. Somehow, even she managed to eradicate the voices of the young women who'd come forward in 1993. When I asked her why she hadn't acknowledged that it was women athletes who first spoke out about sexual abuse in sport, she shrugged and told me that we were into the second wave of recognizing what athletes had been going through.

In 1998, less than a year after Kennedy spoke out, a leading Canadian family magazine asked me to write a piece that would help parents ensure a harassment-free environment in sport. In the article that resulted, I asked parents to consider for a moment what it says about

Canada that when women reveal they have been sexually assaulted by their coaches for years, virtually no one takes notice, but when boys are abused, it's a national catastrophe. When the article appeared, this question had been deleted without my knowledge or permission.

Why do we have such a hard time accepting that girls and young women are at great risk of sexual abuse at the hands of their coaches? Today, concern about sexual abuse in sport is framed in a very specific way. The 1994 document recognized the power a coach can exercise over an athlete, but current material frames the issue as one that affects children, not women. All too often, the perpetrator is cast as "the other"—someone who isn't from sport, but rather infiltrates it. The proverbial man in a trench coat, hiding behind the bushes. The stranger. The pedophile. The fag.

And why has this happened? If we acknowledged that it isn't "men out there" we have to worry about, but instead "men in here," the façade of the inherent goodness of the sporting world might start to crack. These men aren't outsiders. Noel Dockery was one of the old boys in the horse world; he was also a "good Catholic" who went to mass every Saturday night. The coaches of the women I interviewed for "Crossing the Line" had similar profiles. They were charismatic, sociable, and high-profile. In many ways, they *were* their sport. In fact, if we simply went by what women were saying, we would have to examine many of the men who sit on the do-good boards and fair-play committees who are coaching athletes across the country. How many of them have had sexual relationships with their female athletes? More than we can even imagine. How many, like Noel Dockery, married athletes who were still very young, impressionable, and under their control? Again, the answer would likely shock us. But this is simply too close for comfort, so the voices of the women who spoke out in 1993—and all those who followed them—have been conveniently ignored.

In the Canadian Hockey Association's September 2000 *Speak Out!* workbook for coaches, more than 50 pages outline why any kind of abuse—emotional, physical, or sexual—against children is wrong, how to prevent it, and what to do about it if you suspect it has occurred. This is a positive step, and the workbook makes it very clear that "it is never appropriate for a coach to form a sexual relationship with a young player—under the age of majority." On the subject of players over the age of majority, however, the book is not so unequivocal. "Coaches and other staff and volunteers on university, college and high-performance teams should be discouraged from beginning a relationship with adult players who are under their control," advises the workbook. Note the soft qualifier "should be discouraged" and the phrase "under their control." Does this mean a coach can have a relationship with a player on an opposing team?

Only one paragraph follows this wishy-washy directive, and it does nothing to recognize the fact that because of sport's hierarchical nature, *all* coaches have power over *all* athletes. And since most coaches are heterosexual males, most of these sexual relationships—in hockey and other sports—will be between male coaches and female athletes. The CHA could have decided that any coach who has a sexual relationship with any athlete would lose his or her certification, but it chose to backpedal on the issue—and the same thing has happened in virtually every other sport in Canada. And let me be clear here that I am not talking about situations where women rent the ice to play pickup and one of their husbands volunteers to coach. I am talking only about coaching situations where there is a true power differential.

Even though the gender politics of sexual abuse in sport have been replaced by a do-good concern for the safety of children (which is in itself a good thing), many positive changes for women have been implemented. In 1994, the Canadian Olympic Association drafted a harassment policy that has been included in all athlete orientation packages since then. Today, sports associations must have a harassment policy before they can receive Sport Canada funding. The National Sports Centre in Calgary and the University of Calgary's sexual harassment office now offer a workshop called "Out of Bounds" to athletes who train in that jurisdiction, and the workshop's creators, Karen Strong and Shirley Voyna-Wilson, even brought the campaign to the Salt Lake City Olympic organizing team. Unfortunately, in her master's thesis at the University of New Brunswick, Laura Misener, a former national team gymnast, found very little follow-up on these new policies. There is still no implementation strategy put in place by Sport Canada, she argues, to ensure that athletes are protected.[2] And while all this has been going on, women in countries around the world have been attempting to create a worldwide network for harassment-free sport that would place a much stronger emphasis on a political analysis of power, gender, and sexuality.

When the Law Catches Up

At about the same time that Sheldon Kennedy's charges against Graham James surfaced, prompting the start of the soon-to-be well-publicized movement to address harassment, something else was happening that didn't make the news at all. The pieces in the Noel Dockery case began to fall into place. At last, Dockery's façade began to crack.

Elizabeth had abandoned riding because of the abuse she had suffered, so she didn't know Dockery had returned from Nebraska to southern Ontario after a few years and set up a practice similar to the one he'd had in 1970. He would go to a farm and sell the owners on his great training and coaching techniques, suggesting they trade room, board, and a small salary for his expertise. By this time, he had married Susan, another teenage girl who had originally come to him to be coached. Like Elizabeth, Susan believed the kind of abusive sexual behaviour Dockery exhibited toward her was called love. And he now had the credibility a wife offers a man who might otherwise seem rootless and untrustworthy.

Susan says she came from a family situation that made her very vulnerable to Dockery's manipulation and big promises. "He paid attention and listened to what I had to say, and I didn't get that at home," she told me. "But looking back, I realize he was so sneaky— incredibly bright, but not overt at first about what he was doing."

Susan ended up being one of the complainants who charged Dockery with sexual assault in 1996. During her married years, however, she was easily intimidated and silenced by an angry man. "I didn't miss the signals," she said, referring to her suspicions that her husband was abusing girls he was teaching, "but I rationalized. He was also very good at misconstruing what you see. Noel had these big, elaborate excuses as to why I might think that way if I questioned him about anything. I'd get so confused when he accused me of misreading a situation. He was so charming to others, and eventually I'd tell myself I must have it all wrong. ... Your head gets really messed up. On the one hand, your instincts are screaming at you. On the other hand, these things are right under your nose. You say to yourself, 'Nobody could be that stupid,' but he really did do this stuff right under our noses. Near the end of the relationship, I used to wander around the house at night. It was like I was on watch, but I didn't know for what."

In 1995, Noel and Susan moved to a farm owned by a woman named Claire. By then, they had a teenage daughter who, like all the other teenage girls, seemed to hang on Dockery's every word. Claire had a thriving boarding stable, and she wanted to start competing seriously on her own horse. Dockery told her he'd make her a champion and beef up her business at the same time. She remembers having an odd feeling about him, but she told herself she was being silly. He was a professional. Also, Claire and Susan formed a fast friendship, and neither wanted to jeopardize that, even when Dockery's behaviour became impossible to rationalize.

But Claire found his presence increasingly troublesome. Instead of bringing more customers to her farm, Dockery seemed to be driving them away. She found him unpredictable, with a temper that went sky high. He didn't have the business acumen she assumed a professional would have, and he appeared to have no other income than what he charged her for his expertise. There were other problems as well.

Out of nowhere, Dockery professed his love for her. Claire was completely taken aback. Susan had become a good friend, and even if Claire had found anything remotely appealing about Dockery, she would never have acted on those feelings. Without knowing why, she started to lock her house at night, which was something she'd never done before. One night, she realized why. When she went to the back door to call her dog, she found Dockery standing there. He immediately turned and ran, but she knew he'd been lurking around her house after dark, trying to see in.

Susan later confirmed this. She told her friend that Dockery would stay out and return to their apartment elsewhere on the property shortly after the lights in Claire's house went out. But when Claire saw him scramble away, she knew she could no longer allow him to stay. All the things she had disliked about Dockery—from his leering glances and his verbal advances to his sneaking about and his uncontrolled temper—now seemed more ominous. Still, she didn't want to lose Susan as a friend, and she also didn't want her to have to fend for herself in what was obviously a dysfunctional marriage.

The morning after Claire caught Dockery at her back door, she and Susan spent the day cleaning Claire's house, since members of the Ontario Quarter Horse Association were coming for a barbecue the next day. Susan could feel that something was up. She was uncomfortable, and because Dockery blamed her for everything, she believed Claire was angry at her. "I said to myself, 'What did I do wrong this time?'" Finally, Claire asked her if she knew where her husband had been the night before, and told her that she'd caught him at her back door. Susan thought she was going to pass out. She immediately understood where Dockery had been all those nights when he disappeared. Together, the two decided they'd have the barbecue and then Claire would tell Dockery he would have to leave the day after that.

Both women avoided him during the social event, but while Susan was fixing breakfast for him the next morning, Dockery announced that he and his daughter were leaving. He told Claire and Susan that all the good customers had left the farm thanks to them and he simply couldn't afford to stay. When they agreed he should leave, he threatened to take the remainder of Claire's clients with him. The women held firm and insisted he go.

Dockery and his daughter moved to an apartment in another town, but his problems were far from over. A girl from his past reappeared in his life. As a 15-year-old, Anna had lived with Dockery and his family so she could ride. Not surprisingly, Dockery assaulted her, just as he had so many others. For years after Anna had left the Dockerys' home, he had continued to be a malevolent psychological force in her life. She had tried to go to university, but often found herself in a fetal position, unable to get out of the closet in her apartment. Eventually, Anna had to abandon school altogether. She believed she would never move forward until she banished Dockery from her life, and the only way to do that, she thought, was to confront the space he occupied. To force herself to face him, she bravely volunteered to take care of the new horses Dockery was training.

When she came to relieve Dockery's daughter, Anna was astonished to learn from her that her mother and Claire had accused him of "sexually fondling people." Anna said later that all she could think was, "Oh, my God, I wasn't the only one." She phoned the police immediately and then went to see Claire and Susan. She initially told them she was looking for a horse to buy. But when Claire told her she would sell her one only if she promised not to train with Dockery, Anna replied, "Don't worry. I'm in the same boat as you." She said later, "For six and a half years, I kept that secret inside—right here."

Within 24 hours of Anna's visit to Claire and Susan, Elizabeth also unexpectedly called, wanting to know if Dockery was still coaching. When she heard Anna's story, she felt terribly guilty; she blamed herself and her silence. But she wasn't going to keep silent any longer. "Count me in," she told the others. It seemed unbelievable, they said later, that after nearly three decades of abuse, this was all falling into place so easily.

The police interviewed 27 women from Dockery's coaching past. They all said that "something" had happened, but most weren't prepared to move forward with a criminal complaint. In the end, six complainants gave statements to the police, and in the fall of 1996 Dockery was charged with 10 counts of sexual assault. He was forbidden to go near the complainants or their property, and he wasn't allowed to attend quarter horse shows or have any contact with minor girls (though his daughter continued to live with him). When Susan and Claire found out he'd approached the 4-H Club and a local horse school for work, they decided to become more proactive. They gave all interested parties copies of the court order restricting his activities, and he was soon cut off.

The case moved relatively swiftly, and on May 16, 1999, it went to trial. Dockery's lawyer tried to have each case tried separately, but the judge ruled that it would move ahead as it was. The complainants supported each other "110%," said Claire. "Once we had given our evidence, we sat in the courtroom to support the next woman. We saw strength in ourselves as a group. Amazing solidarity." After a pause, she added, "There was this big secret we'd been burdened all these years by, and now it was lifted off our shoulders. All of us walked away stronger than when we went in."

Of course, it wasn't quite that easy. Elizabeth says the trial was hell. "It was the worst thing in my life. This lawyer was awful. 'What car did he drive?' From 1970? How would I know at 15? He made me feel like a whore and a liar. ... There were certain nights during the trial [when] I didn't sleep. I think I'd rather be sexually abused again. ... I did get a lot of support from the other women. All of those people with their pain and anger—it was exhausting. I was embarrassed and ashamed. I should be able to be detached, but it's so ingrained; it's like having blue eyes. You really do get bound up in shame. I think I'm pretty healthy, then you're hit with that. His lawyer suggested I was the one with the problem."

"It was the first time in my life I felt like I had a voice," Claire remarked. "My father was very physically abusive. That's why Noel could get away with this. But now we're all sisters. ... I truly believe there are other women, there will be more women who will come forward."

In the end, Dockery was found guilty on all five of the charges that involved girls and none that involved women. "The judge said it's not that he didn't believe the women, it's just that they didn't fight back, and therefore they must have consented," Claire told me in disbelief. "I couldn't believe my ears. I was terrified of Noel—he had such a terrible temper. Who would fight back?"

The Crown wanted to appeal, but the women felt they could lose the convictions they already had and they decided to make do. Dockery received a 36-month sentence, but because part of it could be served concurrently, he really faced only 29 months. Still, the judge said he saw no hope of rehabilitation. This gave some degree of vindication, and the women celebrated.

Looking back on her long journey, Claire said, "You're vulnerable because of your dreams. You have such passion and drive. And then someone says to you, 'I can get your dream to happen.' If they don't destroy your dream, you can use what happened to go forward. Out of the six of us, I am the only one who continues to ride. I've had my best competitive results ever since Noel went to jail. When he coached me, I was mediocre."

Susan wishes she could still ride. "I still love horses and love the sport," she says, "but I need to distance myself. The drive is gone. He takes your dream and turns it into something dirty—a nightmare." She has great concern for her daughter, too. "I feel like I was an iceberg all those years. But feelings are starting to come back now and it's very painful, like when you freeze your hands and then they begin to thaw. It's incredibly hard to work through. I've been on anti depressants for three years now, and still need them. It's a struggle to get up every morning, but I'll make it."

"Susan was his credibility shield," explains Claire. "Look at the happy household they have. You put on the mask because you can't let anyone know what your family life is like."

These exceptional women didn't stop once Dockery had been sent to jail. They worked with the Correctional Service of Canada and Citizenship and Immigration Canada to have him deported, and when he was released from prison on December 5, 2000, he was sent back to Ireland. They also made any associations involved with horses and the training of horses aware of the judge's findings, and some have drafted strict new policies on harassment and abuse as a result.

And of course the women have got on with rebuilding their own lives. Claire has a new horse trainer and a number of new boarders at the farm and is happy with her improved results in competition. Susan has completed a 10-week course to work on a sexual assault helpline and recently enrolled in a three-year college program to learn how to counsel women and children in distress. Unfortunately, her daughter continued to believe her father, even after his conviction. It breaks Susan's heart, but they don't speak anymore.

A Problem That Won't Go Away

Unfortunately, the Dockery case is just one of many cases of abuse in sport. In fact, so many have come to my attention since I first asked Heather Clarke that fateful question that I lost count years ago. Luckily, someone else has been keeping track. In 1996, Athletes CAN sent out a survey on sexual harassment and abuse by people in positions of power. The survey guaranteed confidentiality and anonymity and asked national team athletes to respond on these issues for the first time anywhere in the world. When Dr. Sandi Kirby and women's health expert Lorraine Greaves released some quantitative data on the prevalence of abuse in sport later that year, their findings were startling.

Kirby and Greaves had 266 high-level athletes respond to their questionnaire. The results, says Kirby, "indicate high levels of sexual harassment and abuse, but they certainly do not account for all the sexual harassment and abuse these athletes may have experienced … nor can we report on how frequently particular forms of harassment or abuse of athletes occur within a particular sport. This means our figures underrepresent, in a major way, the actual frequency of athlete abuse."[3]

Of female athletes, 43 respondents said abuse had occurred on trips, while only 18 male athletes reported abuse in this venue; 23 females reported abuse during training sessions, compared to 16 male athletes; 13 female athletes and five males reported abuse in private locations; and three females and two males said abuse occurred in a vehicle or a hotel. One male and one female reported abuse occurring in another, unlisted area. In all, 48 females and 20 males had been abused by a coach, while nine females and three males blamed other athletes. Five females and three males pointed at medical/physio staff, and another five females accused a stranger. Two females also charged administrators, though no males did.[4]

Greaves and Kirby report that, in total, one in five athletes had had what they described as "consensual" sexual intercourse with a person in authority in their sport. The majority of these athletes were female, and the majority of the authority figures were male. Of the 58 athletes who admitted to this, 26% also "reported being insulted, ridiculed, made to feel like a bad person, or slapped, hit, punched or beaten by these authority figures," while 25% of these athletes noted additional physical/emotional abuse.[5] An additional 23 athletes said they had been raped or had survived an attempted rape by a person in a position of authority. Added together, this means a total of 81 athletes, or 30.5% of the respondents, had had some kind of sexual encounter with an authority figure. Given these results, we can conservatively assume that nearly one in three athletes on Canada's national teams has been the victim of some sort of sexual harassment—and remember that the authors believe the study underreported abuse. We also know that female athletes are much more likely to report abuse than male athletes because of the homosexual stigma attached to it, so the rate of abuse must be even higher than 30% among women athletes.[6] A stunning 86% of female respondents said they felt at risk and believed they were vulnerable to sexual abuse and harassment.[7]

When we're confronted by statistics like these, we really must ask ourselves exactly what is happening to girls and women in sport in Canada. And when we view these numbers in conjunction with what we will learn in the next chapter about eating disorders among female athletes—a problem that often goes hand in hand with sexual abuse—we have to admit there is something desperately wrong with sporting culture. Sport can hardly be thought of as a good and healthy experience for girls when so much is so clearly wrong. The question is, will all the sexual harassment policies floating around now make it any better?

7   Starving for the Gold

Athletes and Eating Disorders

Clare Hall-Patch's rise to the podium of the World Junior Road Cycling Championships in 2000 was as swift as her pedalling. Just three years earlier, the then 14-year-old had been, in her own words, "sitting around smoking and having nothing to do with my own life. It was so dumb." When the cycling coach at her school asked her to come out on a ride, everything changed. "I felt like saying, 'Why didn't someone tell me about this before?' I felt so cheated. I immediately loved it. There's such a definite freedom and positive feeling from riding a bike. No matter what happens to me, I hope I never lose these feelings." But she nearly did.

By the end of her second year of high-school racing, she was ready for the national circuit. The Victoria native ended up winning every race she entered, including the junior Canadian mountain bike championship. She had started to have an impressive career as a road rider too, but then it all came to a crashing halt. A serious knee injury caused by misaligned cleats on her shoes and too much training ended up crippling her. "I thought there was a possibility that I may never be able to ride my bike again," she told me in the spring of 2001. "For two months, I couldn't do anything more than walk once around the block."

Hall-Patch was devastated. "I got really depressed," she admitted. "I had to honestly consider what my life would be like without cycling. But I thought, 'Well, right now, my bike is it.' It was difficult for me when I realized I thought like that, because I don't consider myself to be such a narrow person. There were a lot of things happening that I didn't expect. I guess when you're depressed, you don't really feel like eating. Your appetite just shuts down, and it's a bit fuzzy. I guess you don't remember things very well when you're depressed, but I lost a ton of weight. I don't know if I stopped eating. I can't really remember. That time off the bike was, as I mentioned, fuzzy, unfocused. Two and a half months later, in June, when my injury [had] healed, I got back on the bike and I had a totally different body. I'd lost some muscle, but I'd lost almost all body fat. Unfortunately, I really liked my new body."

If she wanted to keep that new body, Hall-Patch knew she would have to alter her eating habits again. She had managed to make it through her sedentary period with little food—no doubt the reason for her "fuzzy, unfocused" thinking—but she realized she couldn't meet the demands of a competitive international circuit on a starvation diet. So she went from anorexic to bulimic. "Things became ugly. There was binge eating, and then I'd become upset with myself, which triggered more binge eating and then purging. Next I'd restrict myself from food. It was a disgusting cycle. I would say to myself, 'Please don't think about it.' But I was thinking about what I ate, constantly."

For Hall-Patch, the preoccupation with food helped her push away thoughts about the future. She was afraid to face a life without cycling, the one thing that had saved her from what she imagined as directionless and unproductive early teenage years. By starving herself, which also starved her mind, she was able to avoid thinking about what lay in store for her. It made things "fuzzy."

"Being a young woman going into this world is kind of a scary thing. To think that we will probably grow up alone, as independent women without partners, is a lot to face. I love my own company, but I know so many people who are afraid to be by themselves. The pressure to be perfect is so intense. Fashion magazines define who we are supposed to be. Reading fashion magazines—that's heinous. My aunt made me a really neat collage from women's magazines:

'Savoury Cinnamon Lips.' 'What Makes a Strong Man Tremble?' 'Beautiful Ritual.' That's most women's lives in a nutshell, [and] not just in a physical sense. We have to read and be helped along to be feminine, so being helpless is also feminine. It's even like failure is feminine because we obviously can't be women on our own. We need so much help all the time.

"We're told [that] what being a woman means is putting on lipstick and worrying about it. It's a grownup thing to do ... to worry all the time about what you look like. A lot of people are running scared because these are dirty tactics used against us. 'Let's have them obsess about things—things that weren't there before, when they were younger. Let's let them obsess about thighs.'"

Hall-Patch was suffering from an eating disorder called anorexia athletica—an intense fear of fatness in already lean people that is characterized by reduced energy intake and an obsession with exercise, sometimes combined with laxatives, vomiting, and diuretics—but she was luckier than most. She was at least able to analyze the situation. She could deconstruct the "beauty myth" culture, and she had a strong family to call on for support. Yet she still couldn't escape her predicament. Ironically, in the world of sport, which is supposed to be beyond the reach of the "heinous" beauty myth, the athlete is increasingly at risk. Female athletes in particular tend to be perfectionists, which makes them more susceptible to eating disorders to begin with.[1] They also compete in a culture that worships the male form, and we've seen in previous chapters that they often find themselves pressured to exploit their own bodies to be accepted. It's a lethal combination.

I would argue that this very troubling trend toward ultra-thinness and the consequent sexual objectification and infantilization of the athlete started at the Munich Olympics in 1972, when the 14-year-old Soviet gymnast Olga Korbut stole the show. Recently, Korbut spoke out about the conditions the Soviet women's team endured when she was in training. In a stunning documentary, she told the BBC that the head coach of the Soviet women's gymnastics team regularly raped the girls—none of whom was old enough to be considered a woman—and denied them food. They were literally his slaves, and they were routinely imprisoned until they performed to his expectations (though they were allowed out to smoke, which helped to stave off hunger pains). In an interview in 1999, she said he manipulated her by convincing her that if she went public with the truth, she would be blamed. "I was afraid that if the truth emerged, it would destroy me as well," Korbut told the *Electronic Telegraph* in the UK. "He was afraid too and used to beat me up. I would come back home covered with bruises and lie that I had suffered a fall."

The little bodies that so many people imagined as beautiful and healthy were in fact ravaged and raped. "The truth is that many of the gymnasts were not just 'sport machines,' but sexual slaves to their trainer," revealed Korbut. "In Russia, many gymnastics coaches hit their pupils. At least Renald [her own coach] never hit me if I didn't do well in competition. He simply said, 'We need to work more to do it better.' That's why he told me to smile all the time—because there's nothing else you can do."

Today, Korbut's smiling pixie-doll look is the norm in sports like gymnastics and figure skating—sports that are fetishized by a culture that has lost the ability to accept the grace, power, and presence of the strong adult female body. The "Code of Points" classifications used by the Federation internationale de gymnastique (FIG) for 2001–2004 list femininity, artistry, beauty, grace, and entertainment value as characteristics judges should reward in gymnasts; value-laden words if there ever were any in an activity that once called itself a sport. And so this derision of the powerful-looking woman—one who doesn't feel compelled to smile constantly—just aggravates the situation for many female athletes, none of whom lives her life in a bubble. As the average athlete sees her thighs growing with training and her calf muscles bulging every time she climbs a hill, she knows she is dragging herself farther and farther away from that tiny, incapable, but compliant body that is so idealized in fashion magazines and certain sports. Clare Hall-Patch remembers feeling terrible every time she'd weight train, a process that increases muscle mass and consequently body weight. "I'd look at the scale, and it would say 117 pounds instead of 115," she recalled, "and I'd go, 'Oh my God, I'm getting fat.'"

Is it any wonder that Hall-Patch so liked her post-injury body? It was exactly the one she was supposed to have: no fat, just lean, sinewy angularity. "In sports," she says, "the ideal body is not a woman's body. The rule is: Lower body fat is good, higher is bad. In cycling, this is especially so. The ideal body is an adolescent male body.

"I've never seen a fat figure skater either," she goes on to say. "They have to be lighter than lightweight. The gym is the ultimate place for this unnatural look. It's frightening. Thin is almost always better. I think athletes are the ultimate when it comes to the desire to be thin. By definition, they are narcissistic. ... You have to be obsessed with yourself to do well. There's good and bad to that. Being a cyclist is about being the subject, but women are expected to focus their attention outward."

It's a psychologically complicated process to try to like your body while the culture you live in is constantly telling you your body is wrong. And if you have an eating disorder, how do you accept the fact that you need help when every message tells you you're doing the right thing? Hall-Patch found that this was one of the hardest parts of facing her condition. "You don't want to admit you have problems," she explained. "There were only a few people I knew who I trusted, but you need to talk to someone who can help you. It took a lot for me to say, 'I have a problem.' I still struggle with it because I liked that body."[2] Eventually, Hall-Patch did seek out a psychiatrist. She still goes for counselling today, and she now recognizes that curing an eating disorder is a long-term project.

Hall-Patch says her counselling sessions and her realization that she had a serious problem made possible her amazing comeback in the 2000 season. A June 2000 Canada Cup mountain bike race was her first one back in the saddle, and she came in sixth—though she says she rode well enough "to put myself in the hospital." (In other words, she pushed herself beyond what she thought she could do and collapsed after the finish line.) At the Canada Cup finals, against

40 top riders, she was sixth once again. But she says, despite the results of the 2000 season, she is still "a work in progress."

"Every experience in life is an opportunity," she told me, "and ethics are in every part of my life. If what you want is a better world, then they are in everything. I knew all the reasons why I should eat properly, and all of that couldn't protect me. I think in the past there was an idea of a good body, but not a perfect body. Women's bodies weren't so processed the way they are now; [today] both men's and women's magazines only have skinny models ... who are missing clothing and [made to pose] in vulnerable positions. They're only adjectives used to describe whatever product it is they're selling.

"Personally, I'm not out of the woods yet, because I still like that body I once had, but I want to get the positive feelings back again. I think I have quite a lot of it back. Still, I want to reclaim not only the physical, but the sexual. ... Sexually, I think women are only allowed to express themselves on someone else's terms and not their own. Look how men fetishize lesbians—they're all disturbingly feminine girls in porn. So it's kind of interesting when a woman wants to express her own sexual self. It's very difficult."

Hall-Patch's 2001 season proved more difficult than the one before it. She said she felt constantly exhausted—as tired after her warmup as she normally was at the end of a race. When she was training on the national mountain bike course in July, she crashed and broke her elbow. Memories of what had happened during the last injury haunted her, but she resisted and was able to ride again after just 10 days of recovery. In August, she went to Colombia to compete in the Pan-Am cycling championships, but the Canadian Cycling Association (CCA) sent her only five days before the competition, which was at high altitude. Her bike took the entire five days to arrive, and she had to borrow someone else's for the time trial (where she placed an astonishing fifth). When her own bike did finally arrive—the night before the road race—its rear wheel was smashed. The replacement she found didn't have the right gear ratios for the steep climbs on the course, and the combination of altitude and the wrong gears put her at a real disadvantage. But she stuck it out and placed seventh—an amazing result considering the circumstances.

When she came home to Victoria, Hall-Patch decided it was time to examine her life. She went to her doctor and said she really wanted to find out why she'd been so fatigued for so much of the season. She really wanted to get better. "It helped me a lot this season to be with other people," she explains. "Instead of saying to myself, 'I'm going to go to my room and binge for the next two hours before I go to sleep,' I'd talk to other people and not binge. I was supposed to go for a fat-percentage test and report the results to the CCA, and I refused. The test is optional, and I opted out." Hall-Patch is questioning all of this—why women have to account to others (mostly men) for their own fat percentage, and even how women athletes are marketed in the first place. "Right now, I know I'm seen as so young, so new in terms of selling my own body. But I think if a female athlete does that, then it's a cure for women's emancipation. She's wiping out our freedom. Cycling gave me a chance to reclaim my body. I can use this body for something positive. I look forward to the times when I can give back. ... I want to find all the other girls who are really into this sport and help them the best I can."

Eating Disorders—In and Out of the Sporting Arena

If Clare Hall-Patch's story sounds heartfelt, complicated, and even contradictory, it's because it is. Today, girls and young women can rhyme off all the reasons behind eating disorders and body-image problems, but they can't control the culture that fosters those problems. As early as 1986, a study of 497 randomly selected Ontario adolescents in their last year of high school showed that two-thirds of the girls were preoccupied with weight and dieting, compared with 15% of the boys.[3] In Australia, 869 schoolgirls aged 14 to 16 were asked to complete a self-reporting questionnaire. The results showed that 33% had disordered eating, 57% engaged in unhealthy dieting, and 12% had distorted body images. Another Australian

study showed that dieting was the best predictor of a girl's vulnera-
bility to an eating disorder.[4]

In the summer of 2001, a southern Ontario research team reported
that 27% of the schoolgirls they surveyed had disordered eating attitudes. As the girls became older adolescents, the percentage with
eating disorders increased. And the danger isn't just from the physical and psychological effects of poor nutrition. The authors point
out that these girls are also more likely to smoke, use alcohol and
drugs, suffer from depression, and attempt suicide. The findings
suggested that conventional methods of teaching positive body
image and proper nutrition don't work. The report's authors note:

> [M]any of the programs have typically consisted of
> curriculum-based didactic sessions focused on giving girls
> information about eating disorders, warning about the
> dangers of unhealthy weight loss behaviours, and
> encouraging healthy eating and exercise. Although
> providing information does appear to increase knowledge,
> these programs do not engage participants emotionally and
> appear to do little to change or prevent unhealthy attitudes
> and behaviours.[5]

And the school system isn't the only place where conventional
methods of deterrence seem to be falling short. A 1997 American
report concluded:

> Reducing the risk of disordered eating in the athletic
> environment requires several educational and preventive
> approaches. As these are implemented we must be aware
> that our best efforts in this regard may inadvertently increase
> the likelihood of disordered eating developing in those
> exposed to these attempts at education and prevention. ...
> [P]rogramming may glamorize eating disorders and make
> participants aware of pathogenic behaviors.[6]

Eating disorders in girls and women—and particularly, I believe, among athletes, where one would expect to find healthy eating habits—are the result of psychological problems that are caused by deeply embedded social attitudes. In effect, they are a physical manifestation of what is essentially a woman-hating culture. But sport is even more patriarchal than everyday society, and as women have tried to gain power within the sporting culture, a new set of rules has appeared that places a great emphasis on physical appearance and maintaining certain prescribed standards.

Again, Hall-Patch was one of the lucky ones. The message to lose weight came from society in general, not from her coach. Although she was expected to volunteer a record of her fat percentage to the CCA, she wasn't under the watchful eye of someone who demanded to weigh her on a daily basis. For many athletes, the pressure to lose weight comes directly from the coach, as we will soon see. And of course many female athletes initially perform better when they start to lose weight. Unhealthy practices are rewarded when they start to ascend mountains faster on a bike or execute a higher axel on skates because of their lightness. Unfortunately, there is no end to the quest for perfection in this equation. If five pounds lost produces a positive result, what will 10, or 20, or 30 result in? Soon the ratio of lean muscle to body mass wears thin; muscles start to be eaten by the body because fat reserves and new forms of energy no longer exist.

But while there are plenty of serious physical side-effects to these disorders—including death—it is the psychological and emotional consequences that linger. Society is never going to stop bombarding women with images of so-called perfection, and part of any sufferer's recovery process is learning to live in that kind of culture. Like Hall-Patch, women recovering from eating disorders can try to intellectually understand the "dirty tricks" that society uses on them, and in that way, they can build their emotional and psychological strength so they don't cave in to the constant pressure to be thin. But it's a terrible and potentially deadly situation, full of social, psychological, and physical complexities that wind around each other like the yarn in a baseball. And for athletes, it can be especially lethal.

The Special Nature of Eating Disorders in Sport

As early as 1992, the Coaching Association of Canada (CAC) noted in its Level III training manual for national level coaches that nearly one-third of Canadian female athletes have disordered eating. In many cases, disordered eating combines an obsession with food and exercise—the sneeze before the cold, and often the precursor to a diagnosed eating disorder. When the training manual was released in 1992, Tom Kinsman, then executive director of the CAC, told me the issues it raised "are problems that weren't talked about before." He added, "I hope a new awareness will go a long way in helping people raise the issues with dignity and security. But I can tell you the process won't be nice, clean, and clear-cut." Ten years later, the problem has only got worse, but coaches and administrators still don't discuss it much.

The CAC wasn't the only athletic organization that started to admit in the early 1990s that female athletes, especially those in the aesthetic and endurance sports (where body mass can be a factor), were more likely than non-athletes to develop an eating disorder.[7] In 1997, the American College of Sports Medicine (ACSM) officially acknowledged the existence of something called the Female Athlete Triad. This triad has a domino effect on the body. First, the athlete develops an eating disorder. Then, her exceptionally low fat levels put an end to menstruation. When she misses three periods in a row, or has only three periods in a year, she has amenorrhea. With amenorrhea, she stops producing enough progesterone and estrogen to maintain normal calcium metabolism and good bones. The athlete who has an eating disorder for a long time risks premature skeletal bone loss, the third element of the triad—which is one reason so many young female athletes suffer from broken bones, and chronic stress fractures even when they haven't incurred a traumatic injury. Some sports medicine doctors have measured bone densities in female athletes that are as low as those found in 70-year-old women. Traditionally a disease of the elderly, osteoporosis has in some cases settled in even before a girl experiences her first period. Added to this are the increased risks with anorexia of life-

long fractures and scoliosis, cardiovascular disease, cancer in reproductive organs, infertility, and, of course, death.

That such august and conservative groups as the ACSM, the
Canadian Academy of Sport Medicine (CASM), and the CAC would
admit that sport, which we all like to think of as healthy, could
instead lead to devastating physical disabilities, diseases, and death
speaks to the prevalence of eating disorders among female athletes.
Certain member universities of the National Collegiate Athletic
Association (NCAA), in an attempt to recognize the risk to female
athletes, have banned weigh-ins and body composition assessments.
This is a good start, but we must go so much further to really address
the problem.

A quick glance at the media guide the Canadian Olympic Association hands out at the Pan-Am and Olympic Games shows that they
still believe in listing athletes' height and weight. In September 2001,
Time magazine did a cover feature on Venus and Serena Williams and
the other top-10 stars of the women's tennis circuit. Inside, they
listed everyone's height and weight.

In July 2001, the CASM's Women's Issues in Sport Medicine
(WIISM) Committee called for an end to weigh-ins and body composition assessments for all athletes and dancers in Canada. In September, just one week after the Canadian Medical Association (CMA)
issued some alarming information on girls and eating disorders, the
members of the CASM endorsed the WIISM committee's motion,
adding their voice to that of the national medical lobby. To support
their motion, members of the WIISM presented a paper, "Strategies
to Reduce Disordered Eating Among Female Athletes," in which
they stated:

> It is the position of the Canadian Academy of Sport Medicine
> that routine body composition assessment be abandoned for
> all female athletes and dancers. This can be a valuable
> strategy toward reduction of the incidence of the Female
> Athlete Triad, when supplemented with prevention
> programs aimed at disordered eating and comprehensive

nutritional counseling to athletes or dancers at risk. This
position statement is based on a comprehensive review and
interpretation of scientific literature concerning body
composition assessment, disordered eating and the Female
Athlete Triad.[8]

"Let's not confuse being thin with being fit," said Dr. James
Carson, the lead author of the WIISM report. "Some sports place too
much emphasis on the size of an athlete's body. This compels some
female athletes and dancers to engage in practices that are
unhealthy, and even dangerous, as they struggle to keep their
weight down. We need to change the culture and attitudes that are
prevalent in sports and abandon routine body composition testing
for physically active women."

So how did this extremely unhealthy practice become so embedded in the first place, and not just in the aesthetic sports, but in
sports such as swimming, cycling, Nordic skiing, running, and more
recently, hockey and soccer? In 1992, I travelled with a former
member of Canada's national Nordic ski team to the 25th anniversary of the Silver Spoon Cross-Country Ski Race in Deep River,
Ontario. (We had both won this race in the past, and the organizers
had invited all previous winners back to celebrate the silver anniversary.) This particular skier had raced internationally for Canada
with her sister, but not for long. I followed their careers for only a
short time before their names vanished from the results list. During
the drive to the race, I learned that both had moved on to study
science at university and were about to become medical students.
When I asked my companion why she and her sister had retired
from skiing before they had reached their potential, the conversation stopped dead. After a pause, she replied, "We both had eating
disorders."

The discussion that followed sent me to other members of the
team who had shone for a season or two in the 1980s and then disappeared. Seven of the women had kept in contact with each other,
and of those seven, four had eventually written kinesiology papers

at university on eating disorders in cross-country skiing. Amazingly, none had mentioned to the others that she had decided to take this direction in her studies.

One—who dropped off the team before the 1988 Olympics, when she weighed less than 110 pounds—found in her research that 37.5% of the former members of the national team who replied to her survey had "a serious eating disorder," while another 12.5% reported they had "a somewhat intense and obsessive preoccupation with thinness." In total, 50% of the respondents "had a symptom of anorexia nervosa," while 35.7% indicated they definitely had an eating disorder. Only two of the 14 women in the survey said they didn't diet, and only one replied that she hadn't been concerned about body weight during her skiing career.[9] One respondent wrote, "I found myself in a binge–exercise pattern, which I recognized as a problem I wanted to get under control. I did stop menstruating for two years. ... Looking back, perhaps it wasn't such a healthy thing! There is a lot of pressure on females to be skinny, and I see this as a problem."

The young woman who wrote the report says it was the then coaches of the team who pressed her to lose weight (an allegation backed up by four other former team members). When she was on the junior national team, a coach took her aside and told her she should "think about" losing weight. "I was 5'5" and weighed 135 pounds, but he said, 'Look, all the top women, all the senior women, are thin.' So I thought, 'Maybe I am a little chubby.' Even though my high-school coach didn't say it directly, we learned even at that level that it was better if we were thin. The national team coach said, 'Look at the two fastest women right now and look at how thin they are.'

"I started training for the Calgary Olympics. By late 1987, I weighed less than 110. I was constantly hungry, but I told myself, 'This is a good feeling.' I lost another five pounds the week before our qualifying competition, but I felt extremely weak and didn't make the team. I'd lost so much strength by then, I believe that's why I didn't make the team." Her standings began to suffer, and two years later, she retired from active competition.

"I certainly had a lot of bitterness over this. It's one of the reasons why I had to quit skiing. That time period undermined my health for the next two to four years. My metabolism was a mess, and I gained quite a bit of weight immediately when I stopped skiing. I'm okay now, but it helped me to write about it in my paper for university. Still, I developed a bitterness towards elite sport in general."

Says another skier, "Looking back, I can see how stupid it was. The coaches were saying, 'Hey, we've got the thinnest team around. The girls are looking great.' We didn't have good results, but that didn't seem to matter. I was just a teenager, and a coach's attitude means everything when you're young. Now I'm angry. They screwed up my mind, and I'll never be able to look at food again the way I did before."

A third athlete added, "Pressure was always felt to be lean, and considerable emphasis was placed on being beneath 12% body-fat composition. Often, it was felt this was more important than actual performance."

The pressure was also applied in other unmistakable ways. One coach instilled a mindset that made the women hold contests to see who could leave the most food on her plate at training camps. Some coaches practised something called pool dunking, where athletes would be submerged in water to measure their body-fat percentage—a procedure that induced anxiety attacks in at least one skier. "After the testing, we'd compare results," she said. "Our coach would announce at dinner who had the lowest fat percentage, and the roller coaster eating would start all over again."

Another athlete observed, "There was always pressure to come back from testing with low fat percentages and low body weights. I can remember some of the senior women not eating or drinking before weigh-ins, in order to be as low as possible." She added, "Trying to force women of different sizes and shapes into a uniform mould takes away from the real goal of producing top athletes. They [Cross Country Canada] should stop trying to produce clones of their idea of the 'ideal' woman body and support the team in their quest to achieve their athletic goals. To my knowledge, the men were never scolded for eating dessert."

Dr. James Carson of the WIISM believes the tests the athletes refer to are degrading and potentially harmful. "Harassment takes many forms," he wrote in the WIISM report, "but can generally be defined as comment, conduct, or gesture directed toward an individual, or group of individuals, which is insulting, intimidating, humiliating, malicious, degrading, or offensive. In most cases, harassment is an attempt by one person to inappropriately exert power over another person. Harassment occurs over a continuum that ranges from mild conduct, such as gestures or comments, to conduct which may be more physical, forceful, or violent. In the absence of proven benefits, a mandatory weigh-in can be equated with harassment."[10]

When I drove with one ski coach to the summer training camp in the Bugaboos of B.C. to interview the cross-country team in 1987, I remember him bragging that "not one of our girls is over 12% fat." When I arrived at the camp, it was obvious this was the case. Athletes were super lean and were putting bran on everything they ate in an attempt to use "legal" laxatives. The women's team members had also limited such fundamental carbohydrates as bread and pasta, which normally form the mainstay of any endurance athlete's diet. And it didn't end there. "It got competitive off the ski trail," one of the athletes told me. "We'd talk about how to lose weight, and look at each other and see if we could lose it quicker than someone else on the team."

There was an uneasy tension at that camp. Skiers I remembered as happy and excited about training had lost their lustre. Two athletes had gone from big, strong young women to tiny, sunken-chested shadows of their former selves. One had had a top-20 finish at the Lake Placid Olympics when she was still a teenager. She never had that high an Olympic result again.

Did this emphasis on low body fat affect the team's performance? You could say that. Our women Nordic skiers had dismal results at the 1988 Calgary Olympics, with everyone finishing at the back of the pack. We barely qualified a women's team for the 1992 Olympics, and not one woman qualified for 1994. When one team member retired after the 1992 Olympics, she developed allergies to virtually every food she ate. Another—a silver medallist at the junior world championships—developed hyperthyroidism and "disappeared off the face of the earth," according to a former teammate. While Cross Country Canada looked in vain for other reasons to explain the team's inability to compete, the four women who had retired before the Calgary Olympics began doing research and writing their papers on eating disorders.

Today, those close to the team say eating disorders are no longer a problem. Instead of measuring fat, skiers now measure muscle—a far more accurate indicator of increased strength. The coaches who had insisted on ultra-thinness are gone from the team. They're not gone from the sport, though, which troubles a good many women. One does TV colour commentary, and in a national broadcast, he announced that a Russian skier looked like she'd gained a few pounds and wasn't skiing so well now.

The facility where the national team trains in Canmore, Alberta, still has a scale front and centre, along with other apparatus meant to test strength. When I was at the facility, I saw athletes being weighed immediately after lunch. The thought of weighing themselves in front of clubmates produced anxiety in many of the women who were being tested that day. I've seen the so-called strength tests in action, and what they are is a perfect example of bad science. A test that supposedly tests abdominal strength is highly affected by the point of fulcrum in the body being tested. The variables of biomechanics negate this test as any true measure of strength. While it's true that the body-fat tests have been done away with, I couldn't help wondering if these new, supposedly more accurate measures weren't just as meaningless.

Eating Disorders and Sexual Abuse

Therapists counselling athletes with eating disorders and body-image problems have found that many of their clients are also survivors of sexual abuse. In 1994, Canada's National Eating Disorder Information Centre identified this link, but cautioned:

It will be a long time before researchers sort out all of these issues. In the meantime, there are some things that we can be certain about. One is that sexual abuse by itself is not sufficient to cause eating problems, because not all women who have been sexually abused develop eating problems. Another is that sexual abuse doesn't necessarily precede the development of eating problems, because not all women with eating problems have a history of sexual abuse. However, we know that a considerable number of women understand their eating problems as meaningfully connected to incidents or long-standing patterns of sexual abuse.[11]

In a 1999 study, "The Relationship Between Eating Disorders and Childhood Trauma," Drs. Janet de Groot and Gary Rodin argue that there is clearly a relationship between childhood sexual abuse (CSA) and "subsequent psychopathologies," which may include anorexia nervosa and/or bulimia nervosa. They cite one Canadian study that showed that 33% of women with eating disorders reported childhood sexual abuse, more than double the rate of abuse (14%) in women who were not suffering from eating disorders. An American study also found that "rape prior to age 12 years had occurred more commonly among women with bulimia nervosa than among women who did not have bulimia nervosa." These studies were seen as significant because they were based on "large, non-clinical samples."[12]

De Groot and Rodin focused on the relationship between eating disorders and childhood sexual abuse. But in the sporting world, coaches who abuse athletes normally start in a girl's teenage years, and they frequently wait until she is above the age of consent (though, in many cases, they will have been grooming the girl for several years so she will easily be emotionally manipulated into a sexual relationship in her later teens). No studies have yet been done to establish a link between eating disorders in female athletes and sexual abuse by coaches, but de Groot and Rodin's study does offer some interesting food for thought.

In discussing the role of the family in childhood sexual abuse, de Groot and Rodin argue, "Indeed, the disclosure of the abuse and the response of the family to this disclosure may be an important determinant of its pathogenic effect. The role of abuse in the development of conditions such as eating disorders is best considered in the family context in which a young girl is raised and in terms of all the other risk factors and protective factors that may be present."[13] In sport, a girl's team often becomes her surrogate family, with the coach taking on the role of father. If this substitute family is dysfunctional and abusive, the effect on the athlete can be devastating.

So where does this leave the young female athlete who believes her coach when he tells her she "could lose a few pounds"? And how does she resist his subsequent sexual advances when she has no self-esteem, rational power, or physical stamina left? She may be an adult in the eyes of the law, but is she really able to consent to a sexual relationship of her own free will?

I subscribe to the definition of sexual abuse in sport Celia Brackenridge sets out in her book *Spoilsports*. She believes the relative power of the abuser is the determining factor, not the age or implied consent of the victim. Brackenridge argues, "The distinction between child and adult athlete is regarded in this book as morally irrelevant. In terms of non-legal definitions, the boundary between the two is unclear. ... Nonetheless the relationship between athlete and coach is one based on power and trust and is considered here to override age distinctions."[14]

In *The Dome of Silence*, Canada's Dr. Sandi Kirby identifies a further complicating factor in sexually abusive relationships between coaches and athletes. "There are often contradictory feelings and emotions regarding the perpetrator and the abuse and its meaning," she writes. "Mixtures of loyalty, commitment, fealty, affection, guilt and shame contribute to denial and work against disclosure. ... While sexual abuse is about power, not sexual activity, when sexual measures become part of the scale of success, trainers and coaches and judges will push to develop these aspects of the athletes under their influence."[15] Both scholars agree that the gendered imbalance in sport awards virtually all power to men and creates a climate where sexual abuse can thrive.

Most literature on sexual abuse in sport refers to situations where the athlete is "non-consenting." I disagree with the use of this term and would argue, as Kirby and Brackenridge do, that any kind of intimate relationship between a coach and an athlete—no matter how consenting or adult she is—is an act of sexual exploitation by a person in a position of authority. When I visited that pre-Olympic camp for the Nordic ski team in 1987, every woman there was either married to, living with, or having a sexual relationship with a coach, technical director, or equipment supplier. One woman was just out of making the top six and thus of representing Canada when she told me it seemed that if you weren't sleeping with an important man, you didn't have a hope of making the team. This woman had married her university coach, who apparently wasn't high enough in the male pecking order for his athlete to matter. (Later, when he was in his late 30s, he left her for an 18-year-old skier he was training.)

Eating disorders, sexual abuse, homophobia, and the sexual objec-tification of athletes all take place in the mix that is women's sport and pile up on one another, sometimes simultaneously, sometimes sequentially, but never in isolation. Unfortunately, Nordic skiing— like cycling, track and field, swimming, volleyball, gymnastics, and no doubt plenty of other sports—has a long tradition of coaches getting sexually involved with athletes. Along with all the other sports I named, it has an equally long tradition of athletes develop-ing eating disorders, severe body-image problems, and psychosexual problems.

After an athlete's teachers, her coach is usually the first adult outside of the family with whom she forms a relationship that is at once power-laden and emotionally loaded. He can be a powerful father figure. Ideally, like good teachers and parents, coaches use lessons, instructions, and their own experiences to teach young people how best to realize who they are and turn their dreams into realities. In effect, a good coach works himself out of a job. Coaches also choose who makes a team, who gets dropped, who plays, who sits on the bench, who gets their undivided attention, and who gets ignored. It's inherently a power imbalance.

Sport is also a highly emotional place, with constant shifts in mood and physical location. When athletes are on the road, they often eat as a group, sometimes sitting with an authority figure at the table. The one constant in all of this kinetic, emotional, and geographical movement is the coach.

When we look at how girls are trained to please from the time they are infants, and admit that sport is still a place where women are only allowed in, as opposed to embraced, we can see that the male coach's power is all-encompassing. As psychiatrist Jennifer Jones argues in a study on eating disorders, "Females are taught that being physically attractive is related to pleasing and serving others and will secure their love. … The development of self-concept in girls is based more on interpersonal and external forces than boys, and girls tend to refer to the views of others to describe themselves. … Pre-pubertal girls report beginning to worry about becoming fat as early as nine years of age."[16]

The athlete-coach relationship is also often established at a time when the athlete is testing the waters of independence and trying to form her own unique sexual identity, and Jones argues that this is the time in adolescent girls when "physical and psychological changes … can amplify concerns regarding weight and shape."[17] Canadian studies show that the coach will frequently have more influence over the athlete than parents do during this crucial period.[18]

If a coach chooses to take advantage of this power disparity, what is the ultimate power he can exercise? He can control an athlete's feelings about her own body. According to Karin Jasper, a Toronto psychotherapist who treats young women with eating disorders, "The athletic look is lean with narrow hips, and we have learned that women dislike the size of their hips, stomachs, and thighs, those areas most connected with pregnancy."[19] Women have learned to adapt to the idealized male aesthetic over the years, particularly in sport, where the mere mention of child-bearing hips is considered a grave insult. All too often, they literally starve themselves in an effort to achieve a slim look that actually desexualizes them.

Of course, there are plenty of costs to this when it's taken to extremes. At least one of the common side-effects of self-starvation is the loss of sex drive. The body's hormonal system all but shuts down because it doesn't have enough fat to stimulate normal production of progesterone and estrogen. And not only does the anorexic athlete not desire sex, she also has no hips, no breasts, no period, and possibly a covering of fine hair that the body has produced to stay warm in the absence of subcutaneous fat. Physically, she looks like a boy—just what the coach was hoping for. There will be no competition from other men now: The athlete doesn't desire them, and they surely don't desire her. The coach has successfully changed a woman into a eunuch, and he has his new girl/boy all to himself.

This may sound like a nightmare scenario, but I remember lining up for a Nordic ski race in the early 1980s and gasping as I looked at the bodies of a certain coach's athletes. Their Lycra suits were baggy and their faces haggard with the tell-tale signs of starvation. Soft white hair covered their skin, and their spindly legs did not meet at the top. Their crotches formed boxes through which I could see winter sun. It was ghastly. And like so many others, they fell out of the racing circuit after a season or two. I learned later that their coach had tried to get them to have sex with him. He was a middle-aged married man, while they were all under the age of 22. When I returned to the Deep River race for the 25th anniversary, that coach was there too. Because my race was at 1:00 p.m., I didn't eat any lunch. By the time it was over and I'd done a warm-down, I wanted something to eat. But as I was biting into a chocolate chip cookie, he admonished me, "Laura, are you sure you need that cookie?"

I was bold enough to believe I could decide for myself whether I should have that cookie, but what of those women who second-guess this most simple decision? As Clare Hall-Patch reported, the world becomes fuzzy when you're starving and depressed. Making complex decisions and guarding against unethical behaviour becomes very difficult; the athlete's own survival system is disarmed. And if an athlete grows up in sport, she often has no outside reference points to call on. Practices that might seem "normal" to her, such as a coach doing a skin-fold caliper fat-percentage test on her inner thigh or buttocks, could constitute sexual assaults in the real world.

The athletes who are most prone to eating disorders also have a heightened need to please, and are thus categorized as highly "coachable."[20] They live for words of approval from their coaches. Many a national team athlete has told me what happened once she agreed with her coach that she could afford to "lose a few pounds." The coach started directing what she could and couldn't eat and interrogating her about what she'd consumed when he wasn't there. Meals ceased being fun and were soon dreaded. Scales became the focal point of the relationship. Once sexual intercourse had also been introduced by the coach, he started to choose what clothes the athlete would wear. He was the filter through which she saw the world. It didn't matter if legally she was an adult—she became "his girl."

The Otherness of the Female Body in Sport

Sport sociology was still a new area of study when Paul Willis first explained how the inferiority of women in sport is entrenched. In 1982, in what was to become an often noted essay, he wrote,

> The fact that no one can deny female difference becomes the
> fact of female sports inferiority, becomes the fact that females
> are innately different from men, becomes the fact that
> women who stray across the defining boundary are in a
> parlous state. An ideological view comes to be deposited in
> our culture as a common sense assumption—of course
> women are different and inferior.[21]

I believe this ideology has created a twisted and complex sporting culture that teaches both men and women to play highly gendered roles that don't upset the patriarchal apple cart. Anyone who has ever been on the outside looking in—Aboriginal people, people of colour, disabled people, gays and lesbians, and women—knows that they must find ways to survive. In her book *The Hungry Self*, Berkeley psychotherapist Kim Chernin describes what those survival methods are like for women:

> We keep our eyes open, our ears take in subtle communications a more secure person could afford to miss. And now we take ourselves in hand, tailoring ourselves to the specifications of this world we are so eager to enter. We strip our bodies of flesh, our hearts of the overflow of feeling, our language of exuberant and dramatic imprecisions. We cut back the flights of our fancy, make our thought rigorous and subject it to measures of demonstration and proof, trying not to talk with our hands, trying hard to subdue our voices, getting our bursts of laughter under control.[22]

In sport, we must put these constraints on ourselves because we can't afford to stand out. If we do, we could be sent back where we came from. And it is important to remember, in all discussion of sport and the female body, that the patriarchal sporting culture focuses almost exclusively on the phallus. In orthodox male-only sport cultures, women exist only to be penetrated by that phallus.

Orthodox male sport is all about staying hard, never going soft, and penetrating until a victory is scored. In my book *Crossing the Line*, I argued that hypermasculine, violent organizations such as men-only junior hockey leagues foster a "rape culture." What is the first rule of a rape culture? The subjugation of women. When women realize this, which for many of us happens only on the subconscious level, we expend a great deal of energy trying to survive that subjugation. Some do it by trying to convince themselves that it's natural, normal, and what God wanted. Women who allow a women's committee to be dominated by men, as women do in the Canadian Hockey Association, are an example of this coping method. The rest of us struggle against it.

What's worse is when mothers internalize their own subjugation so thoroughly that they act in ways that hurt the next generation of females—their daughters. One cross-country ski coach I interviewed told me that one of her athletes had developed an eating disorder because of her mother's need to control her daughter's life. Like hockey fathers who push their sons to realize a dream that they themselves missed out on, some mothers want to live vicariously through their daughters. An eating disorder is one way those daughters can feel they've regained control over their lives.

A second athlete had developed an eating disorder because her parents ignored her accomplishments and focused instead on her brothers' pursuits. In this case, the disorder was a way of gaining control because love and attention were missing. Like many girls with eating disorders, these two athletes were subject to a destructive pattern at home and found this pattern exacerbated by a sporting environment that reinforces it. Some psychotherapists believe that girls who come from homes where they are at a high risk of developing an eating disorder will actually gravitate to sports that mask the disorder as "good athlete" behaviour.[23]

"Her parents put her down by mistake," said the Nordic ski coach (who did not want to be identified) of the second athlete. "Her brothers, who were also in sport, had much better support. She believed she had to excel at everything—sport, school, and be their housekeeper too. If you want to know the truth, the family mainly wanted her as a housekeeper; they weren't very concerned about what else she could do."

This is a story I have heard repeated for years. In the CHA's *Speak Out!* workbook on the abuse of children, they quote a young assistant coach who is worried about a girl on his team. "I am an assistant coach on a girls' hockey team, and there's this girl on my team. The parents wished they had a boy and, therefore, treat their daughter like a boy and favour their son. They say they will be at her game, and then they don't show up. And the whole game she's upset that they aren't there, but [they are] at her brother's hockey game. When they are there, they are always yelling at her and saying that she's bad and doesn't do anything. What do I do?"[24]

When I was investigating sexual abuse in junior hockey, female survivors of abuse by male players often told me that they were ignored within their own families. One girl—who wasn't allowed to play hockey, even though her younger brother did—described the attitude of her parents after she'd alleged that five junior hockey players gang-raped her. "I didn't have any support from my parents; I'm not close to them," she told me. "My mom's not really my mom. I can't talk to her. ... When I phoned her from the police station, she told me it was my fault. 'You dress like a slut,' she said. My parents still go to the [team's] games. Can you imagine the type of parents who would support the team that raped their daughter?" I interviewed this girl at lunchtime. She ate a plate of celery sticks.

These stories show how several issues—worshipping the male body, sexual abuse of the female body, and eating disorders—can collide when we begin to look at the life of the female athlete. If someone is not encouraged to be an athlete in her own right, as happened with the girl who wanted but wasn't allowed to play hockey, she will often attach herself to a worshipped male athlete and effectively use her body sexually to gain access to the sporting culture. When she was ignored in favour of her brother, the very thin, celery-eating girl I interviewed learned quickly to live vicariously through the triumphs of the male body by attaching herself to hockey players. To them, she was nothing more than a "puck bunny." "They passed me from player to player as if I was a puck," she told me.[25]

The Paradox of Self-Fulfilment

Kim Chernin argues that, through terrifying and brutal life experiences like those described above, girls learn that it's a disadvantage to be a daughter. And when we move beyond our families, we find that being female doesn't work in the outside world either. No wonder we strive for a defeminized body:

This anxiety ... makes us yearn to wear male clothes,

regardless of fit, and to work over and worry at and reshape
these females bodies of ours so that they can help us pretend
we have managed to escape from being our mothers'
daughters and have, in our appearance at least, become their
sons. Our mothers' sons—those beings for whom self-
development and the struggle for identity are an entirely
legitimate enterprise.[26]

We may have slowly, incrementally, been able to open some
doors, but we have by no means realized our full potential. And,
ironically, the strides we have made have created new problems, for
as Chernin puts it, "We are a generation who, with every act of self-
assertion as women, with every movement into self-development
and fulfilment, call into question the values by which our mothers
have tried to live."[27] Like the son who has to defeat the father to
come fully into his own, we must accept both the limitations of our
mothers' lives and the possibilities of our own. And this we have not
yet achieved. As Chernin writes,

> Our obsession with losing weight and keeping ourselves
> small, our determination to remake the female body so that
> it suits masculine attire, our retreat into the masculine
> exterior disguise, our desperate eating of large amounts of
> food, our starvation of ourselves, our forced purges and
> evacuations of the food we take into ourselves—they all
> express the immense burden of female self-development. ...
> So far, in our struggle for liberation, we have become women
> dressed in male attire and not yet, by any means, women
> clothed in the full potential of female being.[28]

Chernin goes on to argue that to understand eating disorders,
"We must place [them] in relation to this fateful encounter between
a mother whose life has not been fulfilled and a daughter now
presented with the opportunity for fulfilment."[29] When daughters
jump into the world, they are metaphorically turning their backs

on everything their mothers represent. And the mother who watches her daughter waltz off with only vague thoughts of marriage and children can't help thinking, "Are you telling me that my life of sacrifice and devotion was not living at all?"[30]

In dysfunctional relationships, where mothers and daughters cannot or will not acknowledge the tension between generations, the most powerful force at the mother's disposal is food. Subconsciously she uses this to try to bring her daughter back, to foil her escape. She plies her with brownies, cupcakes, and all the other symbols of the nurturing mother every time she returns home. And if the daughter has learned the script of dysfunction, she will eat them and then purge herself through vomiting, symbolically both eliminating the overbearing mother and sabotaging her own plans for self-fulfilment. When a woman develops an eating disorder, Chernin argues, food replaces her dreams.

For the woman athlete, there is a double whammy. In her quest for a thin body, she is attempting not only to banish the image of the mother, but also to recreate herself as a boy. In sport, the male body has been so predominant for so long it's no wonder that women believe they'll be safer if they look like boys. The roundness of a woman's body is seen as a negative because it makes her easier to single out. And even a hint of our full potential is too unsettling for a certain percentage of men.

Of course, the irony is that as we slim down, we may gain some metaphorical strength, in the form of more open doors and a greater acceptance among men, but we risk losing physical strength. As we have already seen, the trend has been away from hefty muscles and toward a leaner look, especially among elite athletes. This has long been true among figure skaters and gymnasts, but it's also true now among the endurance athletes. Women middle- and long-distance runners, cyclists, Nordic skiers, and swimmers no longer have the hefty thighs and hips that were common in the 1960s and '70s.

We practise a fine balance. We have one foot in the door, keeping it open for the next generation of women, while the other checks for land mines in the very male territory of the playing field. We try to construct our bodies to meet male approval, while not putting ourselves in danger. Most of us genuinely don't want to get too skinny—after all, we can't afford to let men think our bodies are vulnerable—but we often fall in love with our own leaner forms, as Clare Hall-Patch did. And if we can find the perfect balance between lean muscle mass and low body weight, we really do go faster and operate more efficiently. It is possible to be lean and very active, eat a balanced diet, and not suffer from any kind of eating or exercise disorder. This is simply the practice of loving and living in one's own body to the fullest extent. Walking, running, or cycling instead of driving will help us all stay fitter and avoid obesity, which is at least as serious a problem as being dangerously underweight.

Of course, the reality is that slim women are more readily accepted by men. For the most part, larger women, in sport as in other areas of life, are either ignored or barely tolerated, while a woman who's told how "fit" she looks, which almost always means she's very lean, will invariably be accepted. And when the other—the lean female infiltrator—finds favour in the eyes of men, she can go about making changes: getting that door a little more open so those in the next generation don't have to go to such ridiculous lengths just to be let in.

But how do we challenge established norms without putting ourselves in danger from the backlash that inevitably follows? I believe we can undertake both simple little tasks and complex long-term missions. Men need to be deprogrammed from viewing women as outsiders. When we sit in long meetings with them, discussing strategies in coaching, we need to remind them of other issues that must be addressed. Those meetings need to have a minimum of 30% women in them before women will really have a voice, otherwise boards of directors such as the Canadian Hockey Association's, with just three out of 35 delegates being female, will always replicate the male status quo of generations long ago.

It is time to ask questions and work together to provide answers. Why is there still a scale in the physiology lab at the Canmore Nordic Centre? Why do so many governing bodies hire coaches who have had, or are having, sexual relationships with athletes? Why did Swimming/Natation Canada's head coach, Dave Johnson, hire for the Sydney Olympics a young woman who didn't meet the association's own coaching standards, overlooking other, older, more qualified women? Why does a man represent women on the Canadian Hockey Association's executive committee?

The men who run sport have to learn that, while they may feel safe running in a park or on a country road, many of us don't. They have to hear women talk about periods and competitions; pregnancy and returning to racing; childcare and recreation facilities that don't offer any; lesbian leagues; women-only expeditions; new world records; court challenges to ice time; and all the other issues that matter to women athletes.

I believe we must dedicate ourselves to continuing these long and drawn-out fights, for if we do not question the fundamental sexist culture of sport, we are complicit in allowing it to continue. But the easiest way to get men to open that door a crack is by being attractive in their eyes. It's that simple—and that stupid.

This is the realpolitik of feminism, sport, and the media. It feels great to be fit, to be strong, and to know one's body is capable of rising to challenges—but we are always balancing, balancing, balancing.

8   Who Gets to Be a Free Woman?

Sport and the Sweatshop

Alison Sydor is flying along a single-track trail with a bunch of schoolboys on one of the few rain-free days Victoria experienced during the fall of 1999. She tends to let the throttle out when she's riding her bicycle, but today she holds back and lets the kids go first. Her jazzy jersey identifies her as a top pro, but now it blends in with all the store-bought look-alikes around her. Unlike so many of her male counterparts in the world of professional team sports, Sydor exudes an air of quiet humility, tempered by the kind of confidence earned by capturing her fourth overall mountain bike world cup title that year. Underneath the helmet, visor, and loud jersey is a mix of great strength and great empathy—something many human beings, and too many athletes, lack. Soft and strong reside side by side in this woman. She's a great role model for girls, of course, but also for the considerable number of boys and adults who admire her amazing sporting feats.

She has ridden her mountain bike from her home in downtown Victoria to the West Saanich peninsula on a Sunday morning to ride with 107 schoolkids from grades 7 to 12 who have gathered for a morning ride with this West Coast hero and a dozen other B.C. pro mountain bikers. Despite threatening grey skies, there is a palpable excitement in the air. After all, how often does a guy (almost all these kids are boys, a fact that sticks in Sydor's craw) get to ride with a four-time world champion, Olympic silver medalist, and the most frequently crowned world cup rider on the face of the earth?

Sydor and her fat-tire colleagues are volunteers in a school mountain bike program called Sprockids, which has caught on in British Columbia like mud on a rear hub. The professional riders spend much of their off-trail time drumming up backers for this program. Corporate sponsors understand that if one of these bike pros rides for their team, they'll be expected to cough up some bicycles, equipment, and clothing for kids who can't afford any of this stuff for themselves. Well-connected West Coast patrons also endorse and financially support the program, and in 2000, Sprockids gave out the first of its so-called bicycle scholarships to kids who don't have enough money to purchase their own equipment and clothing. Lesley Tomlinson races professionally, and for many years for Canada's national team—and recruited Sydor, her long-time friend, into the program—and her hard work has made the scholarships become a reality.

It's clear that Sydor's involvement in sport also goes beyond what it holds for her. "People are meant to move," she says, offering her philosophy of sport. "It's sad that kids are being sold inactive lifestyles—Nintendo, TV, sitting in school all day. It's hard to get yourself going if you always stay sitting. When kids discover mountain biking, they start riding and riding. Lives have changed because kids get out on bikes. The smile on a kid's face makes my day."

The day I call on Sydor for an interview, NBC has just finished filming her for a documentary on the battle of the Alisons. (Her American counterpart, Alison Dunlap, won the gold at the 1999 Pan-Am Games while Sydor took the silver. Two months later, Sydor beat Dunlap at the world championships.) Nike visited her with a camera crew during the same time period. "You'd hate it," says Sydor of the commercial she made with the shoe company. In fact, I was surprised she'd made it at all. We had talked about Nike in the past, and she had said she'd never endorse a company she felt was unethical. But on this day, Sydor does not want to talk about the world of corporate marketing and merchandising. She will say no more about her Nike endorsement and turns the conversation to the latest developments in Sprockids instead.

The bicycle scholarships, she explains, will make money available for 30 to 40 kids who can't afford bikes on their own. "It's a small step, but the most important one," Sydor says. Her dream is that one day, every kid who wants to ride a bike can borrow or buy one through the program. "This is an amazing sport, but right now it's not available to everyone. It would be nice if every school had a little fleet of bikes for all kids, and we can do something about that."

In another interview, she later tells me, "Winning medals, trophies, is exciting, but they are symbols of how hard you've worked. There's only so much satisfaction in that. Athletes have a huge kind of power, and by that I don't mean competing in high-level sport. I mean I want to totally embrace the role of being a positive image to kids—and adults—of what a healthy lifestyle can be like. Society these days is really stressful and very, very unnatural. The Internet, TV—it's not healthy. Seeing so many kids riding their bikes is a different kind of satisfaction. It's not life or death if you fail. At the end of the day, riding a bike is a non-threatening way to learn a lot about yourself."

It's obvious Sydor has given a lot of thought to the issues she raised. And despite her apparent unease with her Nike commercial, it turns out to be quite un-corporate. "Do I look too masculine?" she asks the viewer. "Do I look too fat in tights? Or too thin? Do I look like a model? Do I look like I care?" The commercial uses edgy images of Sydor in motion—sometimes in black and white, sometimes in colour—but she's in control no matter how steep the slope or the switchback. It's the perfect counterpoint to the McDonald's Barbie brigade, and I actually began to think Nike wasn't so bad—until I saw a two-page spread the company ran just months before the Sydor commercial aired.

In the August 9, 1999, issue of *Sports Illustrated*, the inside front cover and its adjoining page are given over to a Nike ad that has two objects, one line of script, the Nike swoosh, and the Nike Web site address. The catchline reads "Air Is What Makes It Good," and it's surprinted on the two objects. One of these objects is a slick, airbrushed portrait of the Nike AirTunedMax, the company's latest shoe. The other is a little harder to identify because it is all folded up in a clear plastic bag. On closer scrutiny, it becomes obvious that what we are looking at is a picture of a full-sized, anatomically correct inflatable doll. Like Barbie, she is white, blonde, blue-eyed, and ruby-lipped, and even has a beauty mark on her cheek. Here is the ultimate pliable woman. Air makes her "good" because that makes her useful, waiting patiently and quietly for the man who has purchased her to do whatever he pleases. Of course, *he* wears the shoes. Air is something that pumps him up, makes him bigger. On the other hand, she is literally his airhead date.

The Personal and the Political

In the potent early days of modern feminism Gloria Steinem pointed out that "the personal is political." What she meant by that is that the personal lives we lead—the choices we make, the values we live by—are also choices that affect the environment around us; they ripple out. How does this apply to sport? Well, I would argue that even the simple act of running freely in the streets of North America is a political statement—and so, more obviously, is the act of endorsing certain products and corporations.

All too often, one woman's seemingly benign act of free will works against the freedom of another woman somewhere else in the world—and not only her political and economic freedom, but also her sexual freedom. I am referring here not just to the dichotomy between the women who wear running shoes and the women who make them, but also to the dichotomy between the female athletes who endorse certain products and the females who consume them. All of these acts have an especially strong impact on perceptions of sexuality, particularly in girls who are just beginning to define themselves as sexual beings.

Many people will wonder how a run through the streets of a city can be construed as a political act—and especially how it can be connected with sexuality. But women who run are engaging in a public act of freedom. They are also claiming a place in public space—space that has not always been open to women. As recently as 1967, women were barred from running the Boston Marathon. When Kathy Switzer first competed in that race, she was attacked both verbally and physically by race officials. But Switzer and other women like her fought to give us access to that public space. They fought for our right to compete in the Olympic marathon, a right we finally won in 1984. In fact, they fought for our right to run whatever distance we pleased. It wasn't until 1960 that women were allowed to run more than 200 metres. Men, of course, have run all the Olympic distances since the modern Olympics began in 1896.

In my neighbourhoods in Toronto and Calgary, I see groups of women of all shapes and sizes claiming their right to be in public space as they train for upcoming races or just jog to keep healthy. It is an incredibly powerful statement when women take to the streets in their running shoes. They sweat, they spit, they allow their bodies to function freely and their faces to grimace and laugh. No one tries to hide her wrinkles or fix her hair. I hear women giggling and talking as I do my own workouts, and I always feel strengthened by their presence.

But does the combination of publicly and unapologetically being who you are and the empowering feeling you take away from sport really make for a healthier sexuality in women? I would say yes. Anytime we "own" our bodies, especially in a public way, it allows the sexual self to also own the body and spirit. We are sexual beings at the same time as we are runners, canoeists, doctors, lawyers, cashiers, daughters, mothers, and wives. And the unabashedness with which some women claim their right to public space also reinforces a healthy sexuality. When we compare these strong public acts with the message women receive from the media—your thighs are too big, your breasts are too small, your hair is too grey, your weight is too high—the contrast is extraordinary.

Embracing your body and enjoying physical pleasures, which certainly include running on city streets or country trails, is an essential part of a healthy sexuality. Women need to learn that their bodies are there for their pleasure, and they alone can decide what form that pleasure should take.

There is no question in my mind that running is one of the best things some women have going. I'm not a born runner, but there are times when even my feet seem to float along the trails and I feel as if I could run all day long. Running is the most immediately accessible sport there is. No matter where you are, you can slip on your workout clothes and a pair of running shoes and take off. Yet it's not all good news. Most of the big sporting goods corporations have seen the value in promoting running—and all other kinds of physical activity—as freeing for women, but all too often, the marketing campaigns they use act as a smokescreen for the very unfree conditions in which so many of their female employees toil. Some women's freedom is dearly paid for by others—and not just in the developing world, but even in our own backyard.

In the Sweatshops of the World

It's a gorgeous late-summer day in Calgary—the kind of day that has most people heading to the mountains or jogging and cycling around town. But one group of people has decided to take a short walk—around and around again—in front of Forzani's Tech Shop, one of a chain of high-end running and active-wear stores owned by former Canadian Football League player John Forzani, who also owns Sport Chek, Sport Mart, and Coast Mountain Sports.

Forzani's is popular in a city where everyone, it seems, goes jogging, but today, 36 people have gathered to protest the fact that the chain stocks Nike shoes, clothing, and accessories. Human rights advocates have targeted Nike for years, saying the company exploits mainly young female workers in manufacturing its products. This particular demonstration was organized by Estelle Kuzyk, who is in her 10th year as a letter carrier and is co-chair of the Calgary and District Labour Council Human Rights Committee. "I joined the labour council three years ago because I felt we needed a human rights committee," she tells me. "There are so many issues that labour needs to address, and I'm happy to say we walk the walk. The labour council has done good work around things such as sweatshop labour and child labour."

Kuzyk is handing out flyers to customers and runners who use Forzani's store as a base. Most, but not all, take a pamphlet. Just out of Kuzyk's earshot, one woman asks, "Why don't they write letters and join Amnesty International?" I point out to her that the labour council's code of conduct kit includes material from Amnesty International. Workers who try to start unions in undemocratic countries where sweatshops proliferate are often imprisoned, so Amnesty sees them as political prisoners and advocates on their behalf. Oxfam and UNICEF material can also be found in the kit because so much of their mandate concerns the rights and well-being of women and children. And the demonstrators *do* write letters. Plenty of letters. Later, Kuzyk gives me a batch of letters the organization has sent to John Forzani, Nike, and other manufacturers.

One of the women in the parking lot next to Forzani's says she's careful about what she buys. She says that she will find out about the history of a carpet before she buys it, for instance, and that she is selective about the stores she purchases from to avoid buying carpets made by children. But, her friend counters, if people in the developing nations didn't have these jobs, they'd be even worse off.

This refrain is often heard from people in the developed world—that without the benevolent presence of transnational companies, the world's poor would be even poorer. Is there any truth to this credo? It's true that transnationals, and globalization in general, have transformed the economies of the so-called Third World. But is this a good thing? Today, huge tracts of land that were once devoted to agriculture have been turned into industrial farms. Life was never easy in much of the world, but people worked the land and had a relationship to it that allowed them to at least endure, and sometimes flourish. Now these people have little choice but to live by the new rules of the global economy. Many of the young women who work in the sweatshops of El Salvador, for example, are the daughters of farmers who grew corn and coffee. When those farmers could no longer compete with the cheaper crops from massive industrial farms, their daughters had to find work in the city. Ironically, as labour migrates, immigrants from all over the world often find themselves in the United States, toiling as part of the huge production line that continues to put their neighbours in traditional agricultural economies back home out of work.

I am not romanticizing the daily struggle to survive that many people had, and still have, in rural parts of the world. Nor do I think these countries are "poor but pure." The mostly female workforce that makes the clothes and shoes we play in is located, for the most part, in countries that have little or no democratic history. For instance, Indonesia spent 24 years systematically terrorizing and murdering the citizens of East Timor (a country it took over by military force in 1975). Indonesia is now home to many shoe and garment manufacturers, including Nike. With the help of an American-trained military, President Suharto ran Indonesia with an iron fist until 1999, and was later charged in 2000 with defrauding it to the tune of $570 million.

Cicih Sukaesih is an Indonesian woman featured in the Alberta Labour Council's code of conduct kit. She says she was fired from her job at Nike's contractor's plant because of her involvement in union organizing, and members of the Alberta labour council have taken up her cause and included information about her in their handouts at the demonstration. Like so many women, Sukaesih knows it likely won't be her generation that profits from the changes she's working for. She is quoted in the flyer Kuzyk and her colleagues are handing out in front of Forzani's as saying, "The work being done in the North to pressure Nike to treat us fairly might not benefit us tomorrow, but slowly there will be changes."

Sukaesih's concerns are similar to those of women from other Southeast Asian countries who organized unions in the garment and footwear industries in the 1980s. When Nike and Reebok moved their manufacturing from the U.S. to Taiwan and South Korea in the early 1980s, other athletic sportswear manufacturers followed—Adidas, Fila, L.A. Gear, Asics. Pusan, a coastal city of South Korea, soon became the "sneaker capital of the world." In America, 58,000 jobs were lost in the switch, but the sportswear companies could pay their employees considerably less, and they didn't have to concern themselves with North America's pesky workplace safety regulations. Conveniently, places like Indonesia, South Korea, and Taiwan also had military governments that were experienced at quashing dissent among workers. Still, not all Asian women were willing to accept a life with so few benefits—despite the stereotypes of subservience and docility that so comfort the North Americans who believe them. Faced with the dangerous and restrictive practices of the men who held manufacturing contracts with the running-shoe companies, some of the women revolted.

Cynthia Enloe, a professor of government at Clark University in the United States, described in *Ms.* magazine how the South Korean government and the transnational corporations that did business in that country reacted to women who tried to organize there. "At the first sign of trouble," she wrote, "factory managers called in government riot police to break up employees' meetings. Troops sexually assaulted women workers, stripping, fondling, and raping them 'as a control mechanism for suppressing women's engagement in the labour movement.'"[1]

Enloe reports that the women workers continued to fight back and formed the Korean Women Workers Association (KWWA). Eventually, they were able to meet with company managers and address issues such as poverty-level wages, sexual assault by bosses, length of work week, and health care. So effective was the KWWA, in fact, that it is seen as partly responsible for the defeat of South Korea's military government in 1987. (Interestingly, in the summer of 2001, Kim Un-yong, an IOC member from South Korea, placed second in the race for the presidency of the IOC. This man had been the head of South Korea's secret police during the military regime's reign, when so many women workers were fired, jailed, or tortured. This unsavoury past didn't seem to be relevant to the other IOC members.)

And what effect did the KWWA have on the transnationals

themselves? Well, Nike, like so many others, opted to pull up stakes in South Korea in favour of less democratic and more oppressive countries, such as Indonesia and Thailand (where women could not dare organize because of physical threats). In South Korea, out-of-work women soon turned to prostitution as legitimate jobs dried up. Those who had left their hometowns for manufacturing jobs in Pusan found they were generally unwelcome when they tried to go home. A woman who'd been tarnished by "big city life"—even if that life meant working horrendously long hours on an assembly line—was considered "too old and too used" for marriage, and therefore she was no use to her family. And the cycle has continued.

Unfortunately, when manufacturers skip around from country to country, it creates a rift among workers internationally. North American workers often express racist attitudes toward people in the countries where manufacturers have relocated. In Southeast Asia, women whose wages undercut those of women in a neighbouring country are viewed as the enemy. The idea of becoming "one big global family" simply has not brought us together. Globalization is all about a ruthless neo-capitalism—and no one believes their neighbour is family when he is "stealing" their job and their livelihood. Not coincidentally, it is very difficult to build a sisterhood in such an environment.

On the Playing Fields of the World

When Nike pulled out of South Korea, it certainly wasn't to move to a more stable place to do business. Indonesia, one of the company's new homes, has been awash in bloodshed and corruption for years. President Abudurrahman Wahid, who replaced Suharto, was forced to resign in 2001 because of mounting evidence of his direct involvement in the fraudulent transfer of millions of dollars. In the spring of 2001, the IOC's member from Indonesia, Bob Hasan, was found guilty of embezzling $359 million.

In total, Nike contracts its work to 700 factories around the world.

In early January 2001, 800 workers at a plant that made sportswear for Nike went on strike at the Kuk-Dong factory in Atlixco, Mexico. *Globe and Mail* columnist Naomi Klein documented the fallout of the strike in a January 17, 2001, column entitled "Strike Shines a Harsh Light on Nike." Klein reported that the Kuk-Dong garment factory produced sweatshirts with "the insignia of the universities of Michigan, Oregon, Arizona, Indiana and North Carolina." All of these schools, and plenty of others, have contracts with Nike to supply them with merchandise. But university campuses across America have seen larger and larger protests against merchandise produced by exploited workers in the developing world. United Students Against Sweatshops is "now active on 175 campuses," Klein reports, and while students have protested against other manufacturers, "their most public battles have been with sporting goods giant Nike."

The collegiate apparel market is worth $2.5 billion annually, and students and unions believe manufacturers shouldn't be allowed to self-regulate, as they do now, for safety, environmental, and human rights issues, but instead should be monitored by an independent agency that's not "company friendly." Workers and students pressure schools to join the Worker Rights Consortium, which Klein says is "a group that advocates truly independent monitoring, free of company control." The consortium released a video of working conditions at the Kuk-Dong factory so consumers could see for themselves what protesters are talking about. In the video, Klein writes,

> A young Mexican woman speaks of poverty wages, hunger, of getting sick on the job and not being allowed time off. When asked how old she is, she replies, 'Fifteen.' According to Nike's code of conduct, the company will not employ garment workers younger than 16. Nike says she may have falsified documents to land the job. Document fraud is, in fact, widespread in Mexico, but underage workers often claim that they were coached to lie by the local companies' own recruiters.[2]

Workers also complain that the unions, like the monitoring agencies, are controlled by the factory. The workers say that when five of their colleagues protested the "company union," they were fired. Their co-workers protested the firings. One of the fired employees, Josephina Hernandez, said, "What we are asking for is an end to the corrupt union and for an independent union formed by workers." And what was the response of the company that manufactured for Nike? "Riot police, led by the leader of the company union, swept in and put an end to the protest, beating workers and sending 15 to hospital," Klein reported. "The attacks were so brutal that roughly 200 workers have decided not to return to work at the factory even though the strike is over, fearing management retribution. Freedom of association, a right according to Mexican law and Nike's own code of conduct, is clearly not a reality at the Kuk-Dong factory."

A Nike spokesperson said at the time that the company would assess the situation and determine whether to place further orders with the Kuk-Dong factory. But the one thing that neither the factory workers nor the university students want is for Nike to pull up stakes, as it has so often done in the past. "They don't want Nike to flee an ugly scene to save face," wrote Klein, "but to stay and prove that its code of conduct is more than pretty words. 'We want Nike to put pressure on Kuk-Dong to negotiate directly with the workers,'" an anti-sweatshop activist told Klein. "'It's a long term approach, but we think a more lasting one.'"

At the 2001 conference of the North American Society for the Sociology of Sport, veteran sport sociologist George Sage of the University of North Colorado looked at the struggle to force Nike to mend its ways. In a paper titled "Nike: Global Corporate Worker Benefactor or Victim of a Conspiracy of Activists?" Sage revisited the 1990s campaign, led by academics, religious groups, human rights organizations, and labour and development groups, against the company's labour practices. What was his conclusion? Little has changed.

"Remedies proposed for Nike factories were based on social justice: payment of a liveable wage, end forced overtime, stop using child labour, provide safe working conditions, permit independent unions, permit independent monitoring of factories," wrote Sage. "Rather than addressing and resolving the problems raised by the investigations, Nike spent the past decade with public relations 'greenwashing' ploys and massive advertising campaigns in attempts to maintain its corporate credibility. ... Recently, Nike has employed globalization ideology to argue against resistance to its factories' processes by making capitalism seem to be governed by natural laws, and thus unassailable and irrevocable. Such a position is seriously flawed."[3]

But has all this strife and turmoil had much of an impact on Nike's corporate reputation? Sometimes it doesn't seem so. In 2001, Nike Canada Ltd. received the Corporate Excellence Award at the 28th Canadian Sport Awards, partially because of its commitment to the Girls@Play program (which gives small grants of $100 to $200 to women and girls to further their development as athletes and coaches).

Your Friendly Fast-Food Outlet

Meanwhile, McDonald's—one of the most ubiquitous Olympic sponsors—is notorious for its low wages and high employee turnover. Like Coke, another Olympic sponsor, it markets heavily to young people and, in the case of McDonald's, is staffed mostly by women, teenagers, and immigrants. Yet countless women athletes, including Silken Laumann, Amy Van Dyken, Mary Lou Retton, Tara Lipinski, and Michelle Kwan—all marketed as the straight girl next door—have been spokespeople for these companies.

How does the marketing of fast food through traditional heterosexual female stereotypes provide an opaque barrier for the not-so-pleasant protests currently plaguing McDonald's? How does connecting excellence in athleticism to a questionably healthy product change that product's image? And what would happen if these women actually investigated a company before they signed on the dotted line?

Visit any McDonald's and watch how people eat. Is food savoured?

Is it chewed slowly and with pleasure? Do eyes close in delight? How much garbage does each customer create? Are they smiling? Have they just had a Happy Meal? Then ask the people who work there if they're happy. In the U.S., McDonald's has an annual employee turnover rate of 150%.[4] The meal may be called happy, but the employees don't seem to be anything like it.

In his book *Fast Food Nation*, investigative journalist Eric Schlosser conservatively estimates that on any given day, one-quarter of the American adult population is eating fast food, much of it at McDonald's. According to Dr. Martin Collis, a former physical education professor at the University of Victoria who spends a great deal of his retirement time researching nutrition issues, McDonald's spends $1 billion a year internationally on marketing. But Canadian writer Naomi Klein argues in her book *No Logo* that the actual goods being consumed are not the real product for sale. The average hamburger may be made with meat from more than 100 different cows from slaughterhouses of varying degrees of hygiene. It may be shipped frozen, thawed, and heated up three time zones away. The real product, however, is the image that surrounds the product. Klein writes, "What these companies produced primarily were not things … but images of their brands. Their real work lay not in manufacturing but in marketing. … This corporate obsession with brand identity is waging a war on public and individual space: on public institutions such as schools, on youthful identities, on the concept of nationality and on the possibilities of unmarketed space."[5]

As Klein points out, this is a war that is being fought on many fronts. But one of the most lucrative is the sporting arena, and especially the Olympics. McDonald's and Coke, and all the other members of The Olympic Partner (TOP) program—to which corporations pay millions to belong—can make unlimited use of the highly mediated Olympic space. This space includes the actual space provided by Olympic sites for advertisement and retail outlets, the electronic space provided by TV and radio, the print space provided by newspapers and magazines, and the most coveted space of all—the body of an athlete.

But why would someone like Silken Laumann—the second-most-important female Canadian athlete of the century, according to a poll of national sportswriters, and at least at one time an avowed vegetarian—sell her image to help promote McDonald's? In a March 15, 2000, interview in Edmonton's alternative weekly, *Vue*, Laumann defended her choice of sponsorship by stating, "McDonald's is probably one of the most ethical companies out there. They're a class act."

McDonald's a class act? Eric Schlosser is a well-respected journalist whose book was painstakingly researched and his work is in no way sensationalist. In *Fast Food Nation*, he devotes almost an entire chapter to the company and its questionable business practices. McDonald's appears elsewhere in the book as well, in accounts of labour and workplace exploitation, markedly high levels of fat and sugar, and how fast-food chains target children. Is this anyone's idea of an ethical company?

The biggest civil case against McDonald's to date involved British environmentalists. Both Klein and Schlosser have extensively covered the case, for a start, but it merits another look here. Briefly, in September 1990, McDonald's sued several London Greenpeace activists after they gave out leaflets containing the words "McDollars, McGreedy, McCancer, McMurder, McProfits, McGarbage." In its suit, the corporation claimed that "every statement in the leaflet was false," and this claim was the company's undoing. While three activists apologized and bowed out, two others, Helen Steel and Dave Morris, refused to give in. They forged ahead with the trial, even defending themselves when they were declared ineligible for state-assisted counsel. By the end of the trial, they had compiled 40,000 pages of documents and witness statements, along with 18,000 transcript pages.

While some of the charges made by the environmentalists were indeed unfounded, others, such as their claim that "a diet high in fat, sugar, animal products, and salt ... is linked with cancers of the breast and bowel, and heart disease," were based on solid medical research. Although Steel and Morris were ultimately found by the court to have libelled McDonald's, they were able to uncover many unsightly truths about the company during the 11 years of trials and appeals. McDonald's executives were forced to take the stand and answer difficult questions about the nutritional composition of their products and about the exploitation of young people, both as workers and as consumers.

Then, in the summer of 2000, French cheese producer and sheep farmer José Bové went on trial for vandalizing a McDonald's restaurant in the traditionally agricultural town of Millau, France. He became an international hero not only to displaced farm workers—whose livelihoods, he said, had been destroyed by corporate food giants like McDonald's—but to millions of others who admired his stand against a corporate giant. He was accompanied to his trial by 30,000 demonstrators, and today he is in demand around the world as protests against globalization grow. He has even written a best-selling book, *The World Is Not for Sale.*

On May 16, 2001, *The Globe and Mail* reported on another court case involving a McDonald's in France, this time in Albi. An employee, Rémi Millet, had been fired by his manager because "[Millet] said he used his lunch allowance to pay for five cheeseburgers he gave to a woman who came into the restaurant to beg for money to buy food. He said he thought the gesture would be good for McDonald's image." Although this manager seemed particularly hard-hearted—and was fined 6,000 francs for his actions—we have to wonder if his behaviour was really so far removed from the McDonald's corporate mindset.

So what do transnationals such as McDonald's do to counter their negative image? How do they erase the impression left by sticky legal and ethical situations that often involve the well-being of humans, particularly children? They spend even more time, energy, and money creating a false illusion of beauty and good health.

The winning athletic female body is the perfect canvas for consumer goods that have little or no relation to the athlete's success. Images of success are what is really for sale. A hamburger will get you nowhere, but a fantasized dream that connects you to the hamburger will get you into a McDonald's, spending money. So the dynamic athletic body is used to market products that are identical, predictable, mediocre, and terrifically unexciting at best, and dangerously bad for your health at worst.

And how does the global market's emphasis on sameness of product—of every hamburger tasting the same and every hamburger server reciting the same script—affect the diversity that helps to create a healthy sexuality? To answer this question, let's look first at the relationship between the hamburger and Olympic Barbie.

During the 2000 Sydney Olympics, girls who wanted to purchase a discounted Barbie at McDonald's had to purchase a Happy Meal. The connection children make between food and toys is absolutely crucial to this consumption equation, but this is not just any toy. This is Barbie, the most desired—and unattainable—female body in the world. The promotional agreement between Mattel and the Olympics could have been a way to break with this tradition. Yet not only does Olympic Barbie have the same fantasy body as all the Barbies before her, of the 16 Barbies that were available through McDonald's during the Games, 11 didn't even do any sports. None of them—from Olympic Pin Barbie to Rainbow Princess Barbie, Cool Clips Christie to Secret Messages Teresa, or Birthday Party Barbie to Celebration Cake Barbie—raised the diversity bar one iota. (But they look great in their Olympic outfits—all sewn by workers in China.) And McDonald's was also discounting Hot Wheels cars during its Olympic promotion, thus creating the perfect American pop culture pairing: the plastic female fantasy body and the hard male fantasy car.

McDonald's also used the Olympics to emphasize its devotion to internationalism. In the Olympic press package, the company stated that it had "created a new Olympic-themed print ad that can be customized by every country for maximum impact. The universal creative shows a relay runner 'handing off' a box of McDonald's World Famous Fries to his teammate. The tagline reads, 'McDonald's proudly serves the athletes of the Olympic Games. Pass it on.'"

"Five Weeks, Five Continents, Five Burgers" proclaimed the European promotion during the Games. This pitch "reinforces the connection to the five rings of the Olympics and gives customers the opportunity to experience tastes from around the world. Sandwiches include: McAmerica, a combination of two hamburger patties, cheese, onions, lettuce and bacon with bacon sauce; McAustralia, featuring chicken with bacon, tomatoes and special sandwich sauce; McEurope, with pork, cucumber, lettuce, onions and garlic sauce; McAsia, featuring the McRib with curry-ketchup, lettuce, onions and sandwich sauce; and McAfrica, a combination of two hamburger patties, cheese, tomatoes, lettuce and harissa sauce on a pita-like bun. ... McDonald's expects to serve nearly 1.5 million burgers from now [September 15, 2000] through October 4, 2000." Diversity through hamburger condiments?

Unfortunately, many of the children who eat at McDonald's do so because fast food is what their families know. This is one of the few affordable "treats" that allows lower-income people a break away from their difficult and often unpleasant North American lives. In fact, food choice and nutrition is one of the surest ways to differentiate among income levels in North America. And while the company claimed to be interested in "bringing the fun and excitement of the world's premier sporting event to 43 million customers every day," it was in fact promoting poor nutrition and unhealthy eating habits to its customers—many of whom are young, impressionable children.

Fortunately, not everyone responded by chowing down. On September 11, just four days before the Olympic opening ceremonies, tens of thousands of people gathered in Melbourne, Australia, to protest a meeting of the World Economic Forum. At issue was the huge gap between rich and poor, and the role transnationals play in perpetuating that gap worldwide. Paints a pretty picture, doesn't it? While riot police in Melbourne were lining up against people protesting the international power of such corporations as McDonald's and Coca-Cola, the two giants' logos adorned almost everything Olympic in Sydney. The contrast couldn't have been more jarring, but in the Olympic Village, it was business as usual. In a release entitled "Fun Facts," McDonald's boasted:

- 1.5 million sandwiches [would be served] to athletes, coaches, officials, spectators and media during the three weeks the Games were on.
- More than two million meat patties, 188 tons of potatoes, and 12,000 kilos of lettuce would be consumed.
- An average of 13,000 hamburgers would be served each day— just to athletes, coaches, and officials.

At every Olympic press conference, athletes had large bottles of Coca-Cola put in front of them or close by. When the president of the IOC, Juan Antonio Samaranch, hosted the World Heart Day press conference, he and all the other speakers, including several doctors and a health minister, sat behind the ubiquitous bottles of Coca-Cola—the same Coca-Cola that has seven teaspoons of sugar in every 12-ounce can. The press kit for World Heart Day included a page on Coca-Cola and reminded journalists of the company's Web site.

Such product placement has an obvious goal: Make the good cause rub off on the product. That's why transnationals sponsor Mother's Day runs, street hockey tournaments, and school sports championships, to name just a few of the events made possible by so-called corporate largesse. And because governments all over have cut education budgets so drastically, there is now a strong corporate presence at school sports events. There is literally no other money available to run these programs. In *Fast Food Nation*, Eric Schlosser outlines how Coca-Cola has infiltrated the public education system. Some schools even have "Coke in Education Days," where kids can participate in such intellectually and physically stimulating activities as baking a Coca-Cola cake and spelling "Coke" out with their bodies in the parking lot. The students do not have a choice in the matter— such corporate stroking is incorporated into the curriculum.

But can we really blame the schools? Cutbacks and decreased services are now the norm throughout North America, even in places of relative wealth. On September 1, 2000, *The Globe and Mail* published an article entitled "Alberta Revels in Oil Riches." It drew a quick response from Anne Letain, a teacher-librarian in Coaldale, in the

southern part of the province, who wrote a letter to the editor that
stated:

> I have a budget of $2,000 to purchase materials. This includes
> $700 to maintain the software on my six-year-old computer.
> The rest buys books, software, and supplies for 220 students.
> The principal has produced a spreadsheet to monitor our
> paper consumption and we have all been put on a strict
> paper diet. We have one class with 34 students. Because we
> have provincially mandated "site financial management" at
> the school level, we could make the decision to hire another
> teacher (or part thereof) and run a deficit of $20,000 to $50,000.
> However, it is illegal for us to carry a deficit. Has the bounty
> trickled down to me? Maybe. The Alberta Advantage? Yeah,
> sure.

What school in such dire financial straits wouldn't take a corporate donation for sports equipment, even if it felt that students and
educational integrity would be compromised or co-opted in the
process? Yet this is precisely how young people are indoctrinated
into a "corporate logo" lifestyle when they're most impressionable.
They learn that human beings are measured by how efficiently they
consume a product—if they are not themselves a product to be
consumed. These students are literally being sold to the corporations, and as part of the deal, they are expected to ingest unhealthy
products in great quantities. How is it possible for young people to
learn to have autonomy over their own bodies in this game?

When I covered high-school sports as a journalist, I was dismayed
to see so many kids eating pure junk. I saw pop machines spring up
all over as education funding was cut and schools made "partnerships" with Coke or Pepsi. I saw "potato chip Thursdays" and "pizza
Fridays" become the norm as fast-food companies also elbowed their
way in. Children are a "direct hit" market. They are bombarded with
messages to consume, and the stuff they put in their mouths is
doctored with enough salt, sugar, fat, or caffeine to hook them—

just as nicotine would in a cigarette. The equation works beautifully: Get kids—the younger the better—obsessed with the idea of
the perfect but unattainable body, like Barbie's; addict them to products that will never allow them to even approach having that body
themselves; and then connect the two. Somehow, we think, because
this junk is in schools and at the Olympics, it must be good for us.

   This relationship between the cult of the perfect body and the
consumption of unhealthy products is part of a much larger culture
that disrespects the body. We are inundated, especially in film and
television, with images of corrected bodies. I use the word
"corrected" because I believe that any woman who doesn't meet the
ideal image of the female body is viewed as somehow incorrect. In
fact, women are often conditioned to view themselves this way.
Some have literally internalized the ideal, pushing bags of silicone
under their breasts, adding more fat to their lips and vacuuming it
from their thighs and stomachs, or having their noses broken and
reset. In "The Constructed Body," Colette Guillaumin argues that
our attempts to achieve perfection through surgery are in fact muti-
lations. She writes:

> Physical interventions upon the body, most often muti-
> lations, are generally aimed at the female body, or at least
> affect it most profoundly, and include modifying the body
> with surgery, or with the use of tools or objects that induce
> and maintain certain corporal transformations. ... For the
> most part such practices are final and permanent. They are
> the spectacular and heartrending revelations of
> manipulation and social control of the body.[6]

   When will those of us in the Western world begin to see things
such as fat vacuuming, lip "enhancement," and breast implants in
the same context as foot binding in China and the genital mutilation
that still takes place in parts of present-day Africa and the Middle
East? When will we stop trying to achieve an unattainable ideal? And
when will we finally begin to view our bodies, imperfect as they may

be, as more than receptacles for goods and services? Unfortunately, until we learn to stop stuffing ourselves with whatever fast foods the marketing gurus have persuaded us to consume, there will always be a segment of the population who will view cosmetic surgery as the solution to all their physical and emotional problems. Both are about seeing the body as a site for mindless consumption. No wonder girls are messed up about eating. How could they not be?

In this extraordinarily confused and confusing culture, is it possible to find a way to use corporate support in a responsible manner?

Hope for the Future?

When a reporter questioned Silken Laumann about Nike's human rights record in the March 15, 2000, issue of *Vue*—the same one in which she called McDonald's "a class act"—she defended the company like a paid spokesperson. "Nike has definitely had a tough few years," she admitted. "They realize this is really important. It's an issue with consumers, so it should be an issue with them. There's a ton of rumour out there and very little fact base. But certainly, as an athlete, you shouldn't work with a company you think is unethical and you don't feel comfortable with."

While an athlete is on her way up, training as hard as she can for international success, she often lives in poverty and has to accept whatever sponsorship is available. Too often, it's either take the money or quit. But when her sporting success results in financial comfort, as it has for Laumann, she no longer has to accept money from corporations with questionable human rights records. Athletes are more than able to investigate for themselves the companies from which they receive sponsorship money, but they seldom do.

But instead of informing themselves, athletes support the popular but very inexpensive PR programs, such as Girls@Play, that Nike and other transnationals aim at a youthful and/or female market. "It's really evil the way Nike has spiralled into people's lives," says Estelle Kuzyk, back on the picket line in front of Forzani's. Not only has the company stepped into the inner-city, low-income sports scene, it has a strong presence among middle-class athletes as well. Almost all runs are corporate-sponsored charity runs now, and, while that is a good and generous act, it sometimes masks a less charitable set of values.

Unfortunately, women athletes play it safe. When they do support causes, they always seem to choose the ones that are non-controversial, such as the quest to cure cystic fibrosis or muscular dystrophy. These are noble causes, of course—but wouldn't it be nice to see a top female athlete stand up, as American tennis great Billie Jean King did in the 1970s, and say she has had an abortion and believes in the fundamental right of reproductive choice for women? In the September 2001 issue of *Sports Illustrated Women*, she said even more. "I don't care about anyone's sexuality," she said in the Playbook column on the last page. "Being dedicated to my truth is a daily thing, because truth can change. I've been heterosexual, I'm a lesbian, for a long time I was bisexual. I'm glad that we're more accepted, but we really aren't in some ways."

And in another quote she addresses families: "I tell fathers that they really don't know the impact they have on their daughters. It's very important to tell them they're beautiful, they're good, they're strong, they're fast. It's like an imprint on their souls that never leaves them."

And while female athletes sometimes support local women's shelters or rape crisis centres, they have absolutely no national presence. Why don't we see the national rowing team officially supporting the Ontario Association of Interval and Transition Houses? Why doesn't the women's hockey team officially support the National Lesbian and Gay Journalists Association (NLGJA) Canada? Why do athletes display only corporate logos on their bodies, and not slogans that are slightly subversive, such as "Justice Do It, Nike"?

Some athletes in the gay community have made a good and brave start at dealing with tough but important issues. Martina Navratilova got the ball rolling in the United States in the 1980s. In the 1990s, she was followed by basketball player and sportswriter Mariah Burton

Nelson, mountain biker Missy Giove, and tennis star Amélie Mauresmo of France. In Canada, Olympic gold-medal swimmer Mark
Tewksbury opened the door to a publicly honest discussion on sexuality and sport when he came out as a gay athlete in 1999 on national
television. With far less fanfare, shot-putter and bobsledder Georgette Reed and hockey great Angela James also stood up and said,
"I'm gay and will not pretend otherwise."

But for real sexual equality, we need honesty and fairness on all
fronts. While it may feel great to get out of the confines of the closet,
what about those of the sweatshop? Plant foremen and company-
friendly union bosses have the same unfettered power over women
workers that some unscrupulous coaches and sports officials have
over athletes. And it is no coincidence that neither coaching nor
corporate codes of conduct have markedly reduced the frequency of
sexual assault or harassment of women athletes and workers. These
codes are often worth less than the paper they're printed on because
there are no repercussions for those who fail to adhere to them. As
much as we need athletes—both male and female—to speak out
loud and hard against the sexual exploitation of young people in
sport, we need them to speak out equally loudly against sweatshop
labour.

Still, while I can see no evidence that McDonald's has picked up its
corporate socks from the floor, it may be unfair to paint Nike with
the same brush. In the time it took me to research and write this
chapter, Nike commissioned a private investigator's report on workplace standards and publicly said it will address the serious issues it
chronicles, one of which has been systematic sexual harassment. We
must stay on guard to ensure that any changes are permanent. Let's
also hope we see no more blatantly sexist ads. What the company did
in *Sports Illustrated* made its supposed support for and sensitivity to
issues in women's sport seem like nothing more than a transparent
and dishonest marketing ploy.

Nor does it seem that Nike has totally learned its lesson. In
November 2001, the company organized the Run Across America as a
response to the September 11 terrorist attacks on the United States.

This apparently charitable event must surely be seen for what it is: an attempt to capitalize on an upsurge of American nationalism unlike any we have seen before. But what exactly *is* the message we're meant to take away from the image of an affluent American running for a better world in a shoe made by an exploited worker and sold by a multi-million-dollar corporation with a poor track record in human rights?

As I write this, the morning paper tells me that 20 workers in a garment factory in Bangladesh were killed when others trampled them in an attempt to flee a fire alarm. The alarm turned out to be false, but the doors at the end of narrow staircases were locked and people panicked. Almost all the dead workers were female.

When women have no security of the person—something the Canadian Charter of Rights and Freedoms and several international agreements say should be guaranteed—they also have no sexual security. A person who is not allowed to exercise agency—that is, who does not operate according to her own directives and values—is also robbed of sexual agency. And as long as there are widespread sexual exploitation, harassment, and abuse of women workers, they will never be free sexual beings, especially when they have no other options within their culture. Abuse is devastating to the sexual self, and we should use our positions as women athletes to eradicate it everywhere—not just on the playing field.

Now is the time for women in the West to realize that they have more than enough, and that they must work to improve the desperate lives that are the fate of so many other women the world over. It is also time to question the pat little lies we are so often told in the name of sports marketing and nationalism.

In 1980, North American and many European athletes boycotted the Moscow Olympics because of the Soviet invasion of Afghanistan. At that time, the men who would become the Taliban were called freedom fighters by the American government, which armed them to the tune of $3 billion.

Freedom fighters? They did not hide the fact that they were devoted to a fundamentalist Islamic ideology that gave women no rights whatsoever. One only had to look at other fundamentalist countries like Saudi Arabia and Iran to know what was in store for the women of Afghanistan.

But our athletes did what they were told, pledged their allegiance to democracy, and refused to compete in Moscow, the centre of "heartless Communism." In the past 20 years, it seems we have learned nothing more about the importance of educating ourselves, asking questions, and not accepting at face value everything we're told. We've got to do better than this.

Part iii   Restoring the Whole Woman

9 Playing Together

Two Sexes, One Team

I believe one thing is certain: Things won't change if we don't work together—men and women, old and young, gay and straight, able-bodied and disabled—for change. And we must effect a change in attitude toward girls *and* boys.

Lois Sapsford, a Calgary therapist who counsels girls with eating disorders and/or a history of sexual abuse, says, "There are differences between boys and girls, and yahoo for the differences, but there are plenty of similarities. The good things sport gives boys should be available to girls too."

Sapsford believes the development stages identified by psychologist Erik Erikson best illustrate what can go wrong in the way we perceive differences between boys and girls. Erikson theorized that all humans go through a clearly defined series of changes as they grow psychologically. First there is attachment to the mother, then autonomy, then separation, individuation, and forming a partnership with someone else. "In Erikson's books," Sapsford explains, "women were not as good at the individuation process, but [they] did better than men in the relationship part, which is the ultimate goal of the whole process. It's interesting that men could do well in individuation, but not in relationships. What does that tell us about the model? Erikson's model doesn't work for women."

Sapsford says women psychologists have spent years creating a new model of human development. "Women develop the self through relationships with others," she says. "I think men would too if they were allowed to, but we train this impulse out of boys. We teach them they have to look out only for themselves—only to be independent. They have few relationship skills. This new model is a healthy, human model. The stronger the relationships you have with others, the more you know about yourself."

Sapsford believes a new model of human development would benefit boys as well as girls. "We need to teach boys about relationships with people," she says. "If we don't do that, our boys' sport culture is in great danger. As long as we teach children that the model for power is based on bullying and not sharing, then girls will learn to be as bad as boys. ... How we live our lives has great impact on the children around us. We must demand that the culture take responsibility for its behaviour and do something about it. Right now, our culture sexualizes the young female body—the bodies of girls—and that is very disturbing. A strong presence of girls in sports can help counteract that."

Boys need to learn by firsthand experience that the bodies of girls are real, strong, and resilient. Boys need to see girls sweat, spit, take a swig from a water bottle, and then score. Boys need to understand that the female body has as much right to public space as the male body. Until boys learn to respect the female body in truly deep and caring ways, we will continue to have tragically high rates of physical and sexual abuse of women by men. Until boys understand that they have been receiving more than their fair share of facilities and opportunities in the sporting world, they will too often respond in anger, instead of empathy, when girls demand the right to public space.

The cases described in this chapter are not just about the rights of individual girls to participate in their sport of choice; they are about strong and determined people of all ages and both genders trying to create a culture that respects the rights of all human beings.

Melanie Merkley's Story

Three months after Katie Morrison and her father won their case against the city of Coquitlam, the B.C. Human Rights Commission wrapped up another case.

Kitimat is a northern town of approximately 10,000 people, most of whom work in the mining and pulp-and-paper industries. Kitimat winters are long, and life is hard, as in any other northern Canadian town. And for Melanie Merkley, the winters have been longer and life harder than they needed to be, ever since February 1996.

In a small locale like Kitimat, there is only one game in town, and until Merkley came along, it was played almost exclusively by boys. But Merkley had always loved hockey. At seven, she joined a local initiation program run by the Kitimat Minor Hockey Association (KMHA), designed for young kids who want to play hockey when they get older. In her first year, she and one other girl were in a group of 40 to 50 boys. But this didn't faze Merkley. She completed the two-year program in just one year. Then she progressed through the ranks, from novice to atom to peewee. In her second year as a peewee, she was asked to play on a new team of women and girls of all ages and abilities.

"She decided it would be something new and she'd give it a try," says her mother, Monica. "But she was a little hesitant because she was really looking forward to her last year of peewee. Melanie also played for the northern female team at the B.C. Winter Games. She enjoyed it, but it wasn't competitive enough. Before the '95–'96 season started, she told us she wanted to go back to boys' hockey."

Merkley—and four other girls who had joined boys' hockey after her—wanted to spend the next two years honing her skills in preparation for college or university hockey. She had missed her last year of peewee, but with two years in bantam to look forward to, she believed she'd be able to prepare for a successful career after high school. Merkley had grown into a strong young teenager. She was 5'10" and had an aggressive style on defence. "There were times, when Melanie was playing on the girls' team, when she was pulled aside and told not to play so aggressively," says her mother. "On top of this, the closest competition for the team was an eight-hour drive away. Finally she became fed up and said to me, 'Mom, I can't do it anymore.'

"The next year, we signed her up for the bantam house-league team. Melanie was told she would need a letter releasing her from the girls' team, and we applied for it and then took her to her first assessment. She handled the checking and hitting really well. There was no question she could pull her own [weight]. There are three assessments the players receive before they make the team. After the first one ... we were told Melanie was not allowed to play with boys."

The call came from the president of the KMHA, Gwen Seaby, in the fall of 1996. The Merkleys say that Seaby believed that if Merkley and the four other girls who wanted to play on the boys' team left, the girls' team would fold. They were needed to support female hockey as it grew, and the rule book assumed they would sacrifice their own hockey careers for the betterment of others. "The other players and their families supported us," says Monica, "but they didn't file a complaint. We did it on our own. We'd had several discussions with Minor Hockey, but they ended in frustration, and that's when I got in touch with the Human Rights Commission."

Life changed drastically for Melanie Merkley once she'd filed suit in October 1996. She was snubbed by the coach of the girls' team, and some of the kids at school harassed her. "But I also had a lot of support," said Merkley in March 2000. "A petition was started ... and lots of people signed it. People knew I'd been playing with these boys for eight years, but I couldn't go to the arena."

Most of the resistance didn't come from her former teammates on the boys' team, but from the parents of both male and female players. They harassed her whenever she went near the rink and told her she was trying to ruin the female league. "They also thought I was suing Minor Hockey, which wasn't true," Merkley explains. "I didn't do this for money. I wanted to play on my team, and I want all girls to play on the best team for them."

Word travels quickly in small towns, and Seaby lived just a few doors away from the Merkleys. There was considerable tension. "We are not fans of Minor Hockey," says Monica Merkley tersely. The Merkleys believe that the KMHA stalled the process as much as it could, and that Seaby had a great deal of support from Florence Rempel, then president of the British Columbia Amateur Hockey Association (BCAHA). Monica says both women were adamant that girls and boys should play separately.

Seaby says the Merkley case took over her life. "I haven't ever played hockey, but my children do, and I volunteered because I want to help children, get them off the street and give them a place to play. You go through three years that consume you, and you wonder how any of this benefits children. It was stressful for everybody."

Seaby was in her first year of the KMHA presidency when she received Melanie's letter asking her why she couldn't play on a boys' team. "I took the letter to a BCAHA meeting being held up here, and I asked, 'Why? Why does she have to play on the girls' team?' I was looking for guidance from my superiors. Florence Rempel told me it was CHA and BCAHA policy that girls must play on girls' teams if a viable girls' team is available. I actually received a letter from her asking me, 'What is it you don't understand? CHA and BCAHA rules override local rules.'"

Seaby now says she still couldn't figure out why Merkley couldn't play on the boys' team. But she still enforced the CHA and BCAHA rules—even though she now claims she thought they were wrong and the legal advice the KMHA received concluded they were contravening the Human Rights Code. I asked her if she was aware of the treatment Merkley received at the arena, and if she knew at the time that other girls had won similar cases in other parts of the country.

"I have two children, a husband, and a full-time job. I didn't get to the arena very often, so I don't know if she was ostracized. It was stressful for everybody. I had heard about the [Justine] Blainey case in Ontario. Three people told me she won, three people told me she lost." Seaby didn't contact the Human Rights Commission in either B.C. or Ontario to verify which version was correct.

The Merkley case went into its third year before anything was resolved. Then, in June 1999, the BCAHA agreed to settle the issue. The organization's legal adviser, John Waddell, says it was because of a rule change at the CHA level. "It was in the CHA's constitution and bylaws that female players must play on a female team where one existed. The rationale behind this was to stimulate women's hockey. If good female players played on female teams, they would bring the level of play up. The intention of the rule was to make hockey better for women. But there was a tension that existed because of this. Really good players wanted to play with boys. Everyone had the same goal, which was to make the sport better for females, but there was the Human Rights Commission, the individual complainant, the Kitimat [hockey] association, and B.C. Amateur caught in the middle."

At the height of the Blainey case in the mid-1980s, a rule change to the CHA's constitution occurred to encourage the formation and development of female teams while still allowing for exceptions. Girls playing in areas with no female teams could join boys' teams up until the peewee age. Individual branches were allowed to extend the age above peewee in special cases (if, for example, there was no female team in older age groups).

When Melanie Merkley's case first went before the Human Rights Commission, everyone was following the rules, says Waddell. Nothing could change in Kitimat until change occurred at the CHA level. And he acknowledges that there were other tensions at play. The Merkleys felt they had been treated rudely by Rempel. For example, in a letter sent to Monica Merkley in October 1996, in which Rempel stated that Melanie could not play on the boys' team, Rempel concluded: "It would be a shame if Melanie was to give up playing the game that I know she loves but this must be her decision. It sometimes is much easier to quit than to perservere and take advantage of what is offered. "I trust this will put an end to the matter."[1]

Although such exchanges escalated the emotionalism of the conflict, Waddell maintains that the BCAHA was conciliatory from the start. "The point was to deal with the situation as effectively as possible. B.C. Amateur had to get the CHA to soften their position on this. They initiated the change to the rules. Once that was done, they could help Kitimat change their rule to something with which everyone could be satisfied. Ms. Rempel worked with the B.C. Human Rights Commission to come up with a press release and to deal with the direction to the various associations."

If the BCAHA had abided by the spirit of the Blainey decision, the Merkley case would have been wrapped up quickly, and Melanie would have been playing on the bantam boys' team she had legitimately made. Despite the three long years Melanie waited in the fight for her rights, Waddell still claims that the BCAHA acted "quickly, cooperatively and effectively."

The president of the BCAHA in 2000, Mike Henderson, claims that the organization stood in Melanie's way out of a concern for her safety. "We were regarding at the time a situation that we felt was being addressed properly. There were concerns about injury to the girl stepping into bantam, and there may have been an effect on the existing girls' team if she played on the boys' team." When I pointed out to Henderson that Merkley had always played with boys, that she was 5'10", and that she had already proved in a tryout that she could skate at that level, he replied, "I don't recall there being any discussion about her size or anything, but the speed of the game, everything increases at that age group. It is easy to say in 2000, 'Oh, you should have let her play,' but we weren't in 2000. We were doing this three years ago. Who would know that then?"

No one on the BCAHA board of directors, Henderson says, believed the organization was contravening the Human Rights Code—even though they all knew of the Blainey case. "We don't have authority to make decisions for local associations," Henderson told me. "We can't tell them what to do, but I believe we believed the situation was being handled correctly."

Florence Rempel, who was president of the BCAHA when the case first came to light, says she thought Merkley should have been allowed to play on the boys' team, but she maintains that local associations must call the shots on these sorts of issues. "The BCAHA had a policy then that girls and boys could play together until the end of peewee [12 to 13]. After that, it's up to the association to decide whether she can play with boys or not. I suggested very strongly to them that they allow her to play on both teams. They said, 'No. It's stated in the regulations that players must not play on two teams.' Their reasoning was she'd get twice the ice time. I said, 'Fine—charge double.' But they were still determined they weren't going to let her play."

Seaby, Rempel, and Henderson all insist that they simply wanted to strengthen girls' hockey when they barred Merkley from playing on the bantam boys' team. They say they were only following rules—the CHA's rule 250, to be specific. So why did it take so long for the CHA to change a rule that was obviously a breach of human rights? No one at the BCAHA, the KMHA, or the CHA can answer that question. Instead, they argue that not allowing girls to play with boys makes girls' teams better, though there is no empirical data to support this belief. In effect, all three parties spent a great deal of time and energy ensuring that Melanie Merkley would not be allowed to play, and then blamed one another when it became clear that they had systematically discriminated against a child on the basis of her sex.

At the 1999 CHA annual general meeting in Quebec City, rule 250 was finally changed. And it was about time. The list of girls who had had human rights violations committed against them, not only by hockey organizations, but by Canadian sports associations of all kinds, was growing longer, and legal fees were mounting. Holly Grueger, the Merkleys' lawyer, says, "There were a couple of similar cases at the time, and a settlement [on the Merkleys' suit] was reached. I wished it had gone further than it did. I would have preferred it go through [to arbitration]. I would have liked to see the changes they were talking about at the time, but I went with my client's wishes. I have an interest in women's issues, and this case was important. I was in law school during the Blainey case, so it is a familiar story."

Shelley Coolidge, manager of female development for the CHA, believes that members of the BCAHA finally realized they had to let girls play on boys' teams. "A few years back, people said, 'How can we help our female program?' In rural communities, you can't expect a girl to travel 50 miles just to get to a practice or game when there's a boys' team in her own community. There had been cases before other provincial human rights commissions, and one in Regina in the early '90s that made Saskatchewan have to change.

"When I played there, it was around the same time as the Blainey case, and I lived in a little place called Lashburn, outside of Lloydminster. The team I played on won the zone championships, so we went to the provincials. We won our first game there, and they were going through the registration cards for verification and mine wasn't there. They said, 'Girls don't play hockey.'" Coolidge's card had been pulled.

The CHA's new rule should, in theory, prevent what happened to Coolidge from ever happening again. It allows for dual carding for females, which means that girls and women can play on male and female teams at the same time. And on June 10, 1999, three years after Merkley's complaint had first been lodged, the BCAHA agreed to institute a female hockey development program that would remove all "restrictions on the participation of female players within the BCAHA structure." In the understanding drawn up with the B.C. Human Rights Commission, the organization said it would "support female participation on integrated teams, the formation of female teams, and allow dual carding." In this way, talented female athletes would be able to benefit from competing against the best in their community without depleting the talent available for growing female hockey teams.

The BCAHA also cited statistics that showed the lack of representation of women and girls not only as players, but as officials as well. In the 1998–99 season, the joint BCAHA and Human Rights Commission report states, "only 3,822 of the 45,595 registered players in B.C. were female. Female participation in clinics ranged from 10.8% of the 1,339 participants at the Canadian Hockey Safety Program to 0.7% of the 276 participants at the official level III clinic. In order to promote female participation, and to ensure that females are aware of all opportunities that exist within the hockey structure, the BCAHA commits to advising its membership of the purpose of the BCAHA in ensuring equal access to hockey programs and services and of the new BCAHA policy allowing dual carding for minor-aged female hockey players."

Yet for all the promise of its report, the BCAHA still gives the final decision to local organizations when it says that it "does not have the authority to compel [local minor hockey] associations to allow female players on both all-female and integrated teams. ... Granting a girl a card for a boys' team is 'at their discretion.'" Even though every girl who has brought a human rights complaint against a hockey organization has won her case, the CHA still insists on having the final call—a line of thought Florence Rempel likes to parrot. "I think you should always take a strong stand on justice, whether the Human Rights Code applies or not," she told me. "But when you're operating within a hockey structure, you have to go by the rules. There are things that happen in hockey that you may not agree with, but you have to let local associations go with their decision."

Rempel's remarks made me wonder how much the BCAHA's female hockey development program had actually done to make hockey in British Columbia more welcoming for women and girls. In March 2000, I contacted Don Freer, BCAHA's executive director. I asked him for specific examples of what the BCAHA had done to remove restrictions on female players and support female participation, as the organization had said it would do in its accord with the B.C. Human Rights Commission. Freer told me he couldn't remember any such agreement and had "no idea" what it might have said. "It must be downstairs in some other files," he explained.

Well, I asked, how is the BCAHA gathering the information it has to submit to the Human Rights Commission by the end of June? Freer was in the dark once more. He didn't know the organization had any obligations at all to the commission. Did he have a breakdown of the districts that had decided to comply with subsection 42(3) and those that had not? Freer couldn't think of any. "Talk to

Gay Hahn," he said, referring to the volunteer responsible for women's hockey.

Gay Hahn told me that she believes the organization is now geared toward providing more opportunities for girls and women. "We're saying this is the direction we're going. No district has specifically signed up with our program, but if they don't allow girls to be dual carded, they're on their own. We won't pay their legal bills."

At the time, Hahn told me she expected to make a report on the progress of women's hockey to the BCAHA board in May 2000. The board would then submit a report to the B.C. Human Rights Commission, as agreed in the settlement. She said she'd asked Freer to compile data on the number of women and girls involved in B.C. hockey, and had had a bulletin sent out to all BCAHA members a year earlier to make them aware of the implementation of subsection 42(3) and to outline ways they could assist girls' hockey.

The June 2000 deadline for the report to the Human Rights Commission came and went. Three months later, at the end of September, the BCAHA finally sent in a one-page document. It gave the numbers of women and girls involved in various programs, but nothing else—no comment on whether these numbers showed any improvement over previous years, no plan on how to exceed them for the next season, nothing. And no one from the BCAHA returned any of my phone calls about the report.

So what happened to Melanie Merkley? During her three-year ordeal, she contracted chronic fatigue syndrome and infectious mononucleosis. She was unable to attend school for four months, and she became so disillusioned with hockey that she didn't want to play any more. At first she wanted an apology for what the hockey associations had done to her, but eventually she realized that would never come. By the time they settled, she says she couldn't sit in the same room with or look at Seaby and Rempel. "We wonder if it was worth it," says Monica Merkley. "They hurt her so badly. But last September, a man called from Victoria and told us that his daughter was suddenly not allowed to play on a boys' soccer team. He talked to the president of the association and told him about our case, and they changed their minds right away."

More recently, in Kitimat, two girls who followed in Melanie's footsteps played on both the boys' bantam and midget teams and then successfully tried out for the B.C. provincial women's team. In the winter of 2000, they brought home gold medals from the B.C. Northern Winter Games—with their Kitimat team.

The Merkleys are just one of the many families who have had to spend a great deal of time, energy, and money to address human rights violations in sport. But in Melanie's case, those she saw as her prime adversaries were two women—Seaby and Rempel. By "just following the rules," they upheld the status quo and created a hostile environment for a girl who only wanted to be the best hockey player she could be. Unfortunately, Melanie's story is hardly unique.

The Trailblazers

In 1976, two girls lodged complaints with the Ontario Human Rights Commission, citing sex discrimination in their attempts to access sports services and facilities.

Debbie Baszo was a nine-year-old star player on her softball team in Waterford, a rural community in southern Ontario. She was so talented that she made it onto the local squirt all-star boys' team and was able to represent them in tournaments organized by the Ontario Rural Softball Association (ORSA), which is itself under the umbrella of the Ontario Softball Council (OSC). The nearest girls' team was 35 kilometres away.

But when Baszo and her coach sent her certificate of registration to the Erie Minor Softball Association (EMSA)—which all players had to do if they wanted to compete in tournaments—it came back with "Cannot play" written on it. Baszo's coach, Brett Bannerman, received a letter from ORSA that said, "As for the Erie League, if they also wish to stand behind the rules, which I think they will, get busy and have your girls play where they should and boys where they belong or you come and change all our rules to mixed ball and see how soon it falls on its face."

Despite this warning, Bannerman and his team showed up at the Squirt Boys A playoffs with Baszo. A protest letter was filed against her, the entire team was disqualified, and Bannerman lodged a sex-discrimination complaint.

That same year, 12-year-old Gail Cummings was the starting goalie on an atom hockey team in Huntsville, Ontario, when she successfully tried out for the town's all-star team, which was to go to the Ontario Minor Hockey Association (OMHA) playoffs. She played four games with the team before the OMHA's umbrella organization, the Ontario Hockey Association (OHA), pulled her from the tournament. Like Baszo, Cummings had her player registration card returned to her. She was told that her presence contravened the OMHA constitution, whose objectives were "to promote, encourage, and govern … hockey for boys in the province of Ontario." The OMHA's rules and regulations booklet states that the organization is "the result of many years of hard work by men sincerely interested in the welfare of the boys of Ontario and in the game of hockey." Presumably the presence of strong girls put the welfare of boys at risk.

Like Bannerman, Cummings's mother lodged a complaint with the commission, and on October 31, 1977, professor Mary Eberts heard the case. She wasn't persuaded by the OMHA's arguments and decided that

> A selection system based on ability, rather than sex, will as a matter of course eliminate the individuals—boys or girls—who do not have the technical skills, stamina or strength to play at that level of hockey. There may well be exceptional female athletes whose skill at the game and desire to play does not diminish at puberty or in adolescence. That person should not be denied the facilities to develop her talents, and learn new skills in a structured competitive atmosphere, playing with the best of her peers.[2]

The Baszo case, meanwhile, was heard by professor Sidney Lederman, who wrote in his decision, "Debbie Baszo, without question, possessed the requisite skills and indeed appears to have been the best qualified player on the Waterford team. Only discriminatory conduct, contrary to section 2(1)(a) and (b) of the Ontario Human Rights Code, by the Respondent precluded her from playing in the championship playdowns." Like Eberts, Lederman decided in the girl's favour.

Not satisfied, both sport governing bodies appealed the decisions to the Ontario divisional court, and both original decisions were overturned. Both cases were heard by Judge Gregory Evans. In the Cummings case, he wrote:

> The evidence indicated that the OMHA ... carry[s] out
> competitions for championships with the aim of inculcating
> in the boys certain ideals which will make them good
> citizens. Its purpose is obviously designed to encourage
> participation by as large a number of boys as possible and to
> equalize the level of competition. ... Surely a volunteer
> organization of this nature has the right to limit the scope of
> its activities and cannot be compelled to provide a "facility"
> which it has no desire to undertake, for which there is no
> great demand and the implementation of which may well
> destroy an organization which has contributed much to the
> development of young boys in this province.[3]

Baszo and Cummings appealed these decisions, and on May 24, 1979, both were heard in the Ontario Court of Appeal. In the Baszo case, ORSA had argued that softball fields are not places to which the public is customarily admitted. The panel of three judges agreed that it hinged on the "statutory interpretation" of "services and facilities," and on whether or not ORSA provided them "in any place to which the public is customarily admitted." Justice Bertha Wilson, who was later appointed to the Supreme Court of Canada, wrote:

The submission, it seems to me, if accepted, could also have the effect of defeating the object of the legislation. Is it open to the ORSA to say, "We provide softball for whites and we provide softball for blacks and that is the scope of the service we have decided to provide"? I do not think so. I do not believe that the services provided in a public place can be circumscribed on the basis of the prohibited criteria. ... Indeed, there is no suggestion that Debbie Baszo did not meet all the other tests of eligibility for the playoffs. She was refused registration simply because she was a girl. Her case seems to me therefore to be on exactly the same footing under the section as the case of a boy denied registration by ORSA because he is black.[4]

Unfortunately, Justice Wilson's colleagues, Justice Houlden and Justice Weatherston, disagreed. Justice Weatherston wrote that "the Code should not be interpreted in a narrow and pedantic way; on the other hand it should not be given such a broad interpretation as to offend common sense."

Justice Houlden agreed with this position and simply stated that "the activities carried on by ORSA are not 'services or facilities' within the meaning of s. 2(1)(a) of the Code. ... I think that the words should be restricted to 'services or facilities' offered in places such as restaurants, hotels, public parks, and the like." Even though ORSA played games in public parks, they were not supplying a service, in Justice Houlden's opinion. "The principal function of ORSA is the preparation of playoff schedules for the various leagues that are affiliated with it," he argued. "The preparation of playoff schedules is not a service in a public place, therefore services and facilities in a public place were not theirs to deny." The case was disallowed.

The Cummings case was decided against her on a technicality. All three justices found that the OMHA, unlike ORSA, was not an incorporated entity, and therefore, under the definition used in the Code, was not a "person." Justice Wilson advised that the complaint "should have been laid against named officers or directors of the respondent association." This case too was disallowed.

So what was the fallout from the Baszo and Cummings cases? The mere suggestion that girls and boys might play together provoked an overwhelming response in the amateur sports community. Men said they would quit volunteering in droves "if they had to coach little girls." In fact, the reaction was so strong that a lobby group was formed to persuade the government to do something to prevent further erosion of standards in sport. The Ontario government was at the time headed by Bill Davis, a strong supporter of men's sport. The attorney general, Roy McMurtry, had played hockey and football throughout high school and university and would later become the commissioner of the Canadian Football League. And this government listened.

While this lobbying was going on, there was a pivotal change in Canadian law. In April 1982, Prime Minister Pierre Trudeau patriated the Constitution, with its Charter of Rights and Freedoms. For the first time, Canada had a blueprint outlining rights that would supersede all other laws.

To prepare for the changes this central legislation would bring, all levels of government were asked to examine their present laws and make whatever changes would be necessary to bring them in line with the Charter. The Ontario government undertook an amendment of its provincial Human Rights Code, seemingly with these instructions in mind. But when the newly amended code was published that same year, the sports lobbyists had won out over the Charter. Subsection 19(2) had been added, and this effectively exempted sport and physical activity. The section read, "The right under section 1 to equal treatment with respect to services and facilities is not infringed where membership in an athletic organization or participation in an athletic activity is restricted to persons of the same sex." For some reason, even though the Charter explicitly spelled out that the equality of women was guaranteed, Ontario lawmakers believed they could just as explicitly write women athletes out of human rights protection.

At this time, the government also commissioned John Sopinka to prepare a report on equality in sport. Sopinka, a lawyer who would later become a Canadian Supreme Court justice, set about gathering opinions and information on the state of women's sport. The men he cited told him of the dire consequences of allowing girls and boys to play together. And the women he interviewed were equally negative. For the most part, they headed women-only sports associations, and they believed this fight for "so-called human rights" was really meant to "line the pockets of lawyers about to capitalize on a whole new area of human rights in sports."[5] None of the sports organizations Sopinka cited supported integrated sport, and the report was laced with moral overtones of what might happen if girls and boys ended up on the same playing field or, worse, in the same change room. In fact, upholding "public decency" was offered as the official reason behind subsection 19(2).

When he made his conclusions, Sopinka acknowledged that there was inequality but advised the government to keep subsection 19(2), saying it was a necessary protector of women's sport. His report, and the subsection, stood until a 12-year-old hockey player came along in 1985. Her name was Justine Blainey.

Justine Blainey v. the Ontario Hockey Association

Siblings Justine and David Blainey loved hockey. But it took several years for Justine to convince Caroline, their math-teacher mother, to let her play. "At the time, when I was six or seven, I kept asking my mom, 'I want to play hockey,'" Blainey told me in the summer of 2000. "'I don't want to tap dance, ballet, and figure skate.' And she said, 'No. Girls don't play hockey.' So it took three years before my mom said, 'Okay, you've nagged enough. We'll find you a girls' team to play for.'

"By that time, I was 11, and a year later, I knew I wanted to play with the guys. They had more competition, more hours of ice, the rinks were closer [to home], the hours were at better times, and ... there was a more competitive atmosphere, there were more tournaments.

There was definitely a difference, and I wanted to be part of it. I wanted to be part of the highest level possible with people in my own age category. I finally said, 'Well, I want to play with the guys,' and male coaches said to me, 'Well, why don't you pretend you're a guy?' That wasn't for me. I did it for a while, but it wasn't my choice to pretend I was a boy, so eventually I had to fight for equality."

Caroline Blainey had spent a great deal of her time driving both kids to tournaments and hockey schools, so as the 1984–85 season commenced, she breathed a sigh of relief when they both tried out for—and made—the Toronto Olympics A peewee team of what was then the Metro Toronto Hockey League (MTHL; its present name is the Greater Toronto Hockey League [GTHL]). Now she'd be driving both kids to the same arena, to the same team, at the same time. But when the MTHL found out a girl was playing on a boys' team, they barred Justine Blainey, citing the infamous rule 250. It didn't matter that she had always played with her brother and the other boys in street hockey and shinny. Now that she was in organized hockey, the "no girls allowed" sign was posted.

But the MTHL had picked the wrong girl to wage war against. Blainey got herself a lawyer, Anna Fraser, and believed she could straighten this misunderstanding out in no time. She imagined she'd be on the ice in a week or two. Her mother wasn't so sure. "I said, 'This is going to hurt. You are going to run into problems. Would you like to reconsider it? Would you like to wait?' Of course I did. I'm a mother hen because I am a mother. She said, 'Mom, I want to play in boys' hockey.'"

"People always feel that my mother was the pusher, the feminist, someone behind, pushing this little girl," says Justine. "She was the person who listened, and that's what I needed. I was a little girl who knew what I wanted. I was good enough, I made the team, and this was what I wanted to do. ... She supported me in those goals."

So the Blainey team started to form. Caroline, Justine, and her brother, David, supported one another and worked closely with Fraser, their lawyer. The Canadian Association for the Advancement of Women and Sport and Physical Activity (CAAWS) supported the case, as did the Women's Legal Education and Action Fund (LEAF) and a small but strong group of people from sport. But they'd set themselves a mammoth task. They would have to prove that subsection 19(2) of the Ontario Human Rights Code was unconstitutional—no small matter in the as yet untested waters of Canadian constitutional law.

On September 26, 1985, the Blainey team lost the first battle in divisional court. Justice Donald Steele ruled that while subsection 19(2) did violate the Charter of Rights and Freedoms, he believed the intention of those who had drafted the Charter was not to "surrender all their powers to the individual." He concluded that the provincial Code was designed to allow sports organizations to develop, "rather than jeopardizing those very groups by the wishes of an individual."

Blainey supporters were hugely disappointed and immediately appealed the decision. While Blainey was indeed an individual, the collective rights of all girls and women were at stake. In April 1986, two of the three justices at the Ontario Court of Appeal sided with Justine and declared subsection 19(2) unconstitutional. Justice Charles Dubin (who would later write the Dubin Report on performance-enhancing substances in sport) wrote that while the section

> permits membership in an athletic organization or participation in an athletic activity to be denied solely on the basis of sex without regard to any other factors ... the Human Rights Code is still available to all others who complain of discrimination on other grounds, such as race, colour and ethnic origin. Only sexual discrimination is permitted. This renders s. 19(2) clearly discriminatory. ... In substance, it permits the posting of a "no females allowed" sign by every athletic organization in the province. ... I think the appropriate remedy is to declare it to be unconstitutional and of no force or effect.

Justice Morden agreed with Justice Dubin's interpretation, and Blainey was ecstatic when her mother reached her in her grade 7 class to give her the good news. She imagined herself joining her team for the playoffs—but that wasn't about to happen.

The MTHL and the OHA appealed the decision, refused to allow Blainey to play during the appeal, and passed a new rule that barred anyone who wasn't a registered player from being on the ice during practice. Now Blainey was effectively banned from her team's practices too. And generally, life became difficult. Her old girlfriends turned on her at school and she was ostracized. "As a young person, the most painful events occur with your friends," says Blainey. "You know that your family's been turned down for promotions, you know they've been hassled at work, but the most important thing is losing your friends. ... I'd go to my locker, and there'd be slang and slander written on there. That was definitely hurtful.

"When people would not talk to you as you're walking down the halls, but be talking *about* you. When you'd go to talk to teachers and they'd say, 'No, I don't want to talk to you,' and then slam the door in your face. When you were told you were going to have to repeat a year in school, even though your average is 80%, because you missed too much school time going to court. It didn't make any sense at all, so some of those times were very hurtful and very dangerous."

Blainey received death threats and hate mail. Locker-room graffiti depicted her in pornographic positions. One day, a stranger in a subway station recognized her as "that girl who wanted to destroy hockey" and threw her down a set of stairs. But she didn't back down. And soon, things slowly began to turn in her favour.

After 42 years in power, the provincial Tories were replaced by a minority Liberal government, with the NDP holding the balance of power. The Liberals named Ian Scott as attorney general. The well-known Toronto lawyer took a particular interest in the Blainey case. As a student of law in the broadest sense of the term, he wanted to see where the new Charter of Rights and Freedoms would eventually take Canadian justice. He also viewed a law that entrenched discrimination by sex as an important test of the Charter, and in July 1985, he publicly supported the repeal of subsection 19(2).[6]

As attorney general, Scott was responsible for amending provincial laws to ensure that they met the standards of the new Charter. All levels of government had been given three years to do this, and since the Charter had been entrenched in April 1982, Ontario should have straightened out its laws by April 1985, one month before Blainey lodged her complaint. (In fact, the Tories knew when they added subsection 19(2) that it appeared to be in direct contravention of the Charter, but at the time, the hockey lobby had a lot of sway with the Ontario government.) Scott believed subsection 19(2) would be a good place to start.

In January 1986, the all-party Standing Committee on the Administration of Justice met to hear deputations on Bill 7, the Equality Rights Statute Law Amendment Act. Among other things, this act would repeal subsection 19(2) of the Human Rights Code because it was seen to be unconstitutional. Of all the amendments to the Code, this was by far the most contentious. But Scott had told the committee:

> The repeal of subsection 19(2) means that no individual
> should be denied an opportunity because of that person's
> gender. It means also that each individual has a right to be
> judged on the basis of merit and ability. At the same time, the
> affirmative action provisions of the Code and the Charter
> will ensure the continuation of those women's athletic
> programmes which provide opportunities to so many
> women and will provide an underpinning for programs in
> the future which will increase opportunities for all.[7]

Unfortunately, Scott's optimism was not matched by most sports associations. With the exception of the Ontario Cycling Association, most such organizations opposed the repeal of subsection 19(2). Many who made presentations to the committee saw Blainey as a selfish girl who had inflated her ability as a hockey player just so she could say she played with boys, and portrayed women who supported her as seeking to destroy sport and all its moral virtues with their feminist agenda. The opinion expressed by Carl Noble, the father of one female player, was typical. He wrote to the committee,

> CAAWS and LEAF are a group of busy bodies. They have received their millions from the government to fight the lowly volunteer, who doesn't receive a cent[,] and is bankrupting their sporting governing bodies to fight what CAAWS and LEAF feel is an injustice. One girl out of 5,000 wants to play in a boys' programme, but [she] doesn't want to work within the guidelines. ... I can assure you that if you try and regulate and dictate to the volunteer ... if they don't like what is happening[,] they will quit and then what will happen? If things run smooth, leave it alone! It's like a car—if nothing is wrong, don't fix it."[8]

Those who wanted to maintain 19(2) then tried turning the tables. Girls might not want to play boys' hockey, they said, but female hockey would be overrun by men. "Retired NHL players, over-age juniors, or any other males" would take positions on women's teams, they predicted.[9] Other deputations warned of the end of Girl Guides and ringette because "both would be invaded by men."[10]

Within the amateur sports world, few people supported Blainey beyond the CAAWS and such men as Rob Beamish of Queen's University and Bruce Kidd of the University of Toronto. The Canadian Cycling Association and the Ontario Cycling Association did pass a resolution affirming their long-standing policy "that equal opportunity be given to all competitors in cycling on the basis of ability rather than age or sex," but they were alone among amateur sports organizations. Still, Blainey had plenty of supporters beyond sport. In fact, few Canadians could believe such a discriminatory practice was still taking place. Fortunately, the Supreme Court of Canada reflected the beliefs of most Canadians and refused leave to appeal to the OHA, effectively endorsing the appeal court's decision.

But Justine Blainey's battle wasn't over. The court rulings simply gave her the right to argue her case before the Human Rights Commission. Now the OHA said it would prove once and for all that girls should not be allowed to play with boys.

At this time, Michael Bader, a lawyer who worked for the attorney general's office, joined the Blainey team. Bader says that when he was first handed the file, he wasn't sure they could win, but that situation soon changed. "As we gathered our witnesses, I became quite sure we would win," he told me in April 2000. "We needed the kind of witnesses who would quash the negativity the OHA had painted, and we got them.

"When we got to the hearing, the OHA founded their case by saying [that] there was a difference between the sexes, and that physically girls would not perform as well as boys. [This was] the paternalistic argument that girls need to be protected. Obviously so do boys. Any parent of a young son would express the same concerns of her son or his son being injured. Assuming the bar is set equally, you either make the team or you don't. If you have the ability and the skill, sex matters not a whit."

Soon, others had taken up the cause. Abby Hoffman, the then director of Sport Canada and herself a former athlete, came to support the case, as did Diane Palmasson, who at the time was the director of the women's program at Sport Canada and a world-class distance runner in her age group. Doctors Iris Marshall and Marg Kavanagh were expert witnesses in the area of sports medicine, and both had played hockey on men's teams while working as physicians in the military. Dr. Ira Jacobs, an exercise physiologist and the head of the environmental physiology section of the Department of National Defence, rounded out the team.

Among other things, Dr. Marshall was the director of the sports medicine clinic at the Hospital for Sick Children in Toronto. Using physiological charts, she showed that trained female athletes are only a few percentage points behind trained male athletes in the categories of blood volume, haemoglobin, heart volume, VO_2 max, and lower-body strength.[11] In the categories of flexibility and agility, women athletes actually outperform male athletes. In this way, Marshall disputed claims made by the OHA's expert witness, Dr. Charles Bull, who had been Team Canada's as well as the Toronto Maple Leafs' doctor for years, but appeared to have little expertise in the physiology of women. Dr. Bull had initially testified that women had no testosterone, which he called "the fighting hormone." Minutes later, he corrected himself and said, "But females have a tiny bit of testosterone, I think—I'm getting on bad ground here now—but I don't think they have any androgens."

Dr. Bull wasn't the only OHA witness who appeared to be on shaky ground. Carleton Gray, the women's national hockey team coach in the U.S., testified that in girls "who have played with boys longer—later than others—I have found that it has changed their character. They have become a person that I don't believe they originally intended to be in the sense that it was difficult for them, at age 16 and 17, to come back and participate. They were individuals. They were not team members—and this sport is a team sport, and there is a social structure that goes with it, and I mean that in a nice sense. … If you force an individual at age 13 or 14 to stay exclusively with boys, what I have observed is that they have tended to become very individualistic, to the point that they're looking for individual survival in a boys' league at that point, rather than develop[ing] the hockey skills as a team member." It was a ridiculous statement. If girls became individuals—something that can't honestly be considered a problem—what did boys become?

And the unfounded claims continued. Legendary hockey player Angela James stated that it was because she had played with women and girls that she had become a top player. In reality, James played the first seven years of her hockey career with boys. But she was told not to talk about that. "I was pressured to testify," she said years later. "I would never do that again."

Salt Lake City Olympic gold medalist Vicki Sunohara, who was 13 at the time of the hearings, also told the commission how much segregated hockey had helped her career. Years later, as a member of the national team, she admitted the truth. "I was angry when I was told I could no longer play with boys," said Sunohara in the summer of 2000. "But I did what I was told, and then the Ontario Women's Hockey Association (OWHA) told me another girl thought she was too good to play with girls, and they wanted me to testify against her. I wasn't given the right information; I didn't even think about it. It didn't make any difference to me if I testified or not. Later I understood what I had done, and I had a long talk with Justine. She was very upset at the time, and I felt very bad and apologized for what I did."

Not surprisingly, the OHA's arguments didn't hold up. Dr. Marshall corrected Dr. Bull's claim that women do not have androgens. "We certainly do have androgens, and that is not necessarily primarily where you get your aggression and fighting spirit from," she testified. "Both men and women can be aggressive—it is not related to large levels or large differences of testosterone or androgens." She also cited a study that found that "aggression shown by hockey players did not correlate with their ability to play hockey or their ability to be a good hockey player."

Dr. Bull had also testified that women did not possess high enough levels of VO2 max for integrated hockey. VO2 max measures the maximum amount of oxygen a person can utilize, commonly given in millilitres of oxygen consumed per kilogram of body weight per minute, and the point at which the body goes into an anaerobic state (without oxygen). Dr. Bull had testified that the average NHL hockey player had a VO2 max of 55 millilitres of oxygen per kilogram of weight per minute, and that he'd never seen a woman test anywhere near that amount. Dr. Marshall countered that plenty of women athletes had VO2 max values well above the NHL average, and while the measure is important in the endurance sports, such as marathon running and cross-country skiing, hockey, with all its stops and starts, does not demand a high VO2 max. In fact, Dr. Marshall testified, NHL players did not display anywhere near the readings of endurance athletes, who regularly scored in the 70s.

Dr. Marshall also called into question all the data presented about the physiological performances of women. It was too early, she said, to state anything finite about women's strength. "Most experts," she said, "are looking at their past assumptions and realizing that there were a lot of erroneous thoughts and beliefs in them. That is probably still the majority's belief, but the big changes are not made by the majority; they're made by the one person who looks at something and says, 'Something doesn't fit.'"[12]

Dr. Ira Jacobs was equally persuasive in his testimony. He agreed with Dr. Marshall that "there is very little, if any, correlation—I'm not aware of any—between something like hockey-playing performance and VO2 max. ... Part of the reason for that, I'm sure, is because I don't know of anybody who's quantified hockey players' performance—and you have to be able to quantify something to be able to determine whether or not there is an association. Hockey is a very, very complicated task; it consists of a lot of different types of activities, so to say that hockey is dependent upon VO2 max I think is a little bit presumptuous, because there is no scientific data to back that up."[13]

Dr. Jacobs thus reinforced the basic physiological argument of the Blainey camp: Hockey-playing ability is very difficult to quantify with any scientific exactitude. No one had done a study on the correlation between VO2 max and hockey efficiency because it would have been nearly impossible to measure. VO2 max is measured in individuals, while hockey is played by a team. How could anyone determine that a team won because individuals had high VO2 max readings? Why measure VO2 max and not eye-hand reaction time? Why not measure fat percentage, or how long each line spends on the ice? The physical variables, not to mention the psychological and social ones, are so immense that isolating just one factor is extraordinarily difficult.

As Michael Bader commented years later, "Our task was quite simple: Either you can play hockey or you can't. It's the responsibility of the coach who is choosing the team to determine this. According to him, Justine could play hockey." In fact, Blainey's coach, Dan Demario, had said exactly that when he testified. "She was one of the top skaters that we had out there. ... On my team, that year, she was one of my better defence players. Throughout the tournaments, through games, through practices, she increased her level of skill."

Of course, the Blainey case wasn't really about girls not being physically or psychologically able to play with boys. "The OHA brought parent after parent in who said they didn't believe girls should be sent into a game where checking occurred because of the potential harm to them," said Bader. "I asked them, 'Do you have a boy? Do you worry about the potential harm done to him?' They tried to paint this case as one girl wanting her way, but it was about the rights of all girls to reach their potential."

The case dragged on from May 1986 into the fall of 1987, and then, on December 3, 1987, Ian Springate—who had heard the case for the Human Rights Commission—released his verdict. After the mountains of documents and the parade of witnesses, Springate's decision reflected the simplicity Bader was talking about. In a short, six-page decision, Springate not only found subsection 19(2) to be unconstitutional, he also declared women's hockey to be a "special program" that was protected by the Code under subsection 13(1), which recognizes historical disadvantage. This meant that girls could try out for boys' teams, but boys could not try out for girls' teams because girls were still systematically discriminated against in the province's sport system. The OHA had to let Blainey play.

Springate also ruled that

> All pamphlets, books, or other materials containing the rules
> and regulations, and all registration, recruitment and
> advertising material published or caused to be published by
> the OHA, any division of the OHA and any club or team of a
> division of the OHA rather than the OWHA, contain a
> statement prominently displayed therein that eligibility is
> available to members of both sexes ... [and] that the OHA,
> OWHA and MTHL display prominently in all offices to which
> members of the public are invited a copy of the "declaration
> of management policy" issued by the Ontario Human Rights
> Commission.[14]

The OHA, the MTHL, and the OWHA strongly opposed Springate's ruling and requested another hearing to explain why it would be detrimental to the women's game. Essentially, they argued that they didn't want to be held liable if a member organization contravened this part of the ruling. Fortunately, Springate didn't buy their argument, and in August 1988, he issued another decision:

> The MTHL opposed having such a term apply to its individual clubs and teams. Its concern is that the league might be held responsible should a team coach or manager place a newspaper advertisement such as "Need two boys to play peewee hockey. Call Frank at 442-xxxx." In my view, it is the very possibility of advertisements such as this which justifies ensuring that local clubs and teams not be excluded from any order respecting published material. As for MTHL concerns that it might be held responsible for breaches of an order on the part of local team officials, should such a contention be raised, presumably one of the relevant considerations will be whether the MTHL has taken reasonable steps to ensure that the order is being complied with.[15]

The OHA and the MTHL just didn't get it, or simply refused to get it. They must have thought it would be business as usual, with their members actively recruiting boys and ignoring girls. They didn't seem to understand that advertising for two boys to play peewee hockey is no different from asking for two white people or two non-Jews. Unfortunately, the MTHL didn't live up to this part of Springate's decision. To this day, the organization takes a full-page ad in the *Toronto Star* sports section for one day, every week. Nowhere does this ad state that girls can play in the league; in fact, it almost never mentions girls or women at all. And the next time you're in any arena in Ontario, look for the "prominently displayed" declaration from the Human Rights Commission. I certainly have never seen one.

What did it all mean for Justine and her family? They were elated at first, but soon realized that going to the rink meant walking into an environment that was still openly hostile. "When I did win the court decision, I thought, 'This is amazing!'" says Blainey, "But when I phoned my new coach, I said, 'Guess what? I finally won. I can play!' He said, 'No, no. We gave your card away. We gave your card away last night to John.' And I said, 'Well, John didn't make the team. He had never made the team when there were tryouts. How come he made the team [now]?' And he said, 'Well, that's what we chose to do.' And I was devastated. But my brother picked up that phone and said, 'Know what? If there were a spot, would you give it to my sister?' And Mr. Brooks [the new coach, replacing Demario] said yes. And he said, 'Fine. I quit, and my sister can have my spot, 'cause I'll find a team in a week.' And he did, and that's how I ended up on the Eastenders—taking my brother's spot because he had made the team. The biggest supporter was my brother. He always said, 'If I can do it, you can do it too.'"

The More Things Change …

Well, at least the Blainey case changed attitudes in Ontario, right? You would certainly be forgiven for thinking so. Given the stacks of evidence the team compiled showing that girls and boys of the same ability are actually *better off* playing together, it is hard to imagine that anyone—let alone an educational institution—would come along and pretend none of that evidence ever existed. Unfortunately, that's exactly what happened.

In 1998, 13 years after Blainey first lodged her complaint with the Ontario Human Rights Commission, the athletic association of the York Region District School Board added a rule to its constitution barring girls from playing on boys' teams. Two years later, in March 2000, Risa Saraga, a top basketball player at Thornhill Public School, successfully tried out for the boys' team when not enough girls wanted a team of their own. She played in informal boys' tournaments beginning in September, but when the official regional championships came along in March, she was told by Phil Horseman, president of the district's athletic association, that it was against the constitution to let her play.

Horseman won't say what specific incident in 1998 prompted the association to amend its constitution, though when the story broke in March 2000, the media reported that members were concerned that girls would take places away from boys. But when it became known that a school board had acted in contravention of a girl's human rights, Horseman and the athletic association found themselves caught in a media whirlwind. The story was carried across the country, and few Canadians could believe such attitudes still existed. When Justine Blainey read about it, she contacted Risa Saraga immediately and rushed to support this young girl who just wanted to play.

"I could not believe my ears," said an exasperated Blainey. "After all these years, it was the same old lie. I guess the difference now is [that] when I challenged it, all kinds of people from hockey would debate me in the media. CTV lined Risa and I up for a television show, but no one from the board would appear. They're too embarrassed because of their own rules. I guess they didn't think so many people would see how wrong they are. To me, it's as if we'd tried to take the vote away from women. It's that bad."

To rectify the situation, the association amended the constitution at its annual general meeting in May 2000. Now it states:

> The York Region Elementary Schools Athletic Association is strongly committed to the promotion of sport and believes that both boys and girls should be afforded an equal opportunity to participate in regional athletic competition. In order to be maximized for each sport in which competitions are arranged, there shall either be a tournament for each gender or a co-ed competition. In the case of non co-ed sports, girls are only eligible to participate on girls' teams and boys are only eligible to participate on boys' teams. Where a student's school does not have a team representative of the student's gender, the Appeal Committee may permit the student to participate on a team composed of the opposite gender. In the alternative, the Appeal Committee may permit

a student to participate on a team composed of the same gender in a neighbouring school, or the Appeal Committee may make any determination that in the Appeal Committee's opinion is just.

Once again, the control committee surfaces. The final decision was to be based not on the female athlete's ability, but on whatever a group of adults decided would be best for her.

"We have made all these changes, and sure enough, people have changed it back," complained Justine Blainey. "I mean, haven't they read their past legislation? Hadn't they paid attention to the hard-fought battles ahead of time? One fact that is so astounding about this is that they're saying if there is a girls' team, then girls have to play on it. The fact of the matter is it doesn't matter if there's a girls' team. If you're good enough, let's play for the highest level possible. It shouldn't even be called the boys' team. It should be called the varsity team."

Bob Keele, counsel for the York Region District School Board, says his client does recognize the rights of girls. But he maintains that there are always exceptions, and that the appeals process will address them. "For example, if we say there's an exception for girls because of public decency or physical protection, we want to make sure that's being fairly administered and not being administered in a non-discriminatory fashion. So that's the reason for the appeals process—it's not that girls have the obligation to prove that they have the right. No, we acknowledge the right. The right is there. It's been acknowledged by the courts."

While Keele denies there are any religious or moral overtones to the amendment, his reference to concerns about "public decency" speaks volumes. One would almost think we were back in the Victorian age. But Keele says the real issues are "safety when travelling, safety when practising, those kinds of issues. Those are not as big a thing in most schools as the safety issue—actually playing the sport. Each sport has individual requirements, each sport has individual risks. Some sports are higher risk for a girl playing than other sports would be."

He offers football as an example of a sport that is higher risk for girls. "A girl may have great running ability, and pass and catch well, but she only weighs 120 pounds. What if the average weight on the opposing team is 180? When she gets hit, she's really going to get hit. She meets all the criteria as an athlete, but it's a safety issue." Keele does not explain how a 120-pound person—male or female—would make a team playing in a league where the average player is 60 pounds heavier. Surely weight is a criterion a coach would consider, and if he or she decided to put a lightweight athlete on a heavy-weight team, physical safety would be unrelated to gender. That 120-pound athlete would get hit and hurt the same way—male or female.

While Keele insists that the athletic association's constitution in no way contravenes a girl's right to play, it clearly does. If there is a girls' team, a girl *must* play on it. In the Blainey case, and most others like it, there *was* an existing girls' team. Blainey chose not to play on it, and her decision was affirmed at a human rights hearing. And in York region, if there is no girls' team, a girl needs to go to an appeals committee to obtain permission to play with the boys. "A right is not something that is granted," observes Michael Bader. "A right is a given. You don't have to ask a panel if you can have rights. Permission granted can just as easily be denied. The amendment doesn't meet the standards of the provincial Code or the federal Charter in terms of human rights."

Of course, for most people, the issue isn't one of fair play or human rights. When girls begin to demand equal access to the sporting culture, two fears surface.

The first is that they will take what are seen as places boys should legitimately have. One girl in Cape Breton told me that the mother of the boy she beat out for the position of goalie on her team imme-diately complained to hockey officials and had her removed. "Her son didn't even want to play, but just because I was a girl, she thought I'd taken his spot away. My mom called a lawyer, and she called the Human Rights Commission, and finally I was allowed to play."

The second fear is that something unseemly might happen if boys and girls are allowed to share public space in the heat of sport.

What could possibly be indecent about a bunch of young bodies intensely preoccupied with the sweat and strain of deep physical activity? Why shouldn't their bodies be tangled up or running in unison? Why shouldn't their breathing be passionate but measured? Because it's all way too much like sex, that's why. In many ways, we are still Victorians when it comes to bodies and play.

I would argue that the concern expressed by the self-appointed control committees of sport for the personal safety of girls is specious. If girls are allowed to be physically, emotionally, and psychologically strong, it will only make them safer. It is up to educators, sports administrators, and publicly elected officials to ensure safe environments for *all* children. Unfortunately, we are creating a decidedly unsafe environment for girls when we perpetuate a sport system that tells boys they're so special that girls aren't even allowed to play with them. If boys saw girls taking the puck from other boys, skating down centre ice, and scoring in the opposite goal, perhaps they would gain a more complete understanding of the female body.

If sports associations and their member organizations believe excellence is important in women's sport, they should be creating opportunities for girls to play at levels that are continually challenging. If they are concerned about rising levels of obesity and addiction to tobacco among teenage girls, that should give them another good reason to ensure that all girls have the opportunity to play. And if they really want to help girls' teams, they won't force good players to play below their level of ability. Rather, they will spend real money, time, and effort to make sure that opportunities for all girls increase.

And this is a battle that people have been fighting since the 1960s.

Title IX and the Fight for Equality

Congresswoman Patsy Mink, a democrat from Hawaii, is a veteran of the civil rights movement and the mother of Title IX, which ensures that "no person in the United States shall, on the basis of sex, be excluded from participation in, be denied the benefits of, or be subjected to discrimination under any educational program or activity receiving Federal financial assistance."

"The legislation followed a long fury of hearings, discussions, and problems that were being raised on the House education committee in 1967 and '68," remembers the congresswoman, who still represents her electoral district after all these years. "There was this troubling thing we realized, and that was that the government left girls behind when it came to any sort of equitable consideration in education. The vocational schools arm of the U.S. Education Department showed us training videos they were so proud of. In them, female students were told they could become hairdressers, nurses, even the odd teacher, but male students were told they could become astronauts, explorers, scientists, whatever they wanted. We were shocked that a U.S. department could produce such disturbing material based on preconceived notions of gender-appropriate careers. ...

"I started to think that since we were giving them so much money, we should have a say over what happened to it, and that was the start of Title IX legislation. It was meant to simply legislate gender equity in education. It wasn't designed for sport, but people grabbed on to this. When it took hold in colleges, young women went in and started to win gold—even at the Olympics. They were very visible, everyone could see something was changing in America. Every advance of women's sport was there in full view of the television screen."

Mink introduced the bill to the U.S. Congress in 1972. "We did it in the middle of the night," she explains. "No one understood the enormous consequences. They just thought, 'Oh, there they go again ... those women,' and didn't pay any attention. There was next to no debate. They didn't understand it, and it passed."

Title IX is the most important act ever to deal with women's sport in the United States. It prohibits federally funded educational institutions from engaging in sex discrimination. Even private schools are not exempt under Title IX, because very few are absolutely free of federal funding. And the legislation doesn't look only at whether funding is administered in an equitable way. It also addresses issues such as sexual harassment; discrimination in admissions, counselling, employment opportunities, computer education, and financial aid; and student pregnancies, health, and insurance protection.

Under the terms of Title IX, women and girls must have as much opportunity to participate as men and boys—they must be given equal or comparable access to facilities, equipment, and scholarships. And as Mink pointed out, the legislation was not meant specifically for sports; it also covers any other extracurricular activities, such as drama or music programs. But over the years, it has come to be applied largely to sport.

Before 1972, almost no American women received athletic scholarships. Nationally, the amount spent on monetary awards to female student-athletes was just $100,000. By 1999, American universities spent $180 million on women's sport scholarships. And participation levels also skyrocketed. In a 1997 report entitled *Physical Activity in the Lives of Girls*, the President's Council on Physical Fitness and Sports stated: "Prior to Title IX, 300,000 young women participated in interscholastic athletics nationwide; today, that figure has leaped to approximately 2.25 million participants." High-school participation levels have gone from one girl in 27 in 1972 to one in 2.5 in 1999.

Without question, Title IX has opened the door for women athletes. American women's teams dominate international competition today, mainly because the National Collegiate Athletic Association (NCAA) provides amazing support and top competition for university athletes. But it isn't all good news. Before Title IX, 90% of university coaches and administrators in women's sport were themselves women. By 1998, this had dropped to 47.4%. After a 21-year study, professor Linda Jean Carpenter, of the Department of Physical Education and Exercise Science at Brooklyn College in New York, reported that the number of women in leadership roles had decreased in other areas too. In 1972, more than 90% of college-level women's sport programs were administered by women. In 1998, that figure had dropped to a shocking 19.4%. No women at all are in any administrative capacity in just over 20% of programs. It seems that as the popularity of women's sport increased, so did the value of the coach and the sport administrator—so much so that male athletic directors decided these jobs were important enough for men to do (and were even important enough to merit salaries that actually met or surpassed reasonable standards of living).[16]

These figures are very troubling, especially when they are coupled with regular attacks on Title IX, both legislatively and through the courts. In 1984, the U.S. Supreme Court ruled in *Grove City College v. Bell* that only those educational programs and facilities that directly received federal funds were protected by the legislation. Lawyers for the college argued that it didn't receive funds directly from the government—only some of its students did. Therefore, the college was not subject to Title IX and could restrict access to certain courses, housing, sports, and employment opportunities. The Reagan-era court called its clearly discriminatory decision an act supporting "regulatory relief."

The Grove City decision opened the door to other school boards that were trying to claim that, as long as they offered equal numbers of programs for boys and girls, they were not in contravention of the law. One school district even dropped girls' volleyball and claimed that they hadn't breached Title IX because girls could still join the cheerleading team.

Other doors were opened that were better left closed. Because Title IX was related to numerous other civil rights laws that had been passed since the mid-1960s, and because the Grove City decision was a Supreme Court ruling, those other laws were quickly in danger of being dismantled as well. Title VI of the Civil Rights Act of 1964 prohibited discrimination on the basis of race, colour, or national origin in all federally assisted programs or activities; section 504 of the Rehabilitation Act of 1973 prohibited recipients of federal assistance from discriminating against disabled persons; and the Age Discrimination Act of 1975 prohibited discrimination on the basis of age in the delivery of services and benefits supported by federal funds. The Grove City decision jeopardized all of these pieces of legislation and countless others like them.

Civil rights advocates worked for four years to try to restore Title IX's teeth. They drafted the Civil Rights Restoration Act of 1987, a law that was designed to protect all civil rights legislation. But they were up against the ultra-religious right, a powerful lobby at any time, and particularly so during the Reagan administration. The religious right wanted all schools with any religious affiliation to be declared exempt from Title IX—essentially a roundabout way of denying women access to abortions on campus by getting colleges to affiliate, in whatever way possible, with religious organizations. It was a close and ugly fight, but in March 1988, Congress enacted the Civil Rights Restoration Act (despite a veto by President Reagan), and women students were once again protected by basic civil rights legislation.

Over the years, the fights involving Title IX continued. In February 1992, the Supreme Court handed down another decision, this one in favour of the legislation. In *Franklin v. Gwinnett County Public Schools*, the court ruled that girls and women who sue educational institutions for discrimination can claim "compensatory and punitive damages." This was an important decision because it acknowledged that women's rights were worth money, and it also put educational institutions on notice that they would be financially liable for sex discrimination—a message they can all understand.

Today, Patsy Mink believes the fight for Title IX was worth it. "The world is not perfect," she admits, "but as a statement of principle, [Title IX] is very important, and it caught everyone's attention. In 1975, we almost lost it when men who were feeling abused because their favourite sports had to share revenues with 'those women' attacked it. But there was no big affront, just individual spurts of antagonism, and we won out in the end." Unfortunately, since I spoke with Mink, President George W. Bush has declared that he wants the legislation abolished. We will have to see if he uses the cost of the war against terrorism as an excuse to gut the offices that investigate Title IX violations.

The Canadian Situation

Canada has no legislation equivalent to Title IX. In fact, though we now have superior constitutional equity legislation in the Charter of Rights and Freedoms (which includes sections that are equivalent to the Equal Rights Amendment, for which American women have campaigned for decades), our legal options have in the past been more limited. In 1981, the Supreme Court of Canada ruled, in *Seneca College of Applied Arts and Technology v. Bhadauria*, that Canadians could not sue individuals, corporations, or various levels of governments for discrimination because human rights legislation was already available to them.

Pushpa Bhadauria attempted to sue Ontario's Seneca College when she was unable to land a teaching position there. She had a Ph.D. in mathematics, a valid provincial teaching certificate, and seven years' teaching experience in the field. In rendering his decision, Chief Justice Bora Laskin said that although Bhadauria was told she would be contacted for an interview, "she was never given an interview nor any reason for rejection of her applications. She alleged that the positions for which she applied were filled by others without her high qualifications but who were not East Indian in origin. She claimed there was discrimination against her ... [and] that the college was in breach of a duty not to discriminate against her, and also in breach of s. 4 of the Ontario Human Rights Code, as amended." (Section 4 of the Human Rights Code deals with the right to employment "without regard to race, creed, colour, sex, marital status, nationality, ancestry or place of origin.")

Although Chief Justice Laskin agreed that Bhadauria had in fact been discriminated against by the college, he concluded that she should have turned not to a civil court as a remedy to the situation, but to the Human Rights Commission. In his ruling, he said, "I would hold that not only does the Code foreclose any civil action based directly upon a breach thereof but it also excludes any common law action based on an invocation of the public policy expressed in the Code. The Code itself has laid out the procedures for vindication of that public policy, procedures which the plaintiff respondent did not see fit to use."[17]

Unfortunately for Pushpa Bhadauria, Chief Justice Laskin concluded that the existence of a Human Rights Commission meant that she could not use the civil courts as a remedy for racism. But the disadvantages are obvious. Human rights codes, whether provincial or federal, are only quasi-judicial. They are not legally binding beyond the specific situation they address, and financial settlements are completely insignificant. The half-measures of the OHA in the Blainey case and the BCAHA in the Merkley case are just two examples of how organizations disregard decisions rendered by human rights commissions.

The human rights commissions' lack of teeth is compounded by the fact that, both provincially and federally, they are significantly underfunded and understaffed. And even if a girl and her parents are willing to spend several years fighting for a right that theoretically is legally enshrined, the next girl who makes a boys' team would have to wage the battle all over again. Does it seem fair to anyone that girls in every municipality, in every sport imaginable, and at every level of play available should spend three to five years of their lives challenging a sport body for the right to play? It's a ridiculous concept. We could be challenging various sports organizations for well over the next hundred years for only quasi-legal decisions.

But this issue goes far beyond sport. We need to ask what kind of country allows for huge monetary settlements when a person's property or reputation is damaged, yet restricts such settlements when it comes to acts of discrimination. Why do we limit monetary settlements for discriminatory injury concerning race, religion, sex, creed, and physical ability to only a few thousand dollars?

Canada and its provinces should have years ago invoked legislation that would protect girls and women in sport, and not just to avoid cases like Blainey's, but also to put an end to discrimination such as Katie Morrison faced. Most females don't want to try out for male teams, but they do want to be physically active in a community that gives as much consideration to their needs as it does to male needs.

While the Blainey battle was raging in Ontario, an NDP MPP from Ottawa, Evelyn Gigantes, did table a private member's bill that mimicked Title IX. But it died on the Order Paper when the legislature went into recess, and unfortunately, Gigantes was not re-elected in the next provincial election.

Patsy Mink says the most difficult part of Title IX is its administration. "We never have enough officers," she says, meaning those whose job it is to ensure that the legislation is enforced. "We need many, many, many more officers."

Michael Bader, who was the lawyer provided by the Ontario Human Rights Commission to Justine Blainey, believes there's a similar problem in Canada, where there are too few human rights officers to administer commission decisions. "Officers are supposed to uphold the Code in all aspects—race, sex, disability, sexual orientation, religion, etc.—[and] in every facet of life—the workplace, accommodation, public services and facilities, housing, everything—both before complaints have been investigated and after decisions have been made," he explains. "How could we possibly have enough people ensuring this? It's impossible."

Instead, Bader says we need legislation that will allow citizens to watch for human rights breaches on their own. "If you at least empower the public with the right to sue for discrimination based on sex, race, etc., then you allow people to be able to pursue equity through the courts, as they do in the States. *Bhadauria* was decided by the Supreme Court in 1981, and I believe it's time to revisit the notion that human rights are properly addressed by human rights codes. When that decision was made, constitutional law was in its infancy. It's going to take at least one generation of law students to be creative with our constitution, I believe, before we see how it applies to people's lives. We simply don't know right now.

"But if *Bhadauria* was successfully challenged," Bader continues, "it would make it possible to use legislation and the constitution to act on the big cases, which would give you power to set human rights principles in law. This way, people can use jurisprudence to further the law and human rights."

Harinder Mahil, the deputy chief commissioner of the B.C. Human Rights Commission, agrees that, without legislation, the families of girls like Katie Morrison and Melanie Merkley will have to give up years of time and a great deal of effort if they want to challenge the discriminatory nature of sport. "A Charter challenge to these practices would be very interesting," comments Mahil, "but you need a great amount of resources, very committed people, patience, and perseverance. You can't take a Charter challenge lightly."

I believe that using the Charter to challenge men's domination of the sporting world is a necessary and essential move for women to make—but somehow I don't think either Nike or McDonald's will sponsor us.

10   Strong, Sexy, and Smart

Looking Toward the Future

After being involved with equity issues in sport for all these years, I know that the present legal remedies don't work. Challenging sex discrimination through various human rights commissions simply isn't effective, and even if all the cases were decided in favour of women and girls, the judgements would still have only a quasi-legal status. We could easily spend the next 500 years launching legal challenges to open up every sport offered in every municipality and province, but who wants to do that? Of course, the issue would be moot if males and females were just naturally treated equally, but that is obviously not the case. In Canada, as in most countries, there is a demonstrated predisposition to discriminate, so we must design new laws that acknowledge that this isn't always the fair-minded country it imagines itself to be.

Americans have been much more successful at addressing sex discrimination with Title IX, and Canada should have a similar piece of legislation. But we shouldn't stop there. Title IX addresses equity in federal education programs, but the challenges in Canada go well beyond the education system.

The smartest legal solution—at least in Canada, where we have the equivalent to the never implemented and now conveniently forgotten U.S. Equal Rights Amendment in our Charter of Rights and Freedoms—is to launch a Charter challenge using section 15, which states in subsection (1), "Every individual is equal before and under the law and has the right to the equal protection and equal benefit of the law without discrimination and, in particular, without discrimination based on race, national or ethnic origin, colour, religion, sex, age or mental or physical disability."

To challenge sex discrimination in sport using this Charter clause would take several years, and we would likely need an alliance between the Women's Legal Education and Action Fund (LEAF), which supports Charter challenges, and women activists from sport. Like the civil rights activists and lawyers who successfully challenged the "separate but equal" doctrine of racial segregation in the United States through *Brown v. the Board of Education*, these advocates would have to carefully choose a promising test case. They would need a city that has recently funded male sport by subsidizing either a professional sports team or its facilities. Given how common this practice is, that shouldn't be hard to find. The city of Edmonton, which so gallantly bailed out the ailing NHL Oilers and their arena after the former owner, Peter Pocklington, refused to honour any of his debts, would be perfect. Winnipeg, which has just helped subsidize a new $10-million arena for its American Hockey League team, the Manitoba Moose, would also serve well. Just as the Morrisons showed that boys' sport was unfairly favoured in the city of Coquitlam (see chapter 2), those arguing the Charter challenge would show that Edmonton favoured men's professional hockey over the most basic needs of girls and women in sport. But this time, the stakes would be much higher, because the decision would affect all the municipalities and sport governing bodies in the country.

Perhaps it is the competitive athlete in me, but I believe that, with the right team, we would clean up in this legal competition. So entrenched is our culture's belief in professional sport that subsidizing it is rarely seen as a form of sex discrimination. But that is exactly what it is. Once this practice is found to be unconstitutional, every level of government would be forced to change such inequities, and we would eventually have our own version of Title IX. Of course, this wouldn't happen overnight. When you challenge a few thousand years of patriarchy, you can expect to face resistance. Yet ours is a battle instigated not by women and girls, but by those who refuse to change.

Once we have won the legal right to equity in sport, we can look beyond Title IX for other international examples to use as blueprints for the sporting culture of the future. Canada has had for nearly 20 years a national strategy for increasing the number of women in sport, particularly in leadership positions. In certain sports, women are already well represented, and they have gained senior leadership positions within the past 10 years. The Canada Games Council also has had a positive effect. This organization mandates that 50% of provincial coaching positions be filled by women who have Level III coaching certification when coaching at the Games. Because of this, many women are now moving into more advanced coaching positions.

But despite these encouraging changes, the vast majority of Canadian sport decision-makers are still white, male, and able-bodied. And as we saw with Melanie Merkley and Justine Blainey in chapter 9 and the Stepford wives of sport in chapter 3, change will not happen simply because there are some women in some leadership roles. Women need to be committed to achieving equality for all, not just to creating a little niche for themselves. Until that's no longer the case, I fear nothing will have really changed.

The Scandinavian Strategy

Scandinavian countries have had more effective anti-discrimination legislation for some time. In 1987, Sweden passed an Equality Policy, which stated, "Equality means that women and men have the same rights, obligations and opportunities in all the main fields of life; women and men share power, influence and responsibility in all sectors of the community." This umbrella statement was then applied to various individual facets of Swedish life, including sport.

The Swedish Sports Confederation, through the Working Group on Equality in Sport, has been addressing equity issues for more than a decade. The confederation's plan included a strategy for establishing women in leadership roles. Its key points were as follows:

- In advisory and decision-making bodies at all levels, women and men must be represented by at least 40% in 1995.
- Nominating committees at all levels that are elected from 1989 onwards must consist of an equal number of women and men.
- The proportion of female and male trainers must by 1995, at the latest, be equivalent to the distribution of the sexes among those taking an active part in the respective sports.
- The proportion of female personnel holding senior appointments, such as consultants, secretary-general and the like, must be at least 30% in 1995.[1]

The plan also noted that, in other Scandinavian countries, it is common to have quotas for female representation, though this was not necessarily recommended as a solution for sport. Instead, changes were to be carried out by an organization called the Central Secretariat for Equality Issues, which would help regions and districts implement equity representation. And educational campaigns would increase awareness of equity issues among both sexes. Research into equality issues would continue, and special funds would be set aside for projects for female athletes. Promotional campaigns would make Swedes aware of why equality was important, and sports associations would be restructured so they would recognize gender as a factor every time success was measured.[2]

Sweden's plan, which has been implemented over the past 10 years, is much like the plans of most other Scandinavian countries. These countries have also created huge mass sporting events for women in cycling, running, and Nordic skiing. In the Inga-Låmi ski tour in Norway, for example, several thousand women race or tour a 30-kilometre loppet in Lillehammer in early March. In Stockholm, tens of thousands of women join an annual women's mass bike ride. Events like these have increased the profile of women in sport, and that has translated into more women in leadership roles. Still, there has been some backpedalling, especially because some people have been lulled into believing equality has been achieved; yet Scandinavia remains a model for others. Reading the sports section of

Scandinavian newspapers is always a delight, as I mentioned earlier, because women's sport is covered extensively and knowledgeably. And there is just generally a deeper and more profound relationship with the natural world. It is taken for granted that the body is to be lived in. People are not devoted to indoor clubs with fake equipment that allows them to pretend to be skiing, cycling, rowing, or running. Despite the climate, Scandinavians engage in all sports at a level foreign to most North Americans—and all of it happens outside.

All public transit has room for skis. There are tens of thousands of kilometres of ski trails. When I was in Lillehammer in the winter of 2001, I took a city bus to the ski area each day. Imagine a North American municipal transit system dropping off and picking up at every ski area surrounding the city. All the trails are free, and they lead to large public chalets that provide warm drinks and food. In Oslo, the city tram line leads to 1,000 kilometres of ski trails, all dotted with hostels where you can eat, sleep, enjoy a hearty breakfast, and get going again.

These countries also haven't gone to the great lengths that we have to separate boys and girls and men and women. There is an acceptance of the sporting female body that doesn't automatically lead to its sexualization, and there have been more and better opportunities for girls and women for a longer time. Surely this is no coincidence. If we are committed to equality, and I believe most Canadians are (though many don't understand how much work it takes to actually create a culture and environment where equality is possible), we need to look seriously at the Scandinavian model. Of course, we would also have to start designing cities and their surroundings in a way that makes physical activity matter more than automobiles. Trains (with plenty of room for skis, bikes, and packs) would have to replace the horrendously costly, dangerous, and toxic superhighways we have now. This would just be a start, though, because most North Americans have lost touch with the natural world and don't know how to be a part of it anymore. Perhaps we should consider the way Aboriginal people understand nature and their place in it for a more holistic approach to the body as part of and not separate from the natural world.

Strong, Sexy, Smart, and Brave

Despite the massive changes we need to make, women in North America and Europe have many more options than women in other parts of the world. In sport, we may not have all the opportunities men have, but we do *have* opportunities. Lesbians may lose sponsorship deals when they come out, but they *can* come out and still live relatively safely. Athletes like Italy's Paola Pezzo can pose nude or present themselves in glittery unitards and consent to be portrayed only as sex fantasies if they so choose; it's not against any law in Europe or North America to do so. The women from our Canadian Nordic ski team are free to pose naked to raise money to help defray the costs of competing. Some people may think it's a foolish and exploitative thing to do, but it is their choice to do it. Let us hope that Margaret Atwood's dystopian *The Handmaid's Tale* never comes to pass, and that these young women will always have the freedom to portray themselves in all the ways they choose, even if some of us take exception to it.

For many other women in the world, however, life is simply not like this. Islamic and Hindu women in particular must be very careful about how their sexuality is perceived. At the Sydney Olympics, women competitors from Islamic countries such as Senegal and Algeria, and from the mainly Hindu country of India, were able to compete in track and field, albeit in longer, baggier shorts and singlets than most on the field. An Algerian, Nouria Merah-Benida, won the 1,500 metres in such attire—amazingly, she didn't seem to need a bikini bottom to make her run faster. Her compatriot Hassiba Boulmerka, the world champion at the same distance in 1995, also competed in less revealing clothing in her competitive days. Even so, Muslim fundamentalists in her country threatened her life for the dual "crimes" of running and revealing her body.

Boulmerka tried to walk a fine line during her career. She didn't flaunt her body, but she didn't ignore its wonderful abilities. When she returned to Algeria with her world championship win in 1995, men spat at her and threw stones when she tried to train. Eventually she moved to Cuba, where, she says, the sports-mad Cubans "opened their hearts" to her and allowed her to prepare for the Atlanta Olympics.

In 1996, after one of her heats in Atlanta, Boulmerka told me that it wasn't just the religious fundamentalists of her country who discriminated against her. "Sponsors like the girls with the blonde hair and blue eyes," said the North African runner. Despite her superhuman accomplishments, few corporations offered sponsorship.

When I asked how she was able to train in Algeria, she talked first about how dangerous it was for her as a female runner, but then she related those personal experiences to the experiences of all women in that country. She expressed an understanding of the risks she took and how they affected the next generation of women runners. So I wasn't surprised that, five years after Boulmerka's world championship win, another Algerian woman took the gold in the 1,500 metres in Sydney. Boulmerka is without question one of the bravest and strongest women ever to compete, and her courage and talent clearly sent a message to women throughout the world not to give in to violence and inequity.

Meeting Boulmerka was a highlight of my career, as both an athlete and a journalist, and our conversation at the Atlanta Olympics in 1996 will stay with me forever. And I had a similar experience in Sydney. When cyclist Marion Clignet of France won the silver medal in the women's individual pursuit, I asked her at a press conference what she'd tell girls about having a positive body image. She gave me a memorable response. "You know what I'd say?" she began. "I'd say I don't have to talk to girls and women because it's you guys—the fucking media—that make women think we must be thin. The media mess with women's minds. You lose a kilo and people say, 'God, you look good.' You gain a couple, and it's 'God, you look like a cow.'"

Clignet then told the international crowd about her own fight with bulimia. It began when her ability as an athlete increased, she explained, and she became more and more nervous about her results. Binge eating seemed to calm her nerves, but she started putting on the pounds. In the rather ruthless world of cycling, where weight is an almost obsessive topic, members of her first cycling team nicknamed her "the Load." Throwing up remedied this situation.

Amazingly, of the three women on the podium in Clignet's event, the 3,000-metre pursuit, two that night acknowledged having eating disorders, and the third said she was sympathetic to the experiences of the other two. Was the fact that two of the three medalists fought an eating disorder a coincidence? I don't think so. With the photographers in the media bus two nights earlier complaining that they shouldn't have to photograph women athletes who are "dogs" and "cows," one can understand where Clignet's anger comes from. These men were talking about Olympic champions.

As of the Sydney Games, Clignet said, her eating disorder was history. Still, her resolve to fight for equality in her sport remained strong. "We had a race in Switzerland this summer," she told me during an interview. "The women were housed in nuclear fallout shelters. We were in basements with the absolute bare necessities. Can you imagine male cyclists ever having to do this—especially the top cyclists in the world? They get put up in good hotels. As soon as I retire, I am going to spend my energy making things better for women."

More and more often, I hear women athletes talking like this. For instance, I attended the Canadian Olympic rowing team trials at Elk Lake in Victoria 10 months before the Sydney Games began, and the status of women in sport was a big topic of conversation. This didn't surprise me. Although rowing has a long and ugly history of gender discrimination—after all, the Argonaut Rowing Club in Toronto did not open its doors to female members until 1981—it's also now extremely popular with women.

"Rowing offers a variety of different extremes," says multiple world and Olympic champion Marnie McBean. "There are days when it's sunny and calm; there are days when we're out there and it's windy. There are days when there's mist and an evening sunset. There's the whole aesthetic component. There's the beauty of the single sculler, who is lonesome and has a solitude and a quietness about [her]. It's like watching a water spider cross a plate of oil. On a nice day, the water looks flat, like oil.

"But then there's the power of the crew, where you see eight people working so hard but making it look easy. You know they're working hard because you can see their faces and hear them. You just get this incredible sense of effort, and yet the boat is just gliding along as if there's no check and there's no bounce to it. It just seems to be propelled. It's that unison of crew rowing that provides the complexity of beauty."

Veteran cox Lesley Thompson, also a multiple world and Olympic champ, says rowing has some unique qualities that make it attractive to women. "I think when you get out on the water you're allowed to make your own decisions. There's been some ground-breaking women in the past. They've done well, they've showed a lot of young women they can do well. It's a positive experience. … We have a good history, but sport's different now. … I think the women have come a long way. Society has changed. Hopefully, we're becoming a more global and caring society. Hopefully, people are beginning to understand other people's feelings. There used to be comments about women in sport. I think we're a lot more educated now. I think we see that people have value as people. We're more sensitive now."

McBean also says things are different since she and Silken Laumann first started rowing, and old stereotypes have finally been thrown aside. On the day I went to Elk Lake, there were just as many men cheering the women as there were women cheering the men. Laumann and her husband, John Wallace (who won a gold in the men's eight in 1992), came with their two children in tow—two-and-a-half-year-old Will, and Kate, who at just fourteen days was at her first rowing regatta. And they weren't the only family to come out that morning. There was constant noise and movement. The activity on the shore was as dynamic as the movement on the water.

Laumann says families and sport can work together. "In recreational sport, there should be daycare facilities, babysitting facilities. If a rowing club had these, a lot more women would go rowing. I think as women become more involved in decision-making roles, administrative roles in sport, certainly the needs of families and women are going to be prioritized a little bit higher."

Today, membership in the national rowing body, Rowing Canada Aviron, is approximately 70% female. At the University of Victoria, they struggle to put together one men's novice eight while up to 200 women show up to fill 18 novice positions. It is a sport where big, powerful women—women who can wrap their hands around an oar like nobody's business—feel they belong. Strong women do well in this sport, as do women who like the feeling of eight people working together toward a single goal. These kinds of women were born to row.

"We're not Barbie dolls," said Alison Korn, a member of the women's eight, which won the only Canadian rowing medal in Sydney, a bronze. "We're strong, big women who know who we are, and we don't apologize for it. We have big thighs and big shoulders, and I think we look great in bikinis. I wish girls would get the message that it's great to be a strong woman." Six months after the Olympics, the 6', 183-pound Korn joined an all-female team that was attempting to ski from Canada to Russia via the North Pole.

Marnie McBean, at 5'10" and 165 pounds, also doesn't apologize for her size. "I'd have to say I can't wait to stop rowing so my thighs will decrease a little," she said jokingly. "I can't find a pair of jeans that fit. But when I first started rowing, muscles were so uncool. Now you can go to a bar wearing a strappy little tank top and look tall and a little more muscular than the mainstream, and that's cool."

McBean's trapezius muscles, which run from the top of her neck to her shoulder blades, exude power. The muscles of her thighs bulge in tights. Her biceps and triceps are beautifully large, and her back muscles ripple with strength. She is not "a little more muscular" than the average woman. One look at her in a tank top is enough to tell you that she is one of the strongest women in

Canada. There are thousands of hours of weightlifting in her muscles, and even more hours of rowing.

"You look at triathletes," she continued. "There's tons of women doing triathlons; the number of women who are active and fit is growing. There's still the skinny sort of top-heavy person who's in advertisements now, but there's also a push towards a more healthy body.

"When I first started rowing, even when we were covered by the press, I would be described as blue-eyed, and maybe I might have a big smile. Silken was described as a Nordic Valkyrie with a 150-watt smile. Now we're 'aggressive' and 'dynamic' and 'powerful,' and we're 'muscular.' These are words we hoped to have written about us, because 10 years ago they thought we were dykes because we have muscles. Now we're called athletes. Ten years ago, muscles were a sexuality issue for other people. Now it's a fitness issue."

Naturally Strong, Sexy, and Smart

McBean may believe that the world has changed in the past 10 years, and certainly in rowing I believe it has, but we must still remember that we live both a sexual and a gendered life. In other words, we are all still dependent on the approval of men, and we will continue to be so long as they are the political, economic, and social gatekeepers. If we are heterosexual and sexually active, we want to be sexually attractive to certain men as well, and straight or gay, we all want to be desired and loved.

But in sport, as I said in the introduction to this book, it is possible—if we are unencumbered by a gendered world—just to be athletes. It is a freedom few other experiences can give us—especially ones involving the body—and I believe this is when sexuality can really flourish. Women attain a certain ownership when they combine the sexual and the physical. There's plenty of sweating and physical effort going on, and that makes women feel highly sensual. The body feels spontaneous and strong. It is an animalistic feeling.

When you and another person are skiing, cycling, running,

rowing, or canoeing, and both of you are trying hard and sweating hard, an immediate intimacy is created. When you know how hard you are working, you know how hard the person beside you is working, and that fosters admiration and respect. This, for me, is true equality. In a sport like cycling, riders literally share the work as they take turns at the front of the pack and use their bodies to shelter those behind them. Barriers completely disappear as riders become intoxicated by movement and speed. Their bodies transcend individuality and become one moving human entity.

When I was writing much of this book, I was also skiing in the Rocky Mountains and reading *Tracking and the Art of Seeing: How to Read Animal Tracks and Signs*, by American writer Paul Rezendes. I had written a considerable amount by then about the animal nature of women, so it was very exciting when, one day, after a particularly wonderful ski through the most dream-like powder snow imaginable, I found the following passage on "reading" animals:

> The longer you follow the animal, the deeper you enter into
> a perceptual relationship with its life. … If you know an
> animal well, you will know yourself better. … The more
> intimate we become with other lives, the more aware we are
> of how those lives connect with and affect our own.[3]

Rezendes believes that the more we understand the woods the more we understand who we are. In this environment, we allow the animal to surface—it does so naturally. Once we get to this state the possibilities are endless. Eventually, as we track animals, we track ourselves and are able to keep emotional track of those we love.

> If we care about our relationship with nature, or our
> relationship with other human beings, that caring demands
> our attention. Caring is attention. When we really care about
> another person, we want that person's needs to be met. We
> pay attention to them. There is then the possibility of
> sensitivity, intimacy, communication, and harmony. The

tracker in the forest is in love with his or her surroundings. In nature we are open to a larger perspective of self. We learn to walk carefully on this planet. We learn to see it.[4]

Rezendes must be an exceptional man. He sees nature not as something to be triumphed over, but as something to be lived in. He is a human animal who understands the intense intimacy possible in the natural world.

Every once in a while real people find each other. The animal in us catches a scent, then tracks the other until we find him or her. Even in this artificial world, the powerful force of our animal instincts breaks through the façade. It is at this time that the human animal can come back and stay for a nice long visit. Of course we know very little of the process at the time—it's all very primal.

This animal, with its sharpened senses and desires, is searching for honesty, love, and a truly equal partnership. I don't think this communion happens very often, given how men and women have learned how to impersonate themselves. But when it does, watch out. An avalanche is sure to occur.

It took me several months of riding my bike, skiing, thinking, and talking to my best pal, Doug Brown, at the University of Calgary to be able to draw the distinction between gender and sexuality in sport. And I'm still trying to define exactly what a healthy sexuality is. I don't know how we combine all our options, desires, and loves in a way that brings happiness, or if that's even really a possibility for everyone. Pleasure may be all most of us can ask for; perhaps the truest happiness and intimacy, for some, can be found only alone in nature.

I also believe, however, that the arts can bring great pleasure. I'd never experienced anything like writing this book during the day at the Banff Centre, running the Tunnel Mountain trail in the early evening, and attending a concert at night. A performance by a string quartet brought many of us to tears at Banff's St. George's Anglican Church, where the late-day sunlight filtered through the stained glass that depicted hikers and animals. I believe I felt the poetry of the music more acutely because I had started to hone those senses on my Tunnel Mountain run earlier in the day. I can't imagine a more exalting combination of sense stimuli. What foreplay this is!

So my list of what speaks deeply to my sexual and sensual selves continues to grow. And who could make any final pronouncements in this complex area anyway?

But I do know what healthy sexuality isn't. It isn't purging the body through vomiting or starvation. It isn't about dieting, about surgically altering the body, or about mediating the body in ways that objectify or commodify it. Healthy sexuality is not about power differentials between partners—even when both are adults who say they are consenting, as is the case in so many coach–athlete relationships. Healthy sexuality is not about being a good girl and keeping your mouth shut when there are exciting or contentious ideas flying all around you. In challenging the old boys of hockey, Melanie Merkley and Justine Blainey were taking the first steps toward forming healthy sexual identities.

I think healthy sexuality is largely about feeling really comfortable with the self. It's about feeling like you could hug your own body because it gives you so much pleasure. In sport, much of this pleasure has to do with living fully and physically.

So what happens when a woman feels most at home in the full and physical world that is normally considered male territory? What happens when she feels surer on a pair of skates, on a surfboard, in a rowing shell or a canoe, or on a bike than the average man does? Unfortunately, many men look for the nearest exit. And they retreat most often to women who are unfamiliar with this wild territory—safe women.

But shutting out the wildness can't be much fun at all, can it?

They don't know what they're missing.

Acknowledgments

This book would never have taken the shape it has without the great insight of sport historian Doug Brown at the University of Calgary. The conversations, jokes, and bike rides we shared allowed for the kind of exchange of ideas necessary for a book that seeks to question something as culturally inflected as sport. The Markin-Flanagan Distinguished Writers Programme at the University of Calgary gave me time, space, and an entire humanities faculty with which to explore ideas on the body and culture. Special thanks go to the Markin-Flanagan Committee, and particularly to Nicole Markotic, Helen Buss, Jean Perrault, Aritha van Herk, Fred Wah, Shirley Voyna-Wilson, Karen Strong, Susan Bennett, Sandra Vida, and Pierre-Yves Moquais—all of the University of Calgary. Sandi Kirby of the University of Winnipeg, Patricia Vertinsky of the University of British Columbia, Greg Malszecki and Jennifer Joyner of York University, Dr. James Carson of the Canadian Academy of Sports Medicine, Celia Brackenridge of the University of Gloucestershire, and Kari Fasting of the Norwegian University of Sport and Physical Education played similar roles. Many other professors generously shared their work with me for *Black Tights*, and I am indebted to all of them. As usual, the Banff Centre provided a wonderful space for writing and an extraordinary environment in which to think, ride a bike, and ski. Extra thanks to Carol Holmes. I can't imagine life without this great place.

I would also like to thank Mary and Bert Kowaltschuk for believing in this book and giving me a beautiful space on Lake Huron so I could finish it. Special thanks to the Bruers, Warrilows, and Milnes, who put up with my skis, bikes, books, and files in Grey-Bruce as I spent a good deal of time thinking about my thesis while skiing and cycling in that wonderful place. Barbara Moon, Alberto Manguel, Craig Stephenson, Bronwyn Drainie, Sheila McCook, and Myra Davies were there for me as always. They gave great encouragement, made room for much discussion on this subject, and fed me delicious meals from their kitchens. As well, the women of my Toronto book club were stalwart supporters, and have been understanding and hospitable beyond the call of duty.

My relationship with *The Globe and Mail*'s Comment page started in 1990 with editor Jerry Johnson and continued with Val Ross and Patrick Martin, who allowed me to try out many of the arguments in *Black Tights* on their pages. And not only did they provide a place where big ideas first contemplated on a bike could be sorted out into a critical essay, they encouraged them, made them better—and paid for them. It's a relief to know that there is a place in a newspaper for critical essays on sport. Also in this category are Rona Maynard, editor of *Chatelaine* magazine, and my editor at that time, Cathy Callahan, who commissioned "Animal Instinct" and allowed me to delve into the world of the female human/animal in a literary way. Great thanks to Michele Landsberg for being a wonderful mentor all these years. Shannon Boeckner also contributed greatly by volunteering to organize my files, thus achieving sainthood.

The best part of researching this book was the skiing I did with my clubmates Ross, Bob, and Harry—especially Harry. If they only knew how being in the woods with them helped me formulate my thesis. The same can be said for my cycling clubmates Wayne, Mike, and Anthony. And of course I must add Judy Delogne to this list; she is now a good friend and sister. A very special thanks to Michael Lawrenchuk for helping me write the last pages of this book in such a creative way.

The entire *Black Tights* journey took place with my wonderful editor, and great human being, Nicole Langlois at HarperCollins. We make a good team. Many thanks also to my editor, Janice Weaver, as well as legal counsel Vicki White and of course Hilary McMahon and Bruce Westwood of Westwood Creative Artists.

Finally, thank you to all the women whose stories are told in this book. I greatly appreciate your strength, courage, and honesty.

Notes

Chapter 1: Constructing the Stadium: Putting Women in Their Place

1 Patricia Vertinsky, *The Eternally Wounded Woman* (Champaign, Illinois: University of Illinois Press, 1994), p. 5.

2 Eva Keuls, *The Reign of the Phallus: Sexual Politics in Ancient Athens* (Berkeley: University of California Press, 1985), p. 2.

3 Vertinsky, *The Eternally Wounded Woman*.

4 V. Burstyn, *The Rites of Men* (Toronto: University of Toronto Press, 1999), p. 50.

5 It is essential to note that the most at-risk female body has for centuries been the weak domestic body that stays at home. Women are much more likely to have to visit an emergency room because they've been abused by a partner than because they've been injured playing hockey.

Chapter 2: Show Me the Money: How the Economy of Sport Controls Women

1 Cited in Colette Dowling, *The Frailty Myth: Redefining the Physical Potential of Women and Girls* (New York: Random House, 2000), p. 182.

2 Ibid., p. 183.

3 Bruce Kidd, speech presented to the "Ethics in Sport" conference, Maytree Foundation, February 2001.

4 Mark Rosentraub, *Major League Losers: The Real Cost of Sports and Who's Paying for It* (New York: Basic Books, 1999), pp. 48–49.

5 Ibid., pp. 227–45.

6 Dowling, *The Frailty Myth*, p. 188.

7 Memo from Executive Director Tammy Lawrence re: Promotion Plus involvement in Coquitlam Case, April 1999.

8 Dowling, *The Frailty Myth*, pp. 188–89.

Chapter 3: Sex and the Single Chromosome: How a Biological Test Turned into a Social Test

1 Alison Carlson, "When Is a Woman Not a Woman?" *Women's Sport and Fitness Magazine* (July 1991), pp. 51–54.

2 Ibid., p. 198.

3 Berit Skirstad, Norwegian University of Sport [delivered to European College of Sport Science Conference, Rome, 1999]

4 Patricia Vertinsky, "The Social Construction of the Gendered Body: Exercise and the Exercise of Power," *International Journal of the History of Sport* 11, no. 2 (1994), 147–71.

5 Ibid.

6 Nancy Theberge, *Higher Goals: Women's Ice Hockey and the Politics of Gender* (Albany: SUNY Press, 2000), p. 89.

Chapter 4: The Love of a Strong Woman: The Lesbian Athlete

1 Pat Griffin, "Changing the Game: Homophobia, Sexism, and Lesbians in Sport," *Quest* 44 (1992), p. 254.

2 Theberge, *Higher Goals*, p. 81.

3 Mary Jo Kane, "Fictional Denials of Female Empowerment: A Feminist Analysis of Young Adult Sports Fiction," *Sociology of Sport Journal* 15, no. 3 (1998), pp. 231–62.

4 Theberge, *Higher Goals*, p. 99.

5 Danielle Brittain, "The Lesbian Subculture in Sport: A Case

Study of the Dinah Shore Golf Tournament." Master's thesis, Kansas State University, presented to the North American Society for the Sociology of Sport, San Antonio, Texas, November 3, 2001.

Chapter 5: Whose Body Is This? Women Athletes in the Media

1 Michael Ignatieff, *Human Rights as Politics and Idolatry*, ed. Amy Gutmann (Princeton University Press: 2001).

2 "'Crotch Shots' Are Out," *Vancouver Sun*, S4, Jan. 17, 2002 by Sandra Stevenson

3 Colette Dowling, *The Frailty Myth*, p. 153.

4 Research papers of the Amateur Athletic Foundation of Los Angeles: (I) Gender in Televised Sport, 2000; (II) Gender Stereotyping in Televised Sport, 1994; (III) Gender Stereotyping in Televised Sport, 1989; (IV) Coverage of Women's Sport in Four Daily Newspapers. Available at http://www.aafla.org

5 *An Illusory Image.* Report by the Australia Sports Commission, summarized in 1996, Canberra, Australia.

6 Reported at a meeting of the Canadian Sport Council, October 20–22, 2001, Mississauga, Ontario.

7 1998 interview with Greg Malszecki, author of "He Shoots! He Scores! Metaphors of War in Sport and the Political Linguistics of Virility." Ph.D. diss., York University, 1995.

8 Interview with Michael Robidoux, University of Lethbridge, May 2001. Author of *Men at Play: A Working Understanding of Professional Hockey* (Montreal: McGill–Queen's University Press, 2001).

9 Colette Guillaumin, "The Constructed Body," from *Reading the Social Body*, eds. Catherine Burroughs and Jeffrey David Ehrenreich; trans. Diane Griffin Crowder (Iowa City: University of Iowa Press, 1993), p. 46.

10 Ibid., p. 43.

Chapter 6: Cornered by the Coach: The Sexual Abuse of Female Athletes

1 Collective on Harassment, *Harassment and Abuse in Sport Collective Initiatives* (Ottawa: Sport Canada, 1999–2000), "Background," p. 1.

2 Laura Misener, "Exploration of Federal Sport Policy in Youth Elite Sport in Canada: A Case Study of Gymnastics Canada Gymnastiques." Masters thesis, University of New Brunswick, Faculty of Physical Education, 2001.

3 Sandi Kirby, Lorraine Greaves, and Olena Hankivsky, *The Dome of Silence: Sexual Harassment and Abuse in Sport* (Halifax, N.S.: Fernwood Publishing, 2000), p. 36.

4 Ibid., pp. 62–78.

5 Ibid., p. 82.

6 Ibid., p. 83.

7 Ibid., p. 29.

Chapter 7: Starving for the Gold: Athletes and Eating Disorders

1 Ron A. Thompson and Roberta Trattner Sherman, "'Good Athlete' Traits and Characteristics of Anorexia Nervosa: Are They Similar?" *Eating Disorders* 7 (1999), pp. 181–90.

2 The greatest obstacle to helping female athletes with eating disorders is getting them to acknowledge they even have a problem. See Thompson and Sherman, "'Good Athlete,'" p. 182.

3 R. C. Casper and D. Offer, "Weight and Dieting Concerns in Adolescents: Fashion or Symptom?" *Pediatrics* 3 (September 1986), pp. 384–90.

4 M. Grigg, J. Bowman, and S. Redman, "Disordered Eating and Unhealthy Weight Reduction Practices among Adolescent Females," *Preventive Medicine* 25, no. 6 (November–December 1996), pp. 748–56.

5 Jennifer M. Jones *et al.*, "Disordered Eating Attitudes and Behaviours in Teenaged Girls: A School-based Study," *Canadian Medical Association Journal* 165, no. 5 (September 4, 2001), p. 550.

6 Ron Mann et al., "Are Two Interventions Worse Than None? Joint Primary and Secondary Prevention of Eating Disorders in College Females," *Health Psychology* 16 (1997), pp. 215–25.

7 J. Sundgot-Borgen, "Prevalence of Eating Disorders in Elite Female Athletes," *International Journal of Sport Nutrition* 3, no. 1 (March 1993), pp. 29–40.

8 James Carson and Eileen Bridges, "Strategies to Reduce Disordered Eating Among Female Athletes." Report prepared for the Women's Issues in Sport Medicine Committee, Canadian Academy of Sport Medicine, Gloucester, Ontario, August 2001.

9 "Why Canadian Women Retire from High-Performance Cross-Country Ski Racing." Paper, University of Waterloo, April 1994.

10 Carson and Bridges, "Strategies."

11 Karin Jasper, "Sexual Abuse and Eating Problems," *National Eating Disorder Information Centre Bulletin* 9, no. 4 (September 1994), p. 1.

12 Janet de Groot and Gary Rodin, "The Relationship Between Eating Disorders and Childhood Trauma," *Psychiatric Annals* 29, no. 4 (April 1999), p. 226.

13 Ibid.

14 Celia Brackenridge, *Spoilsports: Understanding and Preventing Sexual Exploitation in Sport* (London: Routledge, 2001), p. 29.

15 Kirby, Greaves, and Hankivsky, *The Dome of Silence*, p. 26.

16 Jennifer M. Jones, "Eating Disorders in Adolescent Females with Type 1 Diabetes Mellitus: A Controlled Three-Site Study." Ph.D. diss., University of Toronto, 2000. Abstract in *Dissertation Abstracts International*, B 61/06, p. 2981.

17 Ibid.

18 Paul Tomlinson and Dorothy Strachan, *Power and Ethics in Coaching* (Ottawa: Coaching Association of Canada and Strachan-Tomlinson, 1996), p. 35.

19 Laura Robinson, "Starving for the Gold," *The Globe and Mail*, April 18, 1992, p. F1.

20 Thompson and Sherman, "'Good Athlete,'" p. 183.

21 Paul Willis, "Women in Sport in Ideology," in *Sport, Culture, and Ideology*, ed. Jennifer Hargreaves (London: Routledge and Kegan Paul, 1982), p. 130.

22 Kim Chernin, *The Hungry Self: Women, Eating and Identity* (New York: Times Books, 1985; reprint, New York: HarperPerennial, 1994), p. 33.

23 Ron A. Thompson and Roberta Trattner Sherman, "Athletes, Athletic Performance, and Eating Disorders: Healthier Alternatives," *Journal of Social Issues* 55, no. 2 (1999), pp. 317–37.

24 Jui Fairholm, ed., *Speak Out! A Workbook for Coaches* (Ottawa: Canadian Hockey Association, 2000).

25 For the complete case study, see Laura Robinson, *Crossing the Line: Violence and Sexual Assault in Canada's National Sport* (Toronto: McClelland & Stewart, 1998), pp. 135–52.

26 Chernin, *The Hungry Self*, p. 37.

27 Ibid., p. 42.

28 Ibid., pp. 36–37.

29 Ibid., p. 43.

30 Ibid., p. 44.

Chapter 8: Who Gets to Be a Free Woman? Sport and the Sweatshop

1 Cynthia Enloe, "Globe Trotting Sneaker," *Ms.* (March-April 1995), p. 12.

2 Video available through United Students Against Sweatshops (See Website at www.behindthelabel.org).

3 George Sage, "Nike: Global Corporate Worker Benefactor or Victim of a Conspiracy of Activists?" Paper presented at the Conference of the North American Society for the Sociology of Sport, November 3, 2001, San Antonio, Texas.

4 Eric Schlosser, *Fast Food Nation: The Dark Side of the All-American Meal* (Boston: Houghton Mifflin, 2001), p. 276.

5 Naomi Klein, *No Logo: Taking Aim at the Brand Bullies* (Toronto: Knopf Canada, 2000), p. 30.

6 Guillaumin, "The Constructed Body," p. 48.

Chapter 9: Playing Together: Two Sexes, One Team

1 Personal correspondence from BCAHA president Florence Rempel to Melanie Merkley, November 1996, Kitimat, B.C.

2 "Reasons for Decision," Mary Eberts, November 1, 1977, Ontario Ministry of Labour (Human Rights Commission) R.S.O. 1970, c. 518, p. 19.

3 *Baszo & Cummings*, Ontario Divisional Court.

4 *Baszo*, Ontario Court of Appeal.

5 Brief to the Sopinka Committee on Equality in Sport from the Ontario Women's Softball Association, June 1984, Toronto.

6 Notes to address the Standing Committee on the Administration of Justice, from Attorney General Ian Scott, July 1986, Toronto.

7 Ibid.

8 Submission made to the Standing Committee on the Administration of Justice by Carl Noble, president of the Ontario Women's Hockey Association, January 1986, Toronto. The CAAWS and LEAF both have volunteer boards, and a minimum of paid staff; wording of the brief is verbatim.

9 Submission made to the Standing Committee on the Administration of Justice by the Central Ontario Women's Hockey Association, January 1986, Toronto.

10 Submission made to the Standing Committee on the Administration of Justice by Joe Halstead, director of the Sports and Fitness Branch, Ministry of Tourism and Recreation, January 1986, Toronto.

11 Ken Dyer, *Challenging the Men: The Social Biology of Female Sporting Achievement* (St. Lucia, New York: University of Queensland Press, c. 1982), p. 84.

12 Transcript from Dr. Iris Marshall, expert witness on behalf of Caroline Blainey on behalf of her daughter, Justine Blainey v. the Ontario Hockey Association in the matter of the repeal of Section 19(2) of the Ontario Human Rights Code. September 13, 1987, Toronto, Ontario, pp. 351–354.

13 Transcript from Dr. Ira Jacob, expert witness on behalf of her

daughter, Justine Blainey v. the Ontario Hockey Association in the matter of the repeal of Section 19(2) of the Ontario Human Rights Code. September 13, 1987, Toronto, Ontario, pp. 400–402.

14 *Canadian Human Rights Reporter*, Vol. 9, Decision 774: *Blainey v. Ontario Hockey Association* (no. 2). Date of decision: March 21, 1988; reported August 1988. D4974.

15 Ibid.

16 R. Vivian Acosta and Linda Jean Carpenter, "Women in Inter-collegiate Sport: A Longitudinal Study—Twenty-One-Year Update, 1977–1998." Paper presented at the North American Society for the Sociology of Sport Conference, Cleveland, Ohio, November 1999.

17 *Canadian Human Rights Reporter, Bhadauria v. Seneca College.*

Chapter 10: Strong, Sexy, and Smart: Looking Toward the Future

1 "A Plan for Equality between Women and Men in Sport in the 1990s." Paper delivered by the Swedish delegation to the International Olympic Academy, Olympia, Greece, 1990.

2 Ibid.

3 Paul Rezendes, *Tracking and the Art of Seeing: How to Read Animal Tracks and Signs* (Willowdale, Ontario: Firefly Books, 1999), pp. 15–23.

Index